Empowerment in Everyday Life

of related interest

Learning to Listen
Positive Approaches and People with Difficult Behaviour
Herbert Lovett
ISBN 1 85302 374 4

Children with Autism
Diagnosis and Interventions to Meet Their Needs
Colwyn Trevarthen, Kenneth Aitken, Despina Papoudi and Jacqueline Robarts
ISBN 1 85302 314 0

Autism – An Inside–Out Approach
An innovative look at the mechanics of 'autism'
and its developmental 'cousins'
Donna Williams
ISBN 1 85302 387 6

Care in the Community for Young People
with Learning Disabilities
The Client's Voice
Janice Sinson
ISBN 1 85302 310 8

Home at Last
How Two Young Women with Profound Intellectual
Disabilities Achieved Their Own Home
Pat Fitton, Carol O'Brien and Jean Willson
ISBN 1 85302 254 3

Listen to Me
Communicating the Needs of People with
Profound Intellectual and Multiple Disabilities
Pat Fitton
ISBN 1 85302 244 6

Invisible Victims
Crime and Abuse Against People with Learning Disabilities
Christopher Williams
ISBN 1 85302 309 4

Day Services for People with Learning Disabilities
Edited by Philip Seed
ISBN 1 85302 339 6

Empowerment in Everyday Life
Learning Disability

Edited by Paul Ramcharan, Gwyneth Roberts,
Gordon Grant and John Borland

Jessica Kingsley Publishers
London and Bristol, Pennsylvania

First published in the United Kingdom in 1997 by
Jessica Kingsley Publishers Ltd
116 Pentonville Road
London N1 9JB, England
and
1900 Frost Road, Suite 101
Bristol, PA 19007, U S A

Copyright © 1997 the contributors and the publisher

Library of Congress Cataloging in Publication Data
A CIP catalogue record for this book is available from the Library of Congress

British Library Cataloguing in Publication Data
Empowerment in everyday life: learning disability
1. Learning disabled – Services for 2. Great Britain – Social
policy – 1979–
I. Ramcharan, Paul
371.9'2

ISBN 1-85302-382-5

Printed and Bound in Great Britain by
Athenaeum Press, Gateshead, Tyne and Wear

Contents

Part 1: Empowerment in Informal Settings

Part 2: Empowerment in Formal Settings

Part 3: Empowerment in Different Legal and Policy Contexts

List of Figures

List of Tables

Acknowledgements

This collection of essays about the nature of empowerment reflects a growing international interest and concern about the continued exclusion of people with learning disabilities from participation within the structures of civil society and with their struggle for citizenship. We would like to thank all the contributors for sharing their research, knowledge and personal insights and for their timely and constructive responses to our request for chapters. We join all the contributors in expressing our gratitude to the many people with learning disabilities, their families, friends, advocates and service workers who have provided a window through which we might seek to understand their world. This volume would not have been possible without their knowledge, help and cooperation. We owe a special debt to Sue Howard at the Centre for Social Policy Research and Development at the University of Wales, Bangor, for coping with our often unreasonable editorial demands and for putting this volume together in a calm manner.

Preface

Paul Ramcharan and John Borland

> The failure to empower is not something that will be tolerated in the
> 21st century. Disabled people, all over the world, are struggling to
> confront the processes that exclude and segregate them and to escape
> from the institutions that are part of that. (Oliver 1996, p.93)

It may be argued that the complexion of the term 'empowerment' is largely the
complexion of its user. As with the notion of 'community care' it is associated
with feelings of warmth and with positive images. Under its banner, and
amongst other interpretations, the political Right proclaims the rights of the
consumer within a free market (Saunders 1993). It is seen as a means of
preventing oppression (Ward and Mullender 1991). It is said to be about people
working to gain control of their lives and to maximise their quality of life
(Adams 1990), and doing so through self-help strategies, unencumbered by the
'gift' of power endowed by professional practice (Jack 1995). It is seen as a
means of according full citizenship rights by maximising autonomy and
self-determination and achieving minimum standards of well-being (Rioux
1994). It has been said to involve the democratisation of decision-making and
participation by both people who use health and social services and those who
provide such services (North 1993); and it has entered the language of
professionals, tripping lightly off the tongue as a rationalisation for virtually
any of their work for, or with, people with disabilities.

The aims of this book are relatively modest and have to do with mapping
the terrain of empowerment. By doing so, it may be possible to defuse one
regular criticism of the academic community, that is, of perennially 'reinventing
the wheel' to make its concepts fit the fad of the moment. We hope this text
will assist readers to enter the debate about what constitutes empowerment. We
also hope that, in small measure, it contains a response to Baistow's (1995)
query: 'How do we know if empowerment intentions and practices are really
empowering? How do we know if you are being or have been empowered? Or
that your actions are empowering others?' (p.42); and, 'what will the struc-

ture/institution/service/citizen relation look like in an empowering society?'
(p.44).

Baistow's point underscores one of the ironies of the empowerment field,
for it is often clear how people are disempowered. But simply removing the
barriers to individual examples of disempowerment is not sufficient to produce
an overall sense of empowerment in everyday life. For example, simply extending a person's choice of personal possessions where they have none, or fostering
their participation in service planning, may constitute single acts through which
empowerment is achieved. But these single acts do not in themselves seem to
overcome the overall sense of a disempowered lifestyle. It becomes vitally
important, therefore, not only to remove the barriers to empowered actions and
interactions, but to examine the substantive, ethical and philosophical links
which might provide the grounds for empowerment in practice-based settings
and everyday interactions. In this sense, this book aims to cast light on these
difficult problems.

Beyond the rather esoteric definitional dilemmas outlined above, Baistow
also points to, '...a noticeable lack of analysis of the meanings and practices
that are associated with empowerment' (p.34) whilst Croft and Beresford (1995)
argue that, '...there is not so much a debate or a dialogue about empowerment
and involvement as at least two different discourses' (p.60). In this volume there
are a number of discourses which relate to the concept of empowerment. For
the reasons outlined above these cannot be exhaustive. What we have attempted
to do is bring together a number of voices talking from different perspectives
and positions within the social world about issues of empowerment, and its
meaning in terms of the practices and experiences of people with learning
disabilities. The views of people with learning disabilities speaking about
themselves, therefore, stand side by side with those of an independent consultant on services for people with a learning disability, with those of practitioners
and with those of writers from the academic and policy-related fields.

Whilst each chapter stands by itself, there is a purposeful choice of chapter
ordering so that readers who are inclined to read from cover to cover may
identify emerging themes and issues. There are several reasons for organising
the text in this way. One of the important features which characterises each
chapter is that the author's voice, discourse and argument are internally
consistent and logical. Yet another important feature is that the different voices
we hear are at times disconsonant and contradictory in terms not only of
discourse and language, but in terms of the substantive points that authors are
raising. As Croft and Beresford (1995) argue: 'Existing inequalities between the
discourses need to be challenged if the debate about empowerment and
involvement is to be a progressive one' (p.68).

With this in mind the book has been split into three sections. After each
section, a short inter-linking commentary reflects upon the emerging themes
and elaborates upon the similarities and differences between the various voices.

Whilst drawing on the chapters within each section, the inter-linking commentaries represent the viewpoint of their respective authors. These commentary chapters, together with Chapter 13, have been written so that they can be read consecutively before the substantive chapters.

How the three sections are ordered is the result of purposeful choice and explains to some degree why a separate book on the notion of empowerment as it relates to people with learning disabilities is so important at this juncture. Simply stated, few would disagree that it is morally proper within our society to confer full rights and protection on all citizens, and the concomitant freedom which this implies. As Tawney argued as far back as 1952:

> A society is free in so far, and only in so far as, within the limits set by nature, knowledge, and resources, its institutions and policies are such as to enable all its members to grow to their full stature, to do their duty as they see it, and – since liberty should not be austere – to have their fling when they feel like it. In so far as the opportunity to lead a life worthy of human beings is needlessly confined to a minority, not a few of the conditions applauded as freedom would be more properly denounced as privilege. Action which causes such opportunities to be more widely shared is, therefore, twice blessed. It not only subtracts from inequality, but adds to freedom. (p.268)

But what constitutes such an ethic of citizenship and freedom? The vast majority of people with learning disabilities, for example, start their formal learning in special educational settings, excluded from the mainstream of education as well as from the work place. It might be argued that people with learning disabilities remain one of the most excluded groups within our society. In what sense can it be said that these realities constitute an ethically acceptable experience for any human being? How, and to what extent, do existing arrangements for welfare provision seek to establish or mitigate the effects of such exclusion? And how successful have such policies been? Some of these questions are addressed in Sections 2 and 3 of this volume, which are concerned with empowerment within formal settings and within different legal and policy contexts.

For several reasons, however, we wish to break away from a view of empowerment in terms of Marshall's (1963) concept of citizenship. According to that approach civil society is defined by the freedoms of speech, of faith and the right to justice accorded to the individual. The political dimension is characterised by the right to participate in the political process and a right to suffrage; whilst social rights are, '...most closely connected with...the educational system and social services' (1963, p.74). In some senses Marshall's work reflects a tradition in which the position of the individual and his/her relationship to the state and to civil society predetermine his/her citizenship rights.

But, as Turner (1990) has pointed out, such theory postulates the creation of citizenship from above. Such theories are descendants of the ideas of Plato and Hobbes in which the central question remains what the state owes its citizens and, as a *quid pro quo*, what citizens owe to the state. Turner also argues that top-down definitions of citizenship may produce an understanding of the 'active and public' aspects of citizenship, but they do little to establish the importance of citizenship in the 'passive and private' spheres of everyday life, a point taken up latterly by feminist writers (Lister 1990; Ungerson 1993).

Marshall, (Turner 1993) argues that the gradual evolution of, '…the welfare state would limit the negative impact of class differences on individual life-chances, thereby enhancing the individual's commitment to the system' (p.6). Based as it is on the state and its policies of welfare, Marshall's view, like those of many writers who start from this position in constructing a notion of citizenship, tends to eschew descriptions of everyday life as the basis for claims to citizenship. Moreover, his notion of citizenship leads back to a debate in terms of the structures and functions of the state rather than how these might be developed or changed *on the basis of people's hopes, aspirations, needs and wishes.*

For this reason, we have chosen to start from a bottom-up rather than top-down perspective, so that the chapters in Section 1 provide descriptions of the everyday lives of people with learning disabilities, their wishes, hopes, aspirations and needs. These descriptions do not lie only in the active and public domain of citizenship, with its concomitant solutions in the largely service-ori-ented public sphere. Rather, the chapters in Section 1 illustrate the importance of beginning to address the areas of social rights which Marshall's theory largely avoids, and which lie within private domains such as the family, friends and within the leisure sphere. These are the areas where interventions by the legislative arm of the state are not only difficult to effect, but are ethically questionable in terms of a citizen's right to privacy and autonomy.

However, in addition to raising the debate on empowerment in everyday life, the book goes on to address the relationship between these everyday lives and the state. In doing so it is the intention to address:

> frequent failure to relate discourse about involvement and empowerment to broader political discussion and political theory; to ideas about the role and nature of the state, democracy, citizenship, rights and power…and…to make connections between community care, empowerment and the welfare state more generally. (Croft and Beresford 1995, p.65)

There are additional reasons for singling out people with learning disabilities as the focus of this text. One further reason is that the meaning of empowerment may differ between groups. People with learning disabilities are not only excluded and alienated from the social and economic life and institutions of our society but, more than most other groups, they face these experiences over the whole of their life course. This is not to negate the importance of these issues for each citizen, rather that the problems faced by different groups *may* be of a different order.

In reviewing the development of the social model of disability, Oliver (1996) argues that, 'it is society which disables physically impaired people. Disability is something imposed on top of our impairments by the way we are unnecessarily isolated and excluded from full participation in society' (p.22). The effect of this imposed disability is '…our exclusion from the ability to earn an income on a par with our able-bodied peers…' (*ibid.*), and, '…dependence on the state must increasingly give way to the provision of help so that a living can be earned through employment' (p.24). Yet he is also aware that some forms of impairment may themselves be disabling. If what is valued in the employment market is productivity, and if access is often based on academic or intellectual merit, the notion of equality of opportunity implied by the social model is likely to leave people with learning disabilities in some of the lowest paid employment, if in the employment market at all. In short, people with learning disabilities may be less able to compete on a par with their peers because their impairments may be disabling in terms of the conditions for entry into the employment market as it is organised at present. This raises important questions about whether the market can make room for people with learning disabilities, or, whether, in their present form, such markets represent the best option. This does not deny Oliver's call for the disabling effects of society to be addressed. As Oliver also recognises, '…we must not assume that models in general and the social model in particular can do everything' (p.41). Questions therefore arise as to the limits for inclusion of people whose impairments may not even allow them to make informed choices about the decisions they may face in their lives.

Finally, the interest of many of the writers in this book is in the field of study relating to 'people with learning disabilities' as opposed to other categories of people. In many of the socialisation processes through which we gain our own personal experience, knowledge and interests we are taught to see the world as consisting of different categories of interest, for example, the elderly, people with learning disabilities, people with mental health problems and so forth. Indeed, the majority of contractual and actuarial devices through which existing service and other systems operate are themselves categorised along these lines. From a phenomenological point of view, it is impossible for people not to work with categories. Such categories help us to make sense of our world and make our interests manageable, or our professional work 'do-able'. It is upon such socially constructed categories that professionals rely for their qualifications, upon which governments legislate, and upon which we all seek to argue for one course of action as compared with another. But perhaps what is at issue here is what Ryle (1949) has termed a 'category mistake'. Perhaps by working with these categories we are colluding with and sustaining a system, the very nature of which is in itself disabling and disempowering. Perhaps it is necessary to examine what alternative categories might be used which would overcome the disabling consequences of particular terminology and the categories with which we work.

This is a theme which recurs in the following chapters of this book. We have left the authors to choose their own terminology, although the issue will be visited once again in the concluding chapter. In the main body of the text, reference is made to 'people with learning disabilities', a term now recommended by the Department of Health in Britain; to 'people with learning difficulties', as favoured by the self-advocacy movement; and, indeed, to just 'citizens'. Whatever terms are used, however, we must remember that those about whom this volume has been written are *people first*, as described by Anya Souza in Chapter 1.

References

Adams, R. (1990) *Self-Help, Social Work and Empowerment*. London: Macmillan.

Baistow, K. (1995) 'Liberation or regulation? Some paradoxes of empowerment.' *Critical Social Policy 42*, 34–46.

Croft, S. and Beresford, P. (1995) 'Whose empowerment? Equalising the competing discourses in community care.' In R. Jack (ed) *Empowerment in Community Care*. London: Macmillan.

Jack, R. (1995) 'Empowerment in community care.' In R. Jack (ed) *Empowerment in Community Care*. London: Chapman and Hall.

Lister, R. (1990) 'Women, economic dependency and citizenship.' *Journal of Social Policy 19*, 4, 445–467.

Marshall, T.H. (1963) *Sociology at the Crossroads and Other Essays*. London: Heinemann.

North, N. (1993) 'Empowerment in welfare markets.' *Health and Social Care 1*, 129–137.

Oliver, M. (1996) *Understanding Disability*. London: Macmillan.

Rioux, M. (1994) 'Towards a concept of equality of well-being: overcoming the social and legal construction of inequality.' In M. Rioux and M. Bach (eds) *Disability is not Measles*. Ontario: The Roeher Institute.

Ryle, G. (1949) *The Concept of Mind*. London: Hutchinson (1963 edition).

Saunders, P. (1993) 'Citizenship in a liberal society.' In B.S. Turner (ed) *Citizenship and Social Theory*. London: Sage.

Tawney, R.H. (1952) *Equality*. London: Capricorn (4th edition).

Turner, B.S. (1990) 'Outline of a theory of citizenship.' *Sociology 24*, 2, 189–217.

Turner, B.S. (1993) 'Contemporary problems in the theory of citizenship.' In B.S. Turner (ed) *Citizenship and Social Theory*. London: Sage.

Ungerson, C. (1993) 'Caring and citizenship: a complex relationship.' In J. Bornat, C. Pereira, D. Pilgrim and F. Williams (eds) *Community Care: A Reader*. London: The Macmillan Press in association with The Open University.

Ward, D. and Mullender, A. (1991) 'Empowerment and oppression: an indissoluble paring for contemporary social work.' *Critical Social Policy 32*, Autumn, 21–30.

PART 1

Empowerment in Informal Settings

Everything You Ever Wanted to Know About Down's Syndrome, but Never Bothered to Ask

Anya Souza (with Paul Ramcharan)

How this chapter was put together

A number of meetings between Anya and myself were recorded where we talked about Anya's life. From the tape recordings I initially wrote down the chronology of Anya's life and then visited her again to make sure that I had made no mistakes. As with each of the other stages of putting this chapter together, we read through the draft word for word and discussed each point in detail. At this stage, I also went with a huge number of questions about each part of Anya's life, about her feelings, her views and her ideas. Again this was tape recorded. From this recording I wrote a first draft of the chapter and went back to Anya who made a number of changes and added a number of new ideas. I made sure at each point that the article was saying what Anya herself wanted it to say. I too came with an idea at this stage, that is, the 'four separations' I explained to Anya what it meant and immediately got a positive response about using it in the article. A number of changes were made and I again went away and worked to produce the final draft of the article. A further meeting was held and Anya made some further changes to the article. We also discussed possible titles until Anya's inspirational idea for the title was decided.

Paul Ramcharan

Introduction

My life could have been completely different. There were so many times that I might have entered the long road to a life defined by some people as being worth less than other members of society. I could all too easily have been created by others as a label and not a person. In fact there have been some ways in which this was always, and still is, on the cards. If it had not been for the persons close to me fighting for my individuality and my rights to a normal life when I was young, I would certainly have fallen into this trap. If I had not myself recognised the issues as I grew up I might have been taken along on their tide of prejudice. But I too have fought for my right to an ordinary life.

It takes a lot of courage and strength to fight against people who have the power to define who you are. People who think they can define you also assume they can tell you what your rights are and, because of who they think you are, specify what you should do with your life. They don't specify this by *telling* you what to do with your life only. It's worse than that. They put you in situations where there are only a limited range of things you can do with your life.

If you get placed in a mental hospital or a special school, or an Adult Training Centre, if you haven't got the money to be able to move about freely, if you need others to support you in doing the things you want to do and there is nobody there, and if you need help with transport, then you are denied access to anywhere but the environment of the place where you're put. This means that the opportunities for friendships, for real employment and for long-term relationships are severely limited. The people who make the decision to separate people from society in this way do not see that the minute this separation starts is the minute they begin to make us disabled. They are disabling us in our rightful role in society. And the longer this separation lasts, the more the person comes to see themselves as separate. This is what makes moving back into society so difficult for some people.

As I say, I'm one of the very few lucky ones. I've had support from family and the strength to try to change things for myself. Others may not have been so lucky. I thought I'd tell you a little bit about the 32 years of my life so that you could see the challenges I've faced. That is not to say it has all been negative. There have been successes and although I still have problems in my life I've found something meaningful in having created my life the way it is now.

Before I knew I was different

Every family with children has its stories. For example there are the 'what a lovely baby' stories and the 'little terror' stories, the 'first word and steps' stories and so on. Parenthood and being a child are such an important and stimulating time. But when I was born my mother was told by the doctors that I had Down's Syndrome and would be mentally and physically handicapped for the rest of my life. It was a very negative way to describe me and what my mum could expect from me. If it had not been for a nurse who told my mother that she could expect a lot of joy from me I think my mother would have been totally devastated. This is what I mean by the first separation. All of a sudden the doctor has separated me out, put a label on me, made everything to do with me a negative image. If my mother had believed the doctor and not tried to find something good in me as the nurse suggested, she could have spent the rest of her days trying to find so-called specialist help and services to fit the label. I could have been separated out from society completely at this point.

My mother could have felt the labels of 'Down's Syndrome' and 'handicapped' were a good reason to hide me from society, that it reflected badly on her. She could have hidden me in my pram, lost her friends because I was 'different'. It would have been all too easy for her to take the easy way out of being subjected to society's prejudices. Don't forget this was 32 years ago when the idea of community care was only very young.

But my mother did not do any of these things. She took the nurse's advice and looked for the good in me, she treated me as any other child would be treated. She got joy out of me as she did with all her other children. And when there were stories in the family they were all about the good things that we remembered. My mum had prevented the first separation of myself from society. But she had gone beyond this. She had made a commitment to place me in society where I belonged just like everybody else and she had found in me another individual with their strengths, likes, dislikes and weaknesses.

Knowing what I now know about things, it could all have been so very different and I think it often is for other people who are labelled in the way the doctor labelled me at birth. I know that each person has different needs, and just because those needs may be different from another child does not mean they have to be all negative. If they are made into a negative thing then they will be. But it really does not have to be like that.

My first memory outside my home was the nursery, where I can remember painting on someone's shirt. I didn't go there very long because my mother took me out. I really do not know why that was. I do know that the next place I went to was a special school. I think you might say that this was the 'second separation'. My mother had fought hard to ensure that as I was an infant that I was looked upon by the family and society as just another infant and not a Down's Syndrome baby. Now it was time to start me on the long road of making contact with society.

When I first went to school I was very excited but also frightened, as most children are when they first go to school. My mother had told me about the things I would be learning. I thought it all sounded wonderful. But I really could not understand what I was doing at the school. What I mean is that the teachers seemed to do everything for me. I remember 'making' paper toys, a stuffed fish and two stuffed rabbits on one occasion. What I mean is that it was the nursery nurse who really made them, and not me. Looking back on it I wonder why the children weren't doing anything for themselves. What was school for if it wasn't to learn? Anyway, I took the rabbits and the fish home and I ripped them up because they were not part of me. I hadn't made them. I think my mother realised that I was not happy.

You see I could have carried on with this school forever and moved on to other schools which separated out 'people like me'. But if I had continued with this 'second separation' I would not have learned anything. I would have been treated on the basis of what the teachers thought I could do. Because they didn't think I was able to do certain things they didn't try or need to try to teach me or the others in the school. Because they thought I was 'different' they did not allow me to be the same, to attend an ordinary school, with 'ordinary' children.

Special schools are not suitable for anyone, no matter how disabled they are. They should be at ordinary schools having an ordinary life. A friend of mine has a learning difficulty, she cannot hear very well but she is at an ordinary school. It doesn't matter that we might not learn in the same way as everybody else. What matters is being with everybody else. I began to understand that I was different at that very young age. I was only five but as my actions showed in ripping up the toys, I did not want to be treated as different. I think my mother realised this and saw what the school would have meant had I to have continued there. After a term she took me out. Without that support and advocacy I would probably not have been what I am today.

Learning for life

I had to have an education. My mother managed to get me into the local primary school. I spent eight years there. For anybody else this would have been seven years, so in all I lost a year. I got put back a year but that didn't upset me too much. They had to put me back you know, and I did year five twice. I think I actually gained from this.

When they put me back my mum talked to me first about it and explained that in the long run it would be better for me. I would be able to go on to an ordinary comprehensive school if I did well enough. My mother always talked to me first on these things so I knew what was going to happen and why. She never did anything behind my back. Only after she had talked to me would she then go on to talk with the teachers about the decision we had made.

Now the teachers at this school did treat me a bit differently. They gave me a lot more respect and they were perhaps not quite as firm with me as with other pupils. This didn't harm me. People with Down's Syndrome do need a lot of attention you know. And I did get a lot of attention, not only from the teachers, but also from the other children. I made some friends there and I still have them as acquaintances now.

There are some times in people's lives when they might be separated out from society. My mother and I had worked to prevent this. The third possible separation from the ordinary world was after primary school. I could have gone on to an Adult Training Centre at the age of 19 after years and years in a special school, having 'special' classes, 'special' friends and no real contact with the world. Instead I was a success. I had got into a comprehensive school! All the efforts of my mother and my own efforts had paid off.

Now people might say: 'Well Anya, you are special, you are able to understand classes and do well at school, but it's not the same for others'. But when they say that I think that for a start I would not have learned as much in a special school; I would not have made ordinary friends; I would not have learned to deal with people who made fun of or discriminated against me; I would not have known about society at large; I probably wouldn't have taken the same interest in boys; and so on. I would have been less educated in class-type work and not educated at all about those things that make you a valuable member of society. It doesn't matter if you pass exams. You are really there to find your place in society and the world. To separate people out from society from the start is to say from the start that you are not, and never will be, a part of this society and world.

Comprehensive school was great fun. I had nice teachers, nice friends and had real fun. I went on excursions to the Wye Valley, to Yorkshire and to Boulogne too. I can't remember anybody at this school really picking on me. I had my friends and we did the things we wanted to do together. Everybody has their friends and also the people they don't want to be in contact with and stay away from. It was no different for me than it was for anyone else. I would say that I am a demonstration that integration into schools really works. I've been through it, I've demonstrated it and shown the way. I still keep in contact with one or two of the friends I made at secondary school, and with many of the teachers also.

All that fun doesn't mean that I didn't also do well in classes. Again it took six years instead of five, but I did all my subjects and came out with three CSEs: Drama, French and Housecraft. I really liked the French best of all and it gave me an interest in foreign countries too.

But there was a really sour end to it all. By now I really wanted to stay on to learn more in the sixth form and to do more courses. But there was a new headmistress who said to my mum: 'What is this Mongol person doing at this school?'. Again my mother stepped in for me. I had reached some independence and was doing things by my own choice, but this was not something I could deal with myself. My mother went to the High Court and the school lost at the first hearing. It was something to do with discrimination and contravening the Education Act.

But after that there was no way I could go back. After meeting lovely friends and teachers and doing well for myself this was a pathetic end to all my efforts. Despite the disappointment life never ends and neither does the fighting. It would be nice to be able to say that so much time and effort does not need to be made just to allow people to be a part of the society in which they live. But it never really works out like that does it?

They can't break down my humanity

So I left school before I wanted to and went back to a special school. I was meeting up with a system I had avoided for virtually the whole of my 18 years of life and I could not believe what I saw, nor accept what I was expected to experience.

After the comprehensive this school was a prison cell to me. I have to say this but all the people there were backwards, and so too were the teachers. It just showed what could happen to people if they were labelled and if people don't really care about what happens to them now or in the future.

There was no teaching at all and all the students were mixed together. I can't remember a single thing that I really learned there. The students were very rough and because I came in so late on they picked on me. I had hot custard thrown over me and on another occasion was thrown down and then had my fingers crushed in the playground, ending up in hospital with swollen fingers. Anywhere else and this would not have been allowed. And if it's one thing I can't stand more than anything else it is being ignored. Yet when I went to the teachers to complain they just brushed me off. I went mad about this, but it did not do any good.

It's funny really, but you really have to have friends in a place like that just to survive. The one trip we made whilst I was at this school was to the Isle of Wight. The teachers went to the pub and left us on our own to get back to the hotel, but the others left me and I was lost and on my own. Lorraine, one of the students, asked them where I was and when she found I was missing she came and found me. From that time to this day we have been very close friends. Lorraine was very tough and so despite the fact they were a very rough crowd I had a protector and friend from that time on, and things became easier.

My mother had fought to keep me in mainstream education up until I went to this school. It took my mother a long time to recognise my worries and I think it was the one mistake my mum really made regarding my education. I can remember when the special school was first suggested by a local authority worker that my mum said: 'Not over my dead body!'. But I suppose in the end she must have thought that somewhere was better than nothing. She was wrong. A school like that should not exist anywhere on Earth today.

That school, whether it meant it or not, nearly took away my independence and spoiled all the hard work in my life. It never treated me as an individual, it broke down all I had learned about the ways of making a success of life with other people and it taught me nothing of practical use. It was as if they were preparing the students for a worthless life, because they felt that was all they could expect.

I was 19 at this time and realised I was not going to be broken down to expect nothing from life. I wrote a letter to a theatre explaining that I loved drama very much and wanted to enrol. This was the first time I had done anything like this about my life without the help or knowledge of my mother.

I was accepted, and when I told my mother she was delighted despite the fact that it would cost her to send me there. I think she knew after I had done this that I had to leave the special school.

The theatre course was only part-time and so after leaving the special school my mother and I started to look round for other opportunities. What was most important though was that the special school had not succeeded in taking away my individuality. They had not succeeded in making me expect more out of life and they did not succeed in separating me from society. I was back on the road to a valued place in society despite the efforts of 'those who knew best' to teach me not to expect that I ever could or would be valued.

Finishing my preparation for the work place

Again it was my mother who looked for courses in which I would be doing real training for real work. I think this is very different from Adult Training Centres, where there isn't very much real work training at all.

In the end I was accepted on to a course training me up in office work. I was interviewed for the course and got in on my abilities. They looked upon me as a person and saw my value and potential, just like the eleven others who were taken on. Their confidence in me was not misplaced because I passed the course and became proficient in typing, duplicating, filing, phone skills and so forth. My one regret now is that I did not keep in contact with the one friend I had made during my time there. It's a shame to lose good friends, but I suppose sometimes people do just move on.

During this course I also had an interview for a City and Guilds course in Catering and Food Industry at a well-known college in London. When I went for the interview they looked at me and said: 'You can do the community care course'. I thought, 'I'm not doing that' and looked down the list of courses, saw 'food' and thought: 'Yeah, that's me'. I knew what I wanted to do and didn't want to be told by anyone what I should do or in what I should be interested. I don't know why they'd think I would want to do a course in 'community care'. Anyway, I stood up for myself and the course on food and cooking it was.

The course lived up to all my expectations and was both interesting and useful. I can now cook a mean meal for myself and others and love to host get-togethers like at birthdays and other special occasions. Most of all I like cooking foreign foods. One of the highlights for me was the project I undertook on foreign foods, including French, Italian, Swiss and German. I had to write a balanced menu, ensure food hygiene, the management of the meal, cooking and presentation.

Overall the course lasted two years, but came to a disappointing end when the careers adviser came to visit the students. She did not at first pay any attention to me and so I got up the courage and asked her about opportunities for a job in France where I would dearly have loved to work. Her immediate response was: 'No there isn't any chance of that', made in a very rude manner followed by her walking away from me. She did help some of the others but for myself and one other girl there was just no interest shown in our careers. I don't understand her reaction to me even now. I could have been given the chance like everybody else.

The fourth separation people might go through in their lives is from the work place. This careers officer seemed to react to me on the basis of her prejudice. She did not see the qualified cook, like the other students, but a person with Down's Syndrome. And her view of people with Down's Syndrome was that they were worthless and not worth wasting time on. She did not give me an equal chance to be part of the work place. She separated me out and labelled me.

I still persevered despite the reaction of the careers officer. I might just have accepted that I should be separate and not part of the work place. But I was 21 years old and was beginning to have high hopes for myself now that I had qualifications. At that time the Down's Children Association had expanded from Birmingham to London. None of the workers at that time had Down's Syndrome, nor had children with Down's Syndrome, but my mum had contact with the organisation and it was again through her that a work opportunity was found. As with many jobs for people with Down's Syndrome, though, I was only working part-time so that my pay would not affect my benefits.

When I joined in 1984 I felt very highly valued and was given the chance for an appearance on BBC Radio 4 to talk about the rights of people with Down's Syndrome for a job, and on television talking about a family who had taken the life of their Down's Syndrome baby. I was also interviewed by *The Guardian* newspaper about the latter case. I will return to these issues a little later, but what my experience was beginning to tell me was that what I really wanted to do was to share my experience and knowledge about Down's Syndrome, and about people with Down's Syndrome, with a wider audience. I wanted to tell, to show and to demonstrate the value of disabled people and people with Down's Syndrome especially.

During my time working for the organisation they changed their name to the Down's Syndrome Association and moved to smaller offices, too small for the ten workers really. This latter part of my time whilst employed there was the most productive. I appeared with the Director of the organisation on Channel 4 to show and discuss what people with Down's Syndrome could do and how valuable they were to society. The programme showed me doing ordinary things such as typing, catching a bus, standing up for myself and so forth. I hope it dispelled some of the myths people have about Down's Syndrome.

I later took part in a video production which demonstrated self-advocacy skills. It showed me in different situations such as in an interview, using a bus and being ignored. I showed how important it was for all people, and particularly those who are often ignored, to speak up for themselves. It is not enough to educate the public about Down's Syndrome. It is also essential to teach people with Down's Syndrome to expect more of the public.

Now, despite all this valuable work I wanted to use my clerical skills more fully. I wanted to use my typing skills and, like the other members of the team, to learn to use the phone and computer systems. But my requests, and those of my mother and sister, to extend my responsibilities, seemed to fall on deaf ears. Because of this I did not feel a fully valued member of the team.

Despite these negative feelings I think it was a very productive time in my life and it was a time when I really found myself and my vocation. But it was a very emotional time too. My mother's health meant that I had to give her a lot of care and support. Doing all that I was doing was one way I could show her how much I loved her. It was a very traumatic period and when my mother died the funeral, and my continued living arrangement in my mother's flat, was organised by family and friends.

I did go back to the Down's Syndrome Association after my mother died. But I felt strongly enough about the need to extend my responsibilities and skills that I decided to leave shortly afterwards. I felt guilty leaving, but I also wanted to work in an environment where I could improve myself and one where people recognised the skills I had to offer.

As you will have noted, my mum had a great deal to do with my early life and in making sure I had opportunities like other people. In my later life, too, she always supported me and spoke up for and with me when it was necessary. Losing my mum was a great loss, but because I had lived as ordinary a life as possible with her help I still had friends upon whom I could rely. These included my 'second mum', a friend of my mother's who had always been involved in my life and who wanted to continue being involved once my mum had passed on. I have continued to have the friendship, advice, support and teaching input of my second mum to date.

Another friend of my mum's called me up shortly after mum died and after I had left my job with the Down's Syndrome Association. She suggested there might be a job through a local Society for the Mentally Handicapped (as it was called). I once again succeeded at the interview and worked largely as a receptionist at first. I was employed through Remploy and it was the first time in my life that I'd been paid well, or should that be properly, for the job that I did. The Society had a job preparation scheme one day a week, a gardening project, a mail-out business and two cafés where people with learning difficulties could learn catering skills.

Most important, though, was that they gave me the opportunity for some outreach work for the first time in my life. I befriended a person living in the community, and gave her support and help. The friendship has carried on to this day despite the fact that I stopped working for the Society. It really is very important to keep friends. They rely on you now, but one day you may rely on them. When you lose friends you lose an important part of your life. If friends who really cared about me from my earliest years were not still around I would have less to do, I would have less people to rely on to discuss things of interest, problems and so on, and I would not be able to rely on them when I needed help as they can rely on me. Being able to give to friends in this way is also a very satisfying experience.

I had not worked for the Society for long before they suggested that I might like to try for a job with Young People First which had just been advertised. I thought, 'that's interesting' and asked my second mum, 'why do I want to do this?'. And I suppose she helped me to convince myself that not only the money, but the challenge, the outreach work and the running of self-advocacy groups was right up my street. In short it gave me the chance to do all the things I really believed in and to help others to speak up for themselves too.

As well as this, in all the places I had worked for people with learning difficulties the thing that struck me most was that it was only people without a learning difficulty who, apart from myself, were employed. I felt very strongly that this should change. I don't think they knew at People First that I was a person with Down's Syndrome when I applied for the job. I was therefore over the moon when they picked me for the post after interviews had been held.

My role at People First was wide and varied. I used to co-facilitate two self-advocacy groups for young people with learning disabilities to help them to learn how to get their voice heard. I was involved in producing several information leaflets and contributed to a booklet. I also attended a conference in Barcelona where I was very angry with all the doctors. They kept standing up and talking about tests for Down's Syndrome in the unborn baby and I thought to myself: 'But I'm Down's Syndrome. What's wrong with me?'. I told them that they were treating us like animals, like guinea pigs and that if people aborted a Down's Syndrome baby just because it was Down's Syndrome then I would not be at the conference. The doctors know nothing about the life of someone with Down's Syndrome and they seem to think it is OK to say that their lives are not worthy of living. They also think that they have a right to sterilise people with Down's Syndrome. But we have a right to boyfriends and girlfriends and sex just like everybody else. We are ordinary people just like you who is reading this chapter. And I wouldn't think of suggesting that anybody should sterilise you. I gave these views when I delivered my paper and I hope that at least some people listened.

I also led the organisation of a conference on Down's Syndrome. About a hundred people attended and they took part in six workshops as well as listening to some speakers. I spoke about the history of the medical condition, about plastic surgery which is being used to change the appearance of people with Down's Syndrome and about issues to do with abortion.

I had not had any sex education up to the point when I went to Young People First. Like other young people I had had some boyfriends by that time and was going out with another young man at the time. Nearly 30 years of age and nobody had ever talked to me or taught me about sex! Yet young children in primary school are being taught sex education! What can people be thinking of when they exclude some people from learning about such an important area of life? I felt very strongly about this and helped whilst working there to make a tape about sexuality, sex education and about safe sex.

All in all I was at Young People First for two years and I worked really hard enjoying all the roles I was filling. My only disappointment was in not being allowed to do outreach friendship work, which I think is essential for the lives of people with learning difficulties. I suppose some of this disagreement was behind me losing my job there. We all make mistakes and later regret them. But I'm still here and fighting for my rights as I always have done. I have dedicated a lot of time recently to developing my skills in stained glass making which my second mum is teaching to me. She has also suggested that, with my knowledge, experience and background, one way forward would be for me to set up as a Consultant in Down's Syndrome. That's a difficult step to take though, and I'm still thinking about how it might work.

Conclusion: I am a person first

Well, that is my life to date. As I said at the beginning of this chapter, my life could have been so different. As long as I can remember family, friends and myself have had to fight a battle to prevent my separation from the rest of society and for my rights. You will have noticed that I have not talked about the service sector and in my case that is because they have not really affected my life that much. My mum and I did have some respite care (from each other as much as anything) from time to time, both on a parent-to-parent scheme and in a hostel setting. I have also had social workers in my time. But they are not in a position to be my friends, to be there when I need them, to have a relationship which will last for a lifetime. Maybe other people need more of a service input, but this should not be in a way which separates them from society. That's the most important thing, to keep people a part of their own society and not an artificial one made by others. That can never be as good as having friends and relatives.

Like other people with Down's Syndrome I have been called 'Mongol' and other names. But like everybody else I have chosen my friends and have ignored and stayed away from people who are prejudiced. With the help of others where necessary, I have been able to stand up and speak up for myself. I have my own flat, I am qualified and am keeping optimistic about the future.

What is more I have been very lucky to be able to stand up and speak for myself and others in the media as I am doing now. It would be nice to see more people portrayed by the media who have Down's Syndrome or other learning disabilities being treated as adults and for their worth and value. I hope that the makers of *Brookside*, for instance, will carry on the Down's Syndrome story-line and watch the baby grow into a valuable and valued member of the Close and community, with all the problems and pitfalls that life throws at each and every one of us, Down's Syndrome or not. Nor am I mentally handicapped. The term seems to be saying 'there's a pretty little thing'. I'm not a pretty little thing. I'm a valuable person in my own right. I have a lot to offer. I might have what doctors term Down's Syndrome but I am a person first as is everybody else.

I have rights: to a job, to services when necessary, to a decent standard of living, to know about my medical problems, to speak my mind and make choices and decisions about friends, what time to come and go out, whether to have sex and so forth. To do this means that you also have the right to independence as you grow up. Luckily the people around me realised this from my earliest days. Families, friends and services need to know when to stop giving orders and start discussing, and then to stop discussing and let us live with our decisions. If this does not happen then other people in my position are likely to suffer one or more of the *four separations* I have told you about in this chapter.

CHAPTER 2

Empowering and Relationships

Michael Bayley

Stan Rivers' story

At first sight Stan Rivers' story may be seen as a success. He is 30, has learning difficulties and poor speech, and has been further handicapped by childhood, adolescence and early adulthood spent in care. Stan looks, and feels, noticeably 'different'. Despite these obstacles he leads an active and outwardly ordinary life. He lives in an ordinary house in a quiet neighbourhood, he is a member of the local working men's club where he is well known and liked, he is a member of an ordinary rambling club and cycling group and is usually out with one or the other at weekends and even takes occasional holidays with them. The residential unit he lived in as a young adult is in the neighbourhood so he knows his locality well and in turn he is well known, a familiar local person. He attends a day centre where his important relationships are with members of staff.

Self-conscious about being 'different', he had developed a number of coping strategies. Because he dislikes showing his bus pass ('I am mentally handi-capped') he nearly always cycles rather than uses public transport. He has learned what constitutes an 'under £10 shop' so he can go to the supermarket and not be embarrassed by being asked to give more money than the £10 note he has just confidently handed over. He saves successfully and always seems to have more in the bank than me, even though he lives only on benefit. He enjoys music, has a large tape collection, he enjoys videos – the man at the local video library knows Stan and can recommend films. This avoids the problem of not being able to read the TV listings. He dresses well and gets on well with people, a well thought of member of his community.

All this is managed with only one regular weekly visit from a home help (assistance with cleaning and shopping, company being more important than direct help) and one weekly visit from myself, the social worker, with extra contact if requested.

But sometimes I would walk away from visiting Stan, no problems or difficulties having been expressed, and I would want to cry. I found a deep

15

sense of loneliness or 'aloneness' in Stan which could be nearly unbearable. Stan feels alone in the world without a single true soul mate, close companion, sexual partner, without love. He is confused about his disability, unsure whether it is illness or punishment, supernatural or accident. The media daily thrust images of perfect men and women at him and he wants his own life to match those images – he wants marriage with a beautiful (fantasy) woman, he wants a family (he has been rejected by his own), he wants material success and a car. The media can successfully create such identity problems for most people and Stan has less ability than most to separate fantasy and stylised image from everyday reality. By the standards of the TV advert, Stan judges himself badly. Unable to articulate this in words, he would play me sad music or songs of lost romance and tell me that was how he felt. He is deeply unhappy.

At one point Stan started going into rigid immobile states rather like seizures except that they might last half an hour or more. The seizures often took place at the day centre and seemed often to happen near a key member of staff to whom Stan felt particularly close. He went into hospital many times, had all the usual tests, all negative. Things started to deteriorate. The situation at the day centre approached crisis, the hospital began to get frustrated with what appeared to be a series of false alarms and Stan seemed to be heading for a breakdown. Needless to say, breakdown would have been catastrophic for Stan, a further reinforcement of his poor self-image. My supervisor and I then decided it would be worth exploring the possibility that the 'seizures' were emotional in origin. Stan and I then had a long, intense and moving discussion. He asked questions he had never asked before – I answered as truthfully as I could and the pain was acute. Then came the moment he had been building up to – would he ever get better? He had lived with this question all his life and at last he knew the answer. My words felt hollow (how could I appreciate this man's agony?) but we ended the session with a discussion of Stan's many successes in the face of great difficulties. The seizures stopped after that discussion but Stan still feels alone. A lifetime's damage to personal esteem and self-confidence will not be undone quickly. The realities of Stan's life, the images he aspires to, all remain and are here to stay.

The lesson for me has been the realisation of the central importance of the personal and interpersonal world to us all. The lesson is particularly relevant in The Brave New World of Community Care. By the criteria of care management, here was a man with a successful 'care package', a stable if not improving situation, and progressively lower needs for practical support and formal involvement. You had to dig long and hard to find the problems.

In the language of the formal assessment process, Stan's problems were in the category 'social, spiritual, aesthetic' – the one where people cough, embarrassed, say 'doesn't go to church' and move quickly on. Stan is lonely and unhappy, the work he needs is time-consuming, delicate and personal. He needs to understand himself, value himself and be a friend to himself before he can find true companionship in others. We need to work with his heart and feelings, with his social networks, create new networks which will welcome him if he is to feel he can belong.

This graphic painful story from a social worker portrays the central dilemma with which this chapter is struggling. It is the fundamental human question of 'Who am I?'. It is a question from which none of us is exempt, though people with learning difficulties have to grapple with it with fewer resources than most. But perhaps that is not the point. Perhaps the real point is that they, like the rest of us, do have to grapple with it. We cannot take refuge in the comfortable belief that people with learning difficulties are immune from questions of the meaning and purpose of life. They too, just as the rest of us, struggle with what it means to be a person but they do so in a context which makes it more difficult for many of them to gain a sense of themselves as loved, valued, worthwhile people.

It is more difficult for them but it is certainly not impossible. Whilst it is vital not to ignore the pain of Stan and others like him, so it is equally important not to ignore the profound sense of fulfilment conveyed by 'A Poem to Michael':

A Poem to Michael

From my heart to you,
I want to say
I love you,
Our wedding means to me,
I didn't believe that would be possible to me.

I want to express
My feelings when you shed tears for me,
Your pain is my pain,
And I feel it deeply,
I worry and think a great deal about it.

From the day of our wedding
I have wanted you to know,
That you are very, very close to my heart,
I want our future to be happy,
To always be together,
And to share everything.

I know how you feel,
How tired you get,
Helping me,
Washing me,
Bathing me,
Dressing me,
Feeding me,
Pushing my wheelchair,

Shopping for me,
Looking after me.

For me Michael
My life has meaning with you.

                                    from your wife, Barbara

                                    (Calligan undated)

This chapter is based on a project which came to centre on empowering people
with learning difficulties by addressing the context within which they live, with
a view to enabling them to come closer to Michael's sense of himself rather
than Stan's. It was based in a town in the north of England. I had contact with
41 people but also drew on the experience of other workers in the area.

The friendship barrier

The starting point of the project was a concern about the experience of people
leaving hospitals and hostels. Many of the schemes enabling people to leave
hospitals and hostels have enjoyed a considerable measure of success and have
widened the opportunities for people with learning difficulties in a most
impressive way. Important gains have been made and should not be decried,
but all the schemes run up against the same barrier – integration within the
local community is generally at a superficial level.

Booth, Simons and Booth (1990) seem fully justified in their conclusion
that: 'Study after study has found that a move into the community results in
most people making greater use of community facilities, but few developing
social networks that reach out into the wider society. Our research was no
exception' (p.180).

All this indicates that there are barriers differing in type and resistance to
full and satisfying integration into the community at large that only a few people
with learning difficulties living in the community manage to pass. If the policy
of encouraging and enabling people with learning difficulties to live in the
community is also to enable them to lead satisfying and fulfilled lives, then it
seemed that this was an issue which had to be tackled.

A community development approach

The most fundamental tenet of the community development approach is that
the worker takes time to develop a real understanding of how things look from
the standpoint of those with whom she is working, that is to understand the
culture, the assumptions and the priorities of those whom she is seeking to help.
There is a strong anthropological element to the work. This has been expressed
well by Ramcharan and Grant (1992): 'The researcher will, like the anthropolo-
gist, have to become immersed in the field in order to discover the subject's
meaningful world and their systems of rationality' (p.4).

In this project this has meant taking time to discover past and existing networks of friendships and acquaintances; sorting out the pattern of services and organisations within which the people with learning difficulties, their families and those connected with them live and have lived, and understanding their values, assumptions, strengths, weaknesses and ways of operating. This could be described as taking a broad social history of the person concerned. It could also be described as taking time to discover the *meaning* of various aspects of their life to people with learning difficulties.

The development of understanding

The process of discovering the meaning of various aspects of the lives of the people with learning difficulties with whom I was working went through a number of stages. To start with the emphasis was on integration, with the recognition that one of the key ways in which integration could be achieved was by the development of friendships, that is, overcoming the 'friendship barrier' which was mentioned above. In pursuing the goal of developing friendships I devoted much effort to discovering people's interests and then trying to link them up with other people who shared that interest. Quite early on I realised that the *main* focus needed to shift from integration to friendship. But soon it also became clear that it was not sufficient to focus just on friendships. Friendships are formed and are carried on within the context of a network of relationships:

> The feeling that one is valued, and a sense that one is making a contribution to the lives of others around, can only be gained through personal relationships. Relationships of all kinds help define who we are... Without relationships with others we cannot know what we are like, or what kind of person we would like to be. (Firth and Rapley 1990, p.19)

Thus rather than just focus on friendship it became apparent that, if I wanted to address the issue of how people with learning difficulties can gain a sense of self-esteem and of being valued, I had to address the full *range of relationships* which are needed to give people that sense.

What is the range of relationships needed?

Relationships are not transferable like different nurses taking on the same task when a new shift comes on duty. We have many different needs and different people, and different types of relationships meet those different needs. Therefore the first task is to see what these basic needs might be.

A convincing typology has been put forward by Weiss (1975, 1979) and taken up by Bulmer (1987) in his book *The Social Basis of Community Care*. Weiss, from his research on lone parents, found that relationships were differentiated and one type was not an adequate substitute for another. Bulmer points out how Weiss shows:

> The provisions of marriage could not be supplied by friendship...nor could the provisions of friendship be supplied by marriage... Weiss was led to conclude that individuals have requirements for well-being that can only be met through relationships. But different relational provisions depend upon different, and usually incompatible, relational assumptions. Thus a relationship with a friend, a child or a spouse all rest on different bases, and a degree of specialisation occurs in what is provided by a particular relationship. (p.144)

The great strength of Weiss' typology is that he gets below the questions of what social roles people play and addresses the different emotional and cognitive needs. I quote Bulmer's summary of Weiss' six types:

1. *Attachment and intimacy.* Feelings can be expressed freely and without self-consciousness, and in such relationships individuals feel comfortable and at home. The absence of such relationships is likely to lead to loneliness and restlessness. Attachment is provided by marriage or other sustained sexual partnership, in some close relationships between a woman and a close friend, sister or mother; and for some men in relationships with 'buddies'.

2. *Social integration* is provided by relationships in which participants share concerns because they are in the same situation or striving for similar objectives. These may be provided by friends or work colleagues. In the area of social support, self-help groups may often provide a means for the social integration of the otherwise isolated person.

3. Opportunities for *nurturance* (i.e. giving nurture) where an adult takes responsibility for a child, encourages the development of a sense of being needed.

4. *Reassurance of worth* is provided by relationships that demonstrate an individual's competence in some role. This may be provided by work, or the ability to support and defend a family. The loss of a source of such reassurance is likely to result in decreased self-esteem, as, for example, for unemployed heads of families.

5. *Reliable assistance* through the provision of services or resources being made available. Friends and/or neighbours may be a source at some period and in some circumstances, but it is only among close kin that continued assistance may be expected regardless of the affective ties.

6. *Obtaining guidance* is derived from relationships with respected others, such as priests, doctors, nurses, social workers and counsellors, and

on occasion impersonal advice services which do not involve face-to-face contact.

(Bulmer 1987, p.144)

O'Brien and Lyles' (1987) five accomplishments approach the same question from a rather different angle. They are Community Participation, Community Presence, Choices/Rights, Respect and Competence. They are not strictly comparable, but one of the accomplishments points to something which seems to me to be an omission in Weiss' typology. This is the opportunity to exercise choice. It could be argued that this is implicit in the six existing categories, but lack of choice, lack of the opportunity to decide for themselves, is so much a feature of the lives of so many people with learning difficulties that I think it is vital to have 'exercise of choice' as one of the categories and so I have included it in my range of relationships, or, to be more accurate, the range of what relationships *need to provide* (as shown in the top row of Table 2.1. The dimensions relating to structural factors in the first column will be discussed shortly).

This last point is important. Clearly 'Attachment and intimacy' or 'Reassurance of worth' are not themselves relationships. They are basic needs which relationships can meet. However, it would be rather pedantic to refer all the time to the 'range of what relationships need to provide' and I will instead simply refer to 'the range of relationships'.

Before we continue Weiss' first category, 'Attachment and intimacy' needs further consideration. I have changed this to 'Belonging and attachment', as you can see in Table 2.1. I added 'belonging' because it expresses the emotional content more powerfully than 'attachment' by itself. But I have dropped 'intimacy'. In most cases a real sense of belonging and attachment will be expressed through an intimate relationship. It is important to acknowledge this when considering people with learning difficulties because for too long they have been denied the intimate relationships which many people take for granted and are an essential part of their lives. However, the reason I eventually decided to stay with 'Belonging and attachment' was that, whilst intimacy is often an integral part of such a relationship, it is not an *essential* part. It is possible for people, and not just people with learning difficulties, to gain a sense of 'belonging and attachment' without the relationship being an intimate one. It seemed important to me not to be prescriptive about the way in which a sense of 'belonging and attachment' was gained. Furthermore, I think that intimacy is more a means than an end. It is possible to be intimate with someone without necessarily arriving at a sense of belonging and attachment.

Table 2.1 Needs, structures and relationships

Structural factors, i.e. settings or occasions	Basic human emotional and cognitive needs						
	Belonging and attachment	Social integration	Nurturance	Reassurance of worth	Exercise of choice	Reliable assistance	Guidance from respected others
Residence/home	Relationship with spouse		Relationship with young nephew or nieces				
Work/education/Occupation				Relationships with workmates			
Leisure/social/spiritual		Relationships with people at church or club		Friendships at snooker club			
Supportive services and people					Going shopping with support worker	Relationships with home help	Relationship with social worker

The relationships occur where needs and structural factors (i.e. settings or occasions) intersect. The examples in the table are taken from the case studies presented in this chapter.

Relationship vacuums

The Patterns of Living course talks about 'relationship vacancies' (Atkinson and Ward 1986, p.22) which is a useful concept, but I want to use the word 'vacuum' instead. The seven categories of relationship sketched out in the previous section are not like a selection of sweets from which you can choose one or two which happen to appeal to you. They represent, albeit inadequately, fundamental elements that are necessary for our social, psychological and spiritual health. This is especially the case with 'attachment'.

> Weiss argues that the relationship that provides attachment is of central importance in the organisation of one's life. Individuals will tend to organise their lives around those relationships which provide them with attachment – usually a spouse or partner, but it could be a grown child or a close friend. Other relationships are then integrated with this central relationship. Lack of intimate relationships may have distressing consequences. (Bulmer 1987, p.145)

Stan Rivers, whose story prefaces this chapter, is an example of someone whose life lacked just that central relationship of attachment. But the reason that I prefer the term 'vacuum' to 'vacancy' is that a vacuum is something which is always likely to be filled up. It will suck in from the outside and this is precisely what appears to happen in many instances.

Mark Hastings was a man in his middle twenties. He lived with his elderly widowed mother in a comfortable owner-occupied semi-detached house. In many ways he was quite able, but he could not read or recognise numbers, though from his normal social competence you would have expected him to do both. His mother suffered from a bad back and needed Mark's help with many household tasks such as making the bed and carrying the shopping. He did this without any trouble. But Mark led a very restricted life. He sometimes went out on his own. He loved watching the bowls in the local park but had always stayed on the edge. His relationship with his mother was rather tense and he was very resentful if he thought she was trying to organise his life. In addition, from time to time when he could not cope with a situation, especially when he felt he was made to feel foolish, for example because he could not read, he would explode. In recent years his violence had become only verbal and did not generally involve anything more startling than marching out in a rather dramatic way, but it was enough to be profoundly disruptive when it came to forming relationships.

It looked at one stage as though I had managed to make some progress in enabling Mark to widen his social circle. He started going to a rambling club which was welcoming and understanding. Mark was able to go on his own and very soon he became heavily involved, going to mid week activities and meetings as well as walks at the weekends. His social life was far richer than it had ever been and he was meeting a wide cross-section of people who were disposed to be friendly. There were occasional setbacks when Mark felt slighted but the people in the club were resilient and it looked as though Mark was settling down into becoming an accepted and valued member.

One of the people in the club who was friendly and welcoming was an attractive young woman who was a bit younger than Mark. She would smile at him but her behaviour was indicative of no more than friendliness. She was already going out with another member of the club, though they were not (yet) engaged. However, Mark took her welcoming smile as indicating that she wanted the romantic involvement for which he was longing. It fell to me to go for a long walk with Mark and say that his romantic overtures were unwelcome and that she was already 'committed'. Mark's lack of a close relationship which could give him a sense of attachment and belonging did not just lead to a sense of loss because of the lack of such a relationship, but also led to inappropriate behaviour in a different category of relationship. The relationships within the club would probably fall within the category 'Social integration'. Behaviour which is appropriate in an intimate relationship is not appropriate in a social setting such as a church or club. This is not to say that it is not possible to progress from a friendly relationship in such a social setting to a more intimate relationship. Indeed that is often how intimate relationships start. But if someone like Mark has a relationship vacuum, especially at the level of 'belonging and attachment', there is always going to be a danger of different relationships, especially at the 'social integration' level, being used inappropriately and therefore breaking down.

For Mark and other people in similar situations these issues are made much more difficult by their lack of social experience. All too often they have not had a lifetime of learning the almost imperceptible signals which govern social behaviour. Thus we have the problem of intellectual disability being exacerbated by lack of social experience.

However, the fundamental point I wish to make here is that where a person – and a person with learning difficulties is especially vulnerable – has a vacuum in her or his range of relationships, especially at the 'belonging and attachment' level, there is a real danger of other relationships being sucked into that vacuum, the result being inappropriate social behaviour as happened with Mark. In the event it all proved too difficult and despite everyone's best efforts Mark left the club with a deep sense of rejection. This was sad because they had worked hard at welcoming him.

What relationships are going to give Mark a sense of self-worth? Mark was confronted with one of the most painful situations which confront people with learning difficulties. He would like a romantic relationship with an attractive woman who did not have learning difficulties – which is a very reasonable thing to want, but the harsh reality is that it is most unlikely to happen. What does one say? Try to meet up with someone of roughly your level of ability who may reciprocate your desire for a romantic relationship? Keep trying and keep being disappointed like other people often are, but other people do not start with the odds stacked against them in the same way? How is it possible to enable Mark to accept his limitations and capitalise on his competence? And how is it possible to do this when he is living with a parent who both needs his physical competence and undermines his confidence? What does empowerment mean in this context?

This great hole in the relationships of many people with learning difficulties was picked up by Margaret Flynn (1989) in her study of 88 people who had moved into their own homes from hostels or hospitals. She writes:

> According to social workers, four people had no contact with friends and eleven only had intermittent contact. In the interviews 18 people did not mention contact with others. As a recipient of two marriage invitations and many requests for further contact with the people I met, I have to conclude that some people's networks are wanting. (p.73)

This shows clearly not just the vacuum in relationships but also the inappropriate use of other categories of relationship.

The example I have given and, it would seem, the examples from Margaret Flynn, are where the most acutely felt vacuum is, in 'belonging and attachment', but the same process operates with other levels of relationship. Jack and Eileen Parsons had been married for five years. Jack had no friends at all. He got very angry when, for example, he was beaten at snooker and so drove people away. His relationship with his wife, which the social worker described as obsessive, was *not* an adequate substitute for the weaker ties of ordinary friendship (i.e. in the 'Social integration' and 'Reassurance of worth' categories). Jack needed friends with whom to play snooker and similar activities and this was a need Eileen could not meet.

I went to a support group run by two social workers for people with learning difficulties shortly before Christmas and I found myself immediately classed as a friend who qualified for a Christmas card from most of the people there. This seemed to indicate a vacuum, perhaps in 'reassurance of worth', for to receive Christmas cards is to be reassured that you are the sort of person with whom people like to be friends. Atkinson and Williams (1990) put the point well:

> The absence of friends can lead to an extended definition of friendship. This means, for example, coming to regard neighbours as 'friends' on the flimsy basis of the occasional nod, smile, or kind word... The extended definition of friendship does not remove the feeling of loneliness – but it may disguise the isolation. (p.68)

Atkinson and Williams also mention social workers, home helps and other staff who come to be seen as friends. There are other factors at play here but it is another indication of the need for a full range of relationships to fill the vacuum which many people with learning difficulties have in their relationships and to counteract the tendency to make inappropriate transfers from one category or level of relationship to another. In this case the transfer was from 'Reliable assistance' or 'Guidance' to 'Reassurance of worth' or even 'Belonging and attachment'.

To sum up, a full range of relationships on the lines set out by Weiss is a common human need. If one of those levels or categories is missing in someone's life, they will either just be the poorer for it like Stan Rivers and suffer accordingly, or there is evidence that some people with learning difficulties, especially because of their lack of social skills and experience, are in danger of making inappropriate transfers, especially from the 'social integration' level to the 'belonging and attachment' level. This is likely to foul up relationships, as happened with Mark Hastings.

This should be qualified by the acknowledgement that there did seem to be some people involved in the project who appeared to be content without any obvious intimate relationships, but where this was the case there did generally seem to be compensatory relationships elsewhere. The clearest example I have found of this comes, not from my own work, but from Atkinson and Ward (1986):

> Alan Perkins is 50 years old. He lived in a mental handicap hospital for 31 years, then in a group home for two years. Now he lives in a flat in a small block of modern council flats.

> Now he lives alone and has to seek social engagements outside the house. He abandoned not only his group home, but the rest of the mental handicap trappings, the ATC, and other mentally handicapped people. Of the latter, his social worker commented, 'I've noticed, out in the street, that if anyone comes along who is handicapped, he will not tolerate them, he puts them down. He's trying to make contact with ordinary people. He doesn't want handicapped people.'

> Alan seeks to engage neighbours, tradesmen and people in the street. His relations with his neighbours began badly when his electrical tinkerings, in the first weekend, led to the whole block of flats being plunged into darkness, and all televisions silenced. His social worker had to intervene, to remonstrate with Alan, found hiding, and to soothe neighbours' frayed nerves. He has erased this inauspicious start from the communal memory by his subsequent friendliness. He calls on people to chat, and to check that elderly neighbours are well, and they reciprocate with kindness. The neighbours have donated furniture, donated and hung curtains, and now Alan can leave his rent with neighbours when the rent man is due to call. His social worker commented, 'They have taken him into their hearts!'

> Alan has also expended energy in cultivating tradespeople. The social worker described this investment: 'He is aware that people give drinks at Christmas. He likes to make sure he has plenty of drinks in. Then

he invites people in, for example, the butcher and the greengrocer. I heard them say, "We'll be round for our drinks Alan", and he replied "OK, whenever you like".' Alan engages people out and about in the neighbourhood too, always having time to stop and chat, his social worker observing: 'A lot of people know him. A lot of people stop and talk to him.' His social worker observed that he has devised a 'strategy of coping', an easy and informal manner, and a genuine interest in others, which is reciprocated, and which has led to the construction of his good supporting network. (p.26)

It is interesting and a bit disturbing that Alan rejects anyone who is handicapped. Mark reacted in a similar way.

There was another way of coping and this was by withdrawal. The clearest example of this was Christopher Johnson. He raises the vital question of structures. Relationships are sustained and supported by structures. They cannot exist in a vacuum and this is what we look at in the next section.

Relationships and structures

It was Christopher Johnson who brought home the message that relationships and structures have to be considered together. He was severely handicapped. He did not talk at all and made little response to anything that was said to him. When I first visited the house and talked with his widowed mother all he did was to lie on the floor and play with his sock. It was hard to see how anything creative could be done to enrich his life. However, his key worker at the day centre he used to attend (rather sporadically) mentioned that the one person who was able to get a response out of Christopher was Mary Cartwright. Who, I wondered, was she? A psychologist, a senior day care worker or a communication therapist? She was none of these. She was a quite severely handicapped woman with a little speech, a great sense of fun and inexhaustible energy. Sadly, Mary had been moved to another day centre about two years previously. The relationship with her was by far the most positive relationship that Christopher seemed to have with anyone. Could it be re-established? Could Mary be moved back? No, she was well established in her new centre. Could Christopher be taken on at least one day a week to the centre she was attending now? It was quite close to his home. No, the transport and escort which would be needed were not available and there was no prospect of them being available. (Finding that out took three weeks.) Was there somewhere where they could meet? Mary had Wednesdays at her hostel. That would be a good day for her to see Christopher. The first occasion we arranged Christopher was ill and it had to be cancelled. I was already booked for the next three Wednesdays, but the day eventually came and I took Christopher by car, as arranged with the staff at the hostel, to meet up with Mary. The message had not been passed on and a member of staff had taken Mary out and was not expected back for an hour or so! We did not manage to try again for six weeks but eventually they met. Mary was certainly pleased to see Christopher. His reactions were difficult to gauge but he certainly did not object. However, after making him a cup of tea and drinking it, there was nothing they could do together so the visit seemed rather flat. Was that the end of the road? If Christopher's key worker was right that Mary meant more to Christopher than anyone else (except his mother), and she had known him for a good many years, then it seemed important to continue to pursue this lead and not be put off by this apparently unpromising meeting. It seemed all the more important because Christopher was severely handicapped and it was important to make the most of any relationships that he did have.

It seemed to me that the most hopeful way of making life a bit more interesting for Christopher was via the ebullient Mary. I spent some time with her and her key worker at the day centre to discover what Mary was interested in. She loved going shopping, she loved going to the park, she loved seeing animals. She would respond positively to almost anything. Therefore the plan was to make it possible for Christopher to go along with Mary and share something of her enthusiasm. But for this to happen they needed to be able to meet regularly and that could not depend on me.

I discussed the possibilities with Mrs Johnson and it emerged that she had another son who lived quite close and he had a car and should be able to take Christopher and herself. It did take place once, after many phone calls, and seemed to be enjoyed by all parties. Not only did Christopher go but also his mother and his sister-in-law. I left it with Mrs Johnson that she would fix the next visit and primed the hostel staff to be ready. I suggested that next time it might be worthwhile going out with Mary and enabling Christopher to see something new. But nothing came of it despite a lot of encouragement and eventually I just gave up. The staff at the hostel were not in a position to help much. They were too short-staffed and it did not seem to fit into the way they saw their job. Mrs Johnson was probably just too worn down by the daily slog of looking after Christopher, so apathy, or perhaps it would be more accurate to say my exhaustion, won the day and Christopher's social life collapsed back into consisting of his mother and no one else. The structure that was needed to support wider social contacts was simply not there. To widen the range of Christopher's relationships required attention to the structures of his life. It became clear that if anything effective was going to be done to widen the range of Christopher's relationships, it was the structures which needed attention.

What are the relevant structures?
The experience of the project suggested that the relevant structures are quite straightforward. The main ones are:

1. Residence/home
2. Work/education/occupation

3. Leisure/social/spiritual

4. Supportive services and people

1. RESIDENCE/HOME

Clearly where anyone lives has a considerable impact on their relationships. Christopher's situation was very different to someone living by themselves or with a partner, or in a small group home or in a hostel. In addition it is vital to consider not just where people are living *now*, but where they lived *in the past*. The significance of hostels and hospitals where people lived in the past was striking. The addition of 'home' is to make the point that everyone lived somewhere but not everyone had a home.

2. WORK/EDUCATION/OCCUPATION

These are grouped together because they are what people do in work time even if they do not work. Amongst the people I saw only one person was in an ordinary job. About half spent at least some time in day care at an Adult Training Centre or its new manifestation, a local training centre where there was much more emphasis on people finding activities in the locality such as helping in or attending a lunch club or going to a local pub. Others combined attendance at day care provided by the social services department with going to adult education classes; some just attended adult education classes. A number had no daytime occupation whatsoever. One of the most forcible impressions that came out of this work for me was how many people with learning difficulties spent their time wasting time. For many there seemed to be an almost total lack of meaningful occupation and this included the time that some people spent in day care.

The same point as was made about residence also needs to be made here. Where people attended day or similar centres in the past is also important for understanding people's present relationships.

3. LEISURE/SOCIAL/SPIRITUAL

This is a much wider category. It links with the previous categories because much of the time people are attending day care they are occupied with leisure activities. However, the distinction is still a valid one and it concerns more what people do outside what is usually considered work time. It includes attendance at clubs such as the Gateway Club, the PHAB (Physically Handicapped Abled Bodied) Club, youth clubs, and so on. It also covers matters of the spirit, of which the most obvious example is membership of a church. Flynn and Hirst (1992) point out how important this category can be: 'When access to paid employment is limited, personal relationships, social contacts and leisure assume a much greater importance, not least in providing activity, variety, a sense of identity and self esteem' (p.69).

4. SUPPORTIVE SERVICES AND PEOPLE

This covers services, apart from residential and day care, from whatever source, but in practice they were almost entirely statutory services (mostly health and social services). It includes support from social workers, community nurses and other community support workers and home helps. Some of the key workers in day care stray across this boundary and are also very important as supporters of people in their homes.

In addition parents or other family members sometimes played an important supportive role for people who had moved into their own homes, and occasionally such roles were played purely out of goodwill by people who were not related at all.

Provision of transport is also a vital part of the support that many people with learning difficulties need in order to be able to maintain their relationships.

The need to relate structures to the range of relationships

It is no use considering structures by themselves. The structures which had been set up with and around Stan Rivers appeared to be exemplary but they had left him feeling he had a great hole inside himself. It is no use considering relationships by themselves because without the structure to support them the relationships will not survive. Therefore the two have to be considered in relationship to one another. Only then is it possible to consider such key questions as what structures encourage the development of trusting, intimate relationships, or integration, or self-esteem, or the exercise of choice.

Sustaining and developing relationships

But even that is not enough because both relationships and structures need sustaining and developing. There is nothing mechanistic about the development of relationships. It is one thing to acknowledge the importance of structures in enabling relationships to develop; it is quite another to assume that getting the structures right is all that needs to be done. Structures only provide the setting which makes the development of relationships more possible.

A pattern of service which accepts the priority and importance of sustaining, nurturing and developing the relationships of people with learning difficulties, will have to accept that this requires the commitment of time, energy and resources. People with learning difficulties *have* learning difficulties and therefore will often have a continuing need for support and help with their relationships, as do some of the general population. This is particularly the case where people have had so little normal social experience from which to learn. It is just one example of the way people with learning difficulties are doubly handicapped, first by their learning difficulties then by their lack of social experience.

The basic hypothesis

It is now possible to state my basic hypothesis. For people with learning difficulties to lead fulfilled lives they need to experience a range of relationships in order to meet the range of basic human emotional and cognitive needs on the lines set out by Weiss. Where there is a vacuum in that range of relationships, especially at the level of those that meet the need for 'belonging and attachment', inappropriate transfers of behaviour from that level to other levels may occur. Wherever a person lacks a relationship meeting the need for 'belonging and attachment', the cost in terms of personal anguish to the person concerned may be high.

This range of relationships cannot exist in a vacuum and needs appropriate structures to support it. Relationships should always be considered in the context of the necessary supporting structures. Both the range of relationships and the structures which support them will need sustaining and developing.

Combining needs, structures and relationships

The lynch pin of the model is the recognition that there is a *range* of basic human emotional and cognitive needs which have to be met if life is to be worth living. They are not all equally important but they are all important. These needs can only be met through appropriate relationships. These relationships require a suitable setting or settings in which they can develop, that is, the relationships required to meet the basic human needs have to be considered within the context of the structures or settings that are needed to support those relationships. A simple way to do that is to construct a matrix which relates the two. This has been done in Table 2.1.

Let me emphasise the importance of this matrix. It is a simple means of enabling anyone concerned with the well-being of someone with learning difficulties to consider both the question: 'Is my range of relationships adequate?' and the vital complementary question: 'Does attention need to be paid to the structures to enable the necessary relationships to develop?'. It is designed to show where action needs to be taken to enable someone to have a chance of leading a full and satisfying life. It could be described as a tool for empowerment at the most basic level – the power which comes from realising that you are a loved and valued person.

The four general areas that need to be covered under structural factors are shown in Figure 2.1, that is, residence/home; work/education/ occupation; leisure/social/spiritual; and supportive services and people. The table shows intersection of needs and these structures. Thus the need for belonging and attachment may well be met in the home by a spouse; the need for social integration by friendly people in a church; the need to give nurturance by looking after a young nephew or niece when on a regular weekly visit to a married sister; the need for reassurance of worth in a work place by sympathetic

fellow employees and a good boss; the need for exercise of choice by going on
a regular shopping expedition with a support worker or relative; the need for
reliable assistance by a team of home helps; the need for guidance from
respected others from a volunteer at Mencap or a social worker.

The key issues

1. The overwhelming impact on people's relationships came from where
   they spent a lot of time, thus the dominance of where people lived
   and where they 'worked' which, for most people, was the Adult
   Training Centre. This was also true of where people *used* to live or
   the training centre they went to *in the past* which were often the
   source of long-established relationships. But these friendships had
   often been broken by people being moved around the learning
   difficulties system with little or no regard to their important
   relationships. The restoration and sustaining of these relationships
   would make a major contribution to people's sense of well-being.

   The staff in residential and day care establishments, especially
   people's key workers (i.e. people who were in nearly daily contact),
   were often important figures in people's lives and would be counted,
   quite legitimately, as friends. As they were paid and might move
   these were perilous relationships for people with learning difficulties,
   but some of these workers seemed to be in a key position when it
   came to trying to develop wider social contacts for people with
   learning difficulties.

2. Where adults lived with their parents, it was generally the close
   relationship with their parents which gave them a sense of 'belonging
   and attachment'. This was clearly of great importance but it often
   appeared to be the case that people did not develop *other*
   relationships which also gave a sense of 'belonging and attachment'.
   In particular they did not develop such relationships with people *of
   their own age*. This put them at risk emotionally. In a number of cases
   the relationship with the parents came under strain because it failed
   to mature in the way that was needed to maintain a sound
   relationship between adults. In all cases it was likely that the parents
   would die first. In either case people were in danger of being landed
   in an emotional black hole with no relationship which gave a sense
   of 'belonging and attachment'.

3. The position of those who had left the parental home early in their
   lives could be even more devastating. It appeared that in some cases
   they had little, if any, sense of 'belonging and attachment'. Stan
   Rivers, whose story appears at the beginning, is one example of this.

4. Where people had found partners, whether married or otherwise, they seemed generally to be more emotionally secure. This was so regardless of the stage of life at which they had left the parental home.

5. The structural implications of this last point are important. First there is the question of where people could meet in order to find a partner. This could be particularly difficult for those who rejected contacts with other people with learning difficulties but yearned for a romantic relationship with a 'normal' person which they were unlikely to achieve. Second, such relationships needed sustaining. Support groups/clubs organised by social workers and community nurses played a most effective role in this respect and were one of the richest sources of relationships.

6. Making links via shared leisure interests proved difficult but the Mencap Gateway club was valued, especially the snooker, as an important part of the structure of the week and a source of valuable relationships for a group of more able men, some of whom were living lives quite well integrated into the general community. There was also considerable potential in links with the churches, but there were occasions when these needed help and support from the services if they were going to be able to play their part in enriching the range of relationships of people with learning difficulties.

7. The structural questions that needed to be asked about relationships are not complicated. The starting point is clear:

   • how are we going to respect and honour the choices people have made already and find ways of enabling them to maintain or re-establish existing or past relationships which they do or did find precious?

   But it is important not to stop there but to go on to consider:

   • where are people going to be able to meet the range of people they want to meet?

   • where are different *kinds* of relationships going to be able to develop?

   • how are the relationships going to be *maintained*?

If we are concerned about empowerment in everyday life, surely this offers a good agenda with which to start.

References

Atkinson, D. and Ward, L. (1986) *Mental Handicap: Patterns for Living: Workbook 1: Living and Learning*, p.22. Milton Keynes: Open University Press.

Atkinson, D. and Williams, P. (1990) *Mental Handicap: Changing Perspectives: Workbook 2: Networks*. Milton Keynes: Open University Press.

Booth, T., Simons, K. and Booth, W. (1990) *Outward Bound: Relocation and Community Care for People with Learning Difficulties*. Milton Keynes: Open University Press.

Bulmer, M. (1987) *The Social Basis of Community Care*. London: Allen and Unwin.

Calligan, B. (undated) 'A poem for Michael.' *Calderdale Citizen Advocacy Newsletter*. Halifax.

Firth, H. and Rapley, R.T.J. (1990) *From Acquaintance to Friendship: Issues for People with Learning Disabilities*. Kidderminster: BIMH Publications.

Flynn, M.C. (1989) *Independent Living for Adults with Mental Handicaps: A Place of Our Own*. London: Cassel.

Flynn, M. and Hirst, M. (1992) *This Year, Next Year, Sometime…? Learning Disability and Adulthood*. London: National Development Team.

O'Brien, J. and Lyle, C. (1987) *Framework for Accomplishment*. Decatur, GA, USA: Responsive Systems Associates.

Ramcharan, P. and Grant, G. (1992) *Empowering Persons with a Disadvantage within the Research Process*. Paper presented at 9th IASSMD World Congress, Gold Coast, Australia.

Weiss, R.S. (1975) 'The provisions of social relationships.' In Z. Rubin (ed) *Doing Unto Others*. Englewood Cliffs, NJ: Prentice-Hall.

Weiss, R.S. (1979) 'The fund of sociality.' *Transation/Society 6*, 9, 36–43.

CHAPTER 3

Shouting the Loudest
Self-Advocacy, Power and Diversity

Jan Walmsley and Jackie Downer

About this chapter

This chapter has been produced by two women Jan who is a lecturer and Jackie who is a self-advocacy development worker. This partnership came about because Jan was invited to write a chapter for the book and, as it was about self-advocacy and empowerment, she didn't feel qualified to do so without assistance from an experienced self-advocacy worker. For this reason she asked Jackie to be her co-author. Jan actually wrote it. Jackie's part was to generate ideas from her own experience and her work as a self-advocacy development worker, and to advise Jan on how to improve it once the first draft was written. This explains why Jackie's contributions are in quotation marks. We thought her ideas came over better as direct quotations than they would if Jan rewrote them and put them in 'book language'. It hasn't been easy. Jan was anxious to keep the language and ideas clear so that Jackie could fully understand what she was signing her name to and found the first draft contained more of her than of Jackie Jackie said she wasn't worried because she could trust Jan.

Here is the result of our work together.

Introduction

Self-advocacy is about many things. Gary Bourlet as Chair of People First said: 'Self-advocacy enables us to make choices and make our decisions and control the way that our lives should be made' (quoted in Simons 1992, p.5).

A list produced by members of People First, London and Thames, describes self-advocacy as:

- speaking up
- standing up for your rights
- making choices

- being independent
- taking responsibility for yourself.

Self-advocacy is about people with learning difficulties as a group gaining power to fight for their rights, rather than, as in the past, being passive recipients of the charity, or otherwise, of others. This is illustrated by the fact that people with Down's Syndrome are disputing the right of women who may be carrying a child with Down's Syndrome to decide automatically on abortion. Delegates at People First's conference for people with Down's Syndrome in 1994 described this as 'very wrong' (People First 1995). It is far more difficult to assume that people with Down's Syndrome should be eradicated when media personalities such as Anya Souza are clearly speaking out for the right of individuals like themselves to live. The belief that people with Down's Syndrome are to be pitied, and may therefore be better off never to have been born, is challenged when such 'pitiable' people join in public debate and argue the opposite. Self-advocacy is not only a means by which people can make minor choices. It's about people with learning difficulties challenging current orthodoxies on life and death matters, such as genetic screening and abortion.

Self-advocacy is also about establishing an identity for yourself. Jackie, for example, thinks it's about believing in yourself and what you can do. As a black woman with the label of learning difficulties she has had to struggle to believe she has a contribution to make.

> What made me get there was the strength of the Lord, my mother, a strong black woman, and teachers who believed in me, not at school, oh no, not at school, college teachers. I feel proud now because they think people with learning difficulties can't do anything and I can prove to them that we can do things.

Of others, she says, 'I want to see people respect those of us with a learning difficulty like they respect themselves – if they respect themselves'.

Self-advocacy in the UK started when some people with learning difficulties attended the 1984 People First Conference in the USA and, on their return, decided to set up a People's First branch in London. The development of self-advocacy was slow and patchy. In 1988 Bronach Crawley found that the majority of groups were within services such as day centres and hospitals, and relatively few were independent of services. She argued that independent groups gave their members more opportunity to challenge fundamentals, whilst service-based groups were limited in their scope (Crawley 1988). At the time of writing (1995) we know that there are still many sizeable towns and rural areas where there are no recognised independent self-advocacy groups – whilst in Liverpool, which has a strong tradition of independently funded and supported self-advocacy, lack of funds is imperilling its future. However, self-advocacy as a movement has gained considerable momentum in Britain.

In 1994 an all England People First Conference was held as a means of creating People First for England. Before that date the largest and best resourced People First branch, London and Thames, had created a certain amount of animosity by appearing to speak for People First nationally. The attempt to create an England-wide organisation was a sign of the growing maturity of self-advocacy. The idea had powerful backing. Two government ministers spoke at the Conference and answered delegates' questions, promising to consult with People First for England on matters of interest to them. One minister promised that people applying for Department of Health grants to hold conferences relevant to people with learning difficulties should have to justify any decision to exclude them as delegates or speakers. After the Conference the Department of Health made money available to resource the creation of a national network. The Department also awarded People First a large grant for its 'Making it Easy' project in preference to bids from other, non-user-directed organisations.

Although self-advocacy still has an uncertain foothold in many areas, it has come a long way since the days when it was mainly about setting up day centre user committees and allowing questions to be asked about the siting of coffee machines or the quality of toilet paper (Crawley 1988). Yet gaining a certain amount of political clout raises new questions about self-advocacy and its future direction. A movement which appears to have some power may attract people, with or without learning difficulties, who are more interested in gaining power for themselves than promoting the interests of a broad constituency. And how can self-advocacy ensure that it genuinely represents all kinds of people with learning difficulties, from those who were mistakenly labelled in childhood to people with no speech and with numerous other impairments?

In this chapter we try to do three things:

- we discuss the diverse identities of people with learning difficulties

- we point to some potential conflicts within self-advocacy

- we explore some strategies which can help to ensure that the broad self-advocacy movement represents different interest groups.

Diversity and people with learning difficulties

The label 'learning disabilities' is notoriously hard to define (Jenkins 1991). This means that the term includes people with many different social characteristics and abilities, and sometimes various medical conditions. Research studies have shown that it is more common for people of lower social classes (Rutter and Madge 1976) and for black people (Bryan, Dadzie and Scafe 1985) to be given the label of special educational needs or learning difficulties. However, specific syndromes such as Down's Syndrome affect people from all social classes.

There was until recently a failure by researchers and practitioners to recognise that people with this label also have identities as men and women, black or white people, Jewish or Moslem, and hetero- or homosexual, indeed as working, middle or upper class. The main emphasis in classification has traditionally been 'mild', 'moderate' or 'severe'. The early days of the self-advocacy movement in Britain were dominated by white men who, like Gary Bourlet, were relatively articulate and confident. Recent research into self-advocacy groups suggests that men still tend to dominate (Thomson and McCarthy 1995), a view that Jackie endorses from personal experience. 'In all the groups I go to,' she says, 'men are shouting the loudest.' There is thus a danger that as self-advocacy grows in importance, its leading figures will represent the interests of white men with mild learning difficulties and other groups of people with learning difficulties will not be seen or heard. This is obviously the case when the language of self-advocacy – speaking up, finding a voice – uses imagery which excludes people who communicate in ways other than speech. It is relatively easy to find out the views, experiences and opinions of self-advocates with speech. The recent Open University course 'Working as Equal People' (1996) includes many examples. Where the team found real difficulties was in representing the views of people with little or no speech. Inevitably this was done on their behalf by family members, advocates and other people with learning difficulties.

Although other people with learning difficulties may well have more empathy with their ways of experiencing the world than non-disabled people, it is not safe to assume that people who have the same label will necessarily have identical interests or be able to represent others adequately. What we will argue in this paper is that single interest groups, such as women's groups or black peoples' groups, are an important stage in the development of a truly comprehensive self-advocacy movement. As Jackie puts it: 'At some stage everybody needs their separate groups'. But the 'politics of identity' can only take us so far, and we also argue that ultimately people with learning difficulties have enough in common to unite them, as long as there is mutual respect for, and recognition of, different interests.

Awareness of difference

In their book *Normalisation, a Reader for the Nineties* (1992), Hilary Brown and Helen Smith argue that normalisation has tended to reproduce and reinforce existing gender inequalities in society:

> New services have tended to imitate the nuclear family in grouping people together in small houses, women in these groups are likely to find themselves in a housekeeping role, in this case servicing men whom they have not chosen and with whom they do not have close personal ties. (pp.159–160)

The gender blindness inherent in conceptualisations of normalisation, such as social role valorisation (Wolfensberger and Thomas 1983), denied women with learning difficulties access to a knowledge of feminism, and tied them into conventional, often subordinate, roles. We would add that normalisation has done little to eradicate, and sometimes has fostered, racism and heterosexism, as well as sexism.

Furthermore, 'normalisation' implies that disabled people are not normal. Jackie put it like this: 'I disagree with normal because I don't think because you've got a disability you're not normal'. The emphasis in normalisation on the value of relationships with people who are not disabled tends to devalue disabled people. Yet the reality of life in institutions or in the community is often that relationships with other disabled people are very important. Not only may they be the only people available for relationships, they may be the people with whom other disabled people have most in common, an issue explored graphically in the film *We Don't Want to Talk About It*, where the mother of a dwarf refuses to acknowledge that her daughter is in any way different to other people. The film ends with a powerful image – the young woman runs away with the travelling circus where she for the first time came into contact with people like her.

Silence often surrounds the stigma of having the learning difficulties label. Staff and families try to shield people they are close to from a knowledge of being different because it may be hurtful. Jackie remembered how this felt: 'I was a slow learner at school. I felt embarrassed about it and I never talked to anyone about having a learning difficulty. Everyone called my school 'spastic school you dunce'. I felt ashamed. I thought I was going to work in a toilet when I left school'. The impression that people with learning difficulties are often unwilling, or unable, to acknowledge that they have a label is given weight by the findings from research studies which indicate that many people do not readily identify with it (Aull Davies and Jenkins 1991; Walmsley 1995).

In contrast to normalisation which, at least in its cruder forms, tends to minimise and deny difference (Perrin and Nirje 1989) people who join self-advocacy groups openly acknowledge their identity as people with learning difficulties. Ken Simons (1992) found in his research with self-advocates that many were fully aware of having a label, and its implications. Like feminism, Black Power and Gay Pride, self-advocacy can be seen as a way of celebrating difference rather than denying it, and opens the way for a recognition of people with learning difficulties as a group with an identity of its own, an identity to own publicly, not hide.

However, being a person with a learning difficulty is not an all-encompassing identity. People also have a race, a class, a gender and a sexual orientation. How far are people aware of these identities? In the rest of this chapter we examine issues pertaining to particular groups, and cite some examples of ways in which their ability to make their views and needs known can be fostered.

Women's issues

Although research and our own experiences suggest that men often set the agenda in self-advocacy, awareness of women's issues within self-advocacy groups is increasing. Our own knowledge of practice suggests that there are numerous women's groups with a variety of aims, mostly within service settings. Several prominent members of People First of London and Thames are women, including, at the time of writing, the Chair, and People First also have a worker and supporter responsible for women's issues. The England People First Conference organisers stipulated that each geographical area should choose one man and one woman to represent them, and this meant that women were numerically equal.

The modest success that women have had in making themselves a visible and influential presence in some leading self-advocacy organisations has followed some hard work in women-only settings. We draw on the reports from two national conferences for women, Women First in Nottingham in 1992 (see Walmsley 1993), and Women in Learning Disability (WILD) in London in 1994 to demonstrate that some issues addressed in women-only settings are specific to women, whilst others appear to affect most people regardless of gender.

Women First claimed to be the first national conference for women with learning difficulties. Women with learning difficulties were in a majority because non-disabled women were only allowed to attend if two disabled women agreed to accompany them. On its agenda were two major themes, celebrating women and sexuality. One of the most impressive events was the workshop on abuse, called Body Strong, attended by over 40 women, some of whom had never before spoken about being abused (Walmsley 1993). The sheer size of the response surprised the organisers, and it seems unlikely that in a mixed event so many women would have the confidence to speak out.

The *WILD Conference Report* (Etherington, Flynn and Platts 1994) highlights the importance of separate spaces to discuss sexuality, relationships and women's health issues. Other parts of the *Report*, such as references to the importance of work and money, the need for someone to talk to about bereavement and opportunities for travel, leisure and getting out and about independently, are things which women have in common with men.

How can self-advocacy groups best take women's issues forward? Jackie identifies the problem as one of agenda-setting. Mixed groups, she says, 'don't concentrate on sexuality or lesbian issues for women'. The Powerhouse, a London-based group, was created specifically to focus on a pressing issue for women, the need to feel safe from abuse. The discovery in a women's class at a college in east London that the majority of students felt unsafe on the streets, in their homes and in service settings, led them to create the Powerhouse to campaign for a safe house for women who had experienced sexual abuse. The importance of single issue campaigning is underlined by their success in opening the Beverley Lewis House in 1995, a facility that is unashamedly and unambiguously for women. Whether a self-advocacy organisation that was less specifically concerned with women's issues could have taken on such a project and brought it to fruition is debatable.

These examples show that women-only events and organisations give women the space and the confidence to define what is important to them as women. As Jackie says: 'If you're doing a movement for women you've got to know them'. There are areas of common ground where men and women can helpfully work together, but there are equally clearly areas which are of particular importance to women, and self-advocacy as a whole must be strengthened by the existence of diverse groups, some with specific women-only agendas.

Issues of race and culture

People with learning difficulties are born into particular races and cultures. Services and practitioners ignored this for many years (Baxter *et al* 1990). In hospitals particularly, people of different races were forcibly anglicised. Ashuk, an Asian man, was renamed Brian by the staff in the hospital where he lived (Cambridge, Hays and Knapp 1994). Dalip Mahrra, a Moslem, attended church services in his hospital. It was only after leaving that staff helped him to make contact with the local Moslem community (King 1991).

The Black People First Conference (Black People First 1993) highlighted some key issues for black people with learning difficulties. The Conference produced a charter which included reference to the need for services to be sensitive to language, culture and diet. However, creating an awareness of a black identity amongst people who have not had the opportunity even to recognise their difference from the majority white culture requires, Jackie argues, long-term strategies. We now look at some ways of helping people to assess the importance of their racial identity.

The Black Friendly Group is a group of black people with learning difficulties who meet fortnightly in south London. The group was started by Jackie and is co-run by her and another black woman, Debbie. This account is taken from Jackie's contribution to an audio tape made with the group. First of all Jackie explains that self-advocacy for black people needs to begin with their own recognition that they are black, and that can take a long time:

> When we are children we grow up and our parents don't talk about being black or having learning difficulties, and it's like if they'd have given them [the children] the chance they could have talked more about it, even communicated more, but not in words sometimes. They're learning now, after 20 years, all the development has gone and it's going to take time. All they know about being black is being called 'nigger' or 'blackie', you know, and some of them find it hard being

black even now and they've been in the Black Friendly Group for at least three to four years now. There's no positive image of black people, there's no culture, there's nothing to say I'm different to somebody else, only if someone calls you a name, and you're so used to white society, everything is white, what do you expect? Even people who are professionals want to be white, they don't like their colour, and it's not just learning difficulties, it's other black people too.

Jackie and her co-worker, Debbie, have developed strategies to help the members of the group recognise that they are black:

Every time when we come here I ask, 'Is anybody in this group white? Stand up anybody who is white'. And everybody looks at the colour of their skin and says, 'I'm darker' or 'I'm lighter, but I'm not white'. So we usually do that every time we come just to feel positive about ourselves as black people.

Another strategy is simple role play. The supporters call people racist names and urge them to respond. The most common response is to turn away. The role plays are followed by discussion of different strategies people can adopt when faced with this type of racist abuse.

The group is also a comfortable place to be, a chance to enjoy relaxing with other black people and to visit local black cultural events together, despite considerable problems with transport as most members have never learned to use public transport.

The lesson from the Black Friendly Group is that many black people with learning difficulties are used to dealing in a passive way with the double discrimination they experience. Because of this, immediate integration with mainstream self-advocacy won't necessarily get black people's issues recognised. Groups where people can learn about being black appear to be an important stage in developing a solid base for the participation of black people in the wider self-advocacy movement.

Working for a recognition of their black identity can pose difficulties for the facilitators. It can be frustrating that the pace of change is slow. As Jackie says, 'I find myself in difficult times with myself. Sometimes I push them, but do I push them too hard?'.

Despite Jackie's reservations, there is evidence for the success of this approach in the achievements of the Black Friendly Group. Seven of its members went as delegates to the National Self-Advocacy Conference at Bangor in 1994 where they were the largest single group of black people.

There are, however, pitfalls if we assume that everyone must claim an ethnic or religious identity if they were born into a particular community. Some people make a conscious decision to turn their backs on their ethnic group. Simone Aspis, for example, says: 'As a person with learning difficulties I feel ashamed of being part of the Jewish community'. Simone argues that the Jewish community is disablist in its outlook, and she does not wish to be part of it (Aspis, personal communication). Of course, this does not mean that Jewish self-advocacy is to blame, but it does sound a warning about blanket assumptions that people want to be part of a wider cultural or racial group.

Issues for gay, lesbian and bisexual people with learning difficulties

The possibility that people with learning difficulties may have gay, lesbian or bisexual identities has not been considered until very recently. Hilary Brown (1994) argues that normalisation has emphasised the desirability of fostering heterosexual relationships: 'Sex education for people with learning difficulties tends to have focused on biological rather than social issues and to have assumed a heterosexist preference and a familial context for all relationships' (p.131). Given the well-known difficulties people with learning difficulties experience when trying to establish 'normal' sexual relationships, the option of positively choosing homosexuality is one that few people have been able to entertain. As with issues of race and culture, people may not know that there are alternatives. At the 1992 Women First Conference a workshop for lesbian women was held. Few women with learning difficulties opted for this workshop, and in reviewing the Conference one of the organisers commented that she might have liked a workshop to find out about lesbianism, but knew too little about it to know whether she was entitled to attend a workshop for lesbians (Walmsley 1993).

Undoubtedly there are men with learning difficulties who do have sex with men, but this is usually covert, often exploitative, and people who do so neither have access to safe sex information nor are encouraged to build a positive gay identity (South East London Health Authority Needs Assessment Project, nd). Nigel Bull, sexuality worker at People First in London, and himself a gay man, explains that where people do make the choice of same sex relationships they are excluded from gay and lesbian life through ignorance, through lack of money to go to bars and clubs, through poor access in places where gay men and lesbians meet, and through discriminatory attitudes from non-disabled gay people (Bull, personal communication).

Like much of heterosexist society, self-advocacy groups are unlikely to be places where gay men and lesbians will have the opportunity to identify themselves as such, to explore issues of importance to them and to put their needs across. Peer groups appear to Nigel Bull to be one way forward, but the fact that gay men and lesbians with learning difficulties are invisible, sometimes even to themselves, has meant that to date there is little practice to report.

People with severe disabilities

A significant challenge for self-advocacy, and those who support it, is to find ways of including people who are severely disabled. In using this phrase we include people who have additional impairments, such as deafness or partial sight, and also people who have little or no speech. Self-advocacy organisations are often more aware than many organisations of the needs of people who are physically disabled, but lack of resources may well prevent them from using buildings with wheelchair access and hearing loops, and from employing signers. The technical solutions to including people who are physically disabled are, however, well known. More problematic, because not susceptible to readily available technological answers, is the challenge of 'giving a voice' to people without speech. It is far easier for most of us to work with people with whom we can readily communicate through speech. Jackie observes that people with learning difficulties need to examine their own behaviour in this respect:

> We as disabled people need to look at ourselves. Don't segregate people but try to let them belong in a different way. I find it hard understanding them. We don't know how to do it. I would love people to integrate but I haven't got an answer.

One step to resolving this at the England People First Conference was to use positive discrimination. The organising committee realised that if areas were allowed to send only two delegates they would be unlikely to choose people with severe disabilities. Therefore, they agreed to set aside some additional income obtained from selling the right to video the Conference to pay for the participation of ten people with severe disabilities. Jackie commented on how unusual it was to see people with severe disabilities at a large self-advocacy conference. However, the Conference was run at a pace which suited the more mildly disabled delegates. Speaking of her experience at the Conference, Jack that is, recalled her delight at seeing people with multiple and profound disabilities present, but noted the impossibility of their participating fully: 'I'm so used to saying 'my needs', tough luck about the others. They're somewhere else. I think it can work but it takes time. And we, as people with learning difficulties, we got no time'.

Again, it seems, this group of people have such specific requirements that expecting self-advocacy organisations to incorporate them when better resourced agencies have so signally failed to do so, is unlikely to bear fruit. This is not an argument for exclusion. The presence of multiply disabled people at events like conferences is important for visibility and self-esteem. But we return to our argument that the interests of this group will be best served by arrangements which allow a specific focus on particular needs. CHANGE, like Powerhouse, a London-based organisation controlled by disabled people, campaigns for a recognition by people with learning difficulties and by staff of the rights of people with a sensory loss and the services they might need. CHANGE's work has highlighted the prevalence of hearing and sight loss amongst people with learning difficulties. As many as one in three may be affected, but services are slow to recognise these additional impairments.

People with modes of communication other than speech may be disadvantaged in a self-advocacy movement where great emphasis is on the spoken word. Jackie advocates work in groups where each participant has a supporter who knows them well, and where the group moves at a pace to enable everyone to take part, using drama, art and photography as aids to communication, as well as signing and computer technology. She suggests that a conference where speech is outlawed might help other people with learning difficulties learn how to include people with no speech.

Conclusion

We have explored in this chapter some possible conflicts in the self-advocacy movement arising out of the fact that the group called 'people with learning difficulties' is itself differentiated by gender, race, ethnicity, sexual orientation and degree of disability (to name but a few). This represents a challenge to a self-advocacy movement which is led largely by white, mildly disabled men. We have also explored some of the different issues facing particular groups, and indicated our belief that a period of separate development helps people recognise that they are different, and to define what is important for them, as women or as black people, for example.

However, this politics of identity can only take us so far. As the women's movement has found (Williams forthcoming), strength is both dissipated and regenerated through identifying separate constituencies within the group known as 'women'. Potentially the fragmentation is endless. A black woman would need to choose whether her primary identity is with women, black people or disabled people. Jackie can't split herself like this: 'My view is that I can't separate my blackness or my disability or being a woman, because I'm all of these. I can't separate them. This is me. I relate to them all in different ways'. What we agree on is that at some point everyone needs their separate groups. Already significant progress has been made in women-only settings, and these may, like the Powerhouse, need to continue for specific goals. At the same time, these groups need to find ways of feeding into a broader self-advocacy movement which can genuinely represent everyone with learning difficulties.

To visualise how self-advocacy could and should develop in the future would be presumptuous. We can point to the creation of partnerships, such as the one we set up to write this chapter, as a way of generating ideas which can feed its development. We can acknowledge that in an imperfect world where people with learning difficulties are denied access to information and resources, non-disabled supporters and friends will continue sometimes to have undue influence and power over people's lives. Ideas like circles of support (Sanderson 1995) are well worth exploring because they offer an alternative to reliance on individual advocates or supporters. We can also urge research which takes an honest look at how funding can be managed and relationships created which genuinely vest power in people with learning difficulties rather than supporters, advisers and helpers. We can also consider the advantages for people with learning difficulties in making common cause with other groups of disabled people on particular issues, such as the highly successful 1994 civil rights campaign in Britain.

Self-advocacy by people with learning difficulties has many achievements to its credit. What we hope to see in the future is a movement which can find ways of being united at the same time as respecting and fostering diversity. It may seem an impossibly idealistic vision, and one that is far from realisation, but without such a vision we are much the poorer.

References

Aull Davies, C. and Jenkins, R. (1991) *Social Identity, Community and People with Mental Handicaps.* Paper presented to the British Sociological Association Annual Conference, March 25–28.

Baxter, C., Poonia, K., Ward, L. and Nadirshaw, Z. (1990) *Double Discrimination: Issues and Services for People with Learning Difficulties from Black and Ethnic Minority Communities.* London: Kings Fund and Commission for Racial Equality.

Black People First (1993) *Conference Report.* London: People First.

Brown, H. (1994) 'An ordinary sexual life? A review of the normalisation principle as it applies to the sexual options of people with learning difficulties.' *Disability and Society 9,* 2, 123–44.

Brown, H. and Smith, H. (eds) (1992) *Normalisation: A Reader for the Nineties.* London: Routledge.

Bryan, B., Dadzie, S. and Scafe, S. (1985) *The Heart of the Race: Black Women's Lives in Britain.* London: Virago.

Cambridge, P., Hayes, L. and Knapp, M. (1994) *Care in the Community: Five Years On.* Aldershot: Arena.

Crawley, B. (1988) *The Growing Voice: A Survey of Self-Advocacy Groups in Adult Training Centres and Hospitals in Britain.* London: CMH.

Etherington, A., Flynn, M. and Platts, H. (1994) *WILD Conference Report.* Manchester: NDT.

Jenkins, R. (1991) 'Disability and social stratification.' *British Journal of Sociology 42,* 4, 557–580.

King, J. (1991) 'A case of role reversal.' *Community Care,* 5 September, 20–22.

Open University (1996) *Learning Disability: Working as Equal People.* (a study pack). Milton Keynes: Open University.

People First (1995) *Not Just Painted On: The First Ever Conference Run By and For People with Down's Syndrome.* London: People First.

Perrin, B. and Nirje, B. (1989) 'Setting the record straight: a critique of some common misconceptions of the normalisation principle.' In A. Brechin and J. Walmsley (eds) *Making Connections: Reflecting on the Lives and Experiences of People with Learning Difficulties.* Sevenoaks: Hodder and Stoughton.

Rutter, M. and Madge, N. (1976) *Cycles of Deprivation.* London: Heinemann.

Sanderson, H. (1995) 'Self-advocacy and inclusion: supporting people with profound and multiple disabilities.' In T. Philpot and L. Ward (eds) *Values and Visions: Changing Ideas in Services for People with Learning Difficulties.* London: Butterworth Heinemann.

Simons, K. (1992) *Sticking Up for Yourself: Self-Advocacy and People with Learning Difficulties.* York: Joseph Rowntree Foundation.

South East London Needs Assessment Project (nd) *Men with Learning Difficulties who have Sex with Men in Public Places.* London: SELHA.

Thomson, D. and McCarthy, M. (1995) 'No more double standards: sexuality and people with learning difficulties.' In T. Philpott and L. Ward (eds) *Values and Visions: Changing Ideas in Services for People with Learning Difficulties.* London: Butterworth Heinemann.

Walmsley, J. (1993) 'Women first: lessons in participation.' *Critical Social Policy 38,* 86–99.

Walmsley, J. (1995) *Gender, Caring and Learning Disability* (unpublished PhD thesis). Milton Keynes: Open University.

Williams, F. (forthcoming) 'Postmodernism, feminism and the question of difference.' In N. Parton (ed) *Social Work, Social Theory and Social Change.* London: Routledge.

Wolfensberger, W. and Thomas, S. (1983) 'Social role valorisation: a proposed new term for the principle of normalisation.' *Mental Retardation,* December, 234–239.

CHAPTER 4

Voices and Choices
Mapping Entitlements to Friendships
and Community Contacts

Paul Ramcharan, Morag McGrath and Gordon Grant

Introduction

Disability is not (only) a characteristic of a person's own inability to do or to participate in certain things. Nor is it a characteristic of there not being things in which people with disabilities might participate. Rather, numerous forms of disability are actively accomplished and produced by others: family, service personnel and the community at large.

Rioux (1994) has further elaborated the ways in which 'disability' is a product of the social, economic, political and legal structures rather than an inherent feature of the individual, arguing that the, '...social, legal and economic policies in place at any given time in history reflect the ways that principles of justice have legitimated differential treatment' (p.67). Rioux argues the need for 'equality' and in summary criticises two models of such equality. The 'formal treatment' model which provides for equal treatment between citizens is problematic in that it assumes that people have the same needs and that each person has an equal capacity to exercise their rights, where, 'social dependency remains the justification for disentitlement...', (*ibid.*, p.77). The liberal theory model, or 'equality of opportunity and special treatment' model, works on the assumption that preferential treatment and affirmative action are justified to provide the shortfall in people's lives. The problem here is that such a theory assumes that disability is an intrinsic quality of the individual and not based on inequality that, '...arises from extrinsic factors such as income, employment, housing and services...' (*ibid.*, p.81). With both models the stigmatising, labelling and dependency-creating effects of having to declare disability to access disability-related services remains a necessary prerequisite to being viewed as a member of the 'worthy poor'.

This leads Rioux to propose an 'equality of well-being' model of disability in which equality is based on the 'outcome' for the individual, and is therefore not dependent on an assessment of disability with all its labelling effects. 'Well-being', she argues, must be based on the achievement of self-determination (choice, personhood and dignity), and full participation and inclusion in social life. Such a model proposes equality in outcome despite the differences between individuals. It suggests the need to put in place varying special accommodation measures to provide the conditions and means for participation. This model also implies that political and legal decisions would have to take into account differences in social well-being in order to provide distributive justice and produce equality of outcomes:

> Traditional limits that have circumscribed political obligation to ensure equality become suspect when the meaning of equality incorporates the notion of well-being, with its implications for resource redistribution. Entitlement is based on a comprehensive notion of citizenship...not on one's status as a member of the class of worthy poor, or on inequality of talent and social usefulness. (*ibid.*, p.87)

Despite the attractions of Rioux's argument there seem to be a number of residual problems with the analysis she presents. First and foremost is the relationship implied in this argument between the structures represented by the legal, economic system and social life (Marshall 1950) and the disabled person *qua* citizen. Discussing the relevance of the notion of citizenship in relation to female carers, Ungerson (1993, p.144) argues that:

> ...citizenship is essentially placed in the public domain...carers are physically located in the private domain...particularly when we adopt a notion of citizenship that emphasises rights, we run into difficult water as soon as we try to operate a notion of rights within the domestic and private domain.

In similar fashion, many of the relationships of disabled people occur at an interactional, mundane and everyday level and, as this chapter will demonstrate, it is often at this level that disability is actively produced and accomplished. The difficulty is always going to be that most of us would not wish the state to stretch its fingers into our mundane everyday life, to legislate who our friends might be and how we should act in relation to relatives (excluding issues which have reached extremes to which the law applies) (Ramcharan 1995). It is therefore necessary to examine the extent and nature of the disabling effects of everyday life and interaction, and to begin to address an agenda which may help to overcome these accomplishments of disability.

The second problem with Rioux's argument, and one she recognises, is the difficulty of knowing what constitutes a 'sufficient privilege' in terms of outcomes. The difficulties of operationalising a notion of equality based on distributive justice were beyond the abilities of even Karl Marx. Questions must therefore be asked about how such a notion of entitlement might be operationalised, whether, for example, it is culturally relative or dependent on the wealth of the state (Soder 1993).

It is proposed that one way of examining the notion of 'entitlement' to which Rioux refers is to seek to establish what forms of disability are actively produced and accomplished, and the way in which disentitlement is a product of everyday actions and interactions. What follows is an examination of what makes for trouble in this respect. At the very least this chapter seeks to show how the actions of others may produce disability and hence constrain the 'entitlement' of people with a learning disability to more friends and community contacts. The analysis limits itself to this, rather than examining the nature and meaningfulness of any friendships that people already have, or those that they might have were they not constrained in their actions by others. That focus must be left for another occasion.

Methods

The data for this chapter are drawn from 'interviews' with 54 adults (over 19 years of age) with a learning disability living in Wales, as well as from interviews with service personnel and key workers involved with each person, and with family carers for those living in a family home. Of the sample, 27 were men and 27 women, 28 lived independently of the family home and 26 lived in a family home. The age range was 20 to 74. Twenty of the sample (37%) were aged between 20 and 29; 11 (20.4%) between 30 and 39; 9 (16.7%) were between 40 and 49; 10 (18.5%) were between 50 and 59, and 6 (11.8%) were over 60 years of age.

The data are taken from a much larger study which involved a postal questionnaire to all family carers (n=752) (Grant, Ramcharan and McGrath 1991; Grant, McGrath and Ramcharan 1994) in seven learning disability team districts in Wales. In six of these seven areas (one having dropped out of the research), a random sample of ten adults and ten children with learning disabilities was selected and interviews were undertaken with their families, with their key workers and with other service personnel involved in their lives. Of the ten adults living in a family home, five were randomly selected for 'interview'. A further five who were not in the original cohort because they lived independently of a family home were also randomly selected from each team's register to provide comparison. This gave a total sample of 60 people with a learning disability to be 'interviewed', half living in a family home and half independently. Of these, one of the prospective interviewees declined to be interviewed, in two cases the family carer declined to let their relative participate in the research, one of the sample was described as 'too aggressive' for interview by both family and service personnel, and contact was not made in two further cases. This left a sample of 54 persons with whom 'interviews' were undertaken.

Considerable time and effort were put into establishing rapport and eliciting and deducing information from the respondents. A range of methods was used including: formal and informal questions; conversation; faces (five, showing happy to unhappy expressions) to elicit appraisals and (dis)satisfaction (Simons, Booth and Booth 1989); a pictorial ladder with seven rungs to establish how far wishes were being met; a sign language translator where required; telling and drawing stories to prompt similar responses; drawing pictures of wishes and wants; use of catalogues to establish interests and likes; accompanying the person to their regular haunts; and going out with the person during the day or the evening. The work involved up to seven visits with each person, some of the visits lasting for a full day. The areas we sought to cover in these 'interviews' are shown in Table 4.1.

Table 4.1 Interview themes

Where you live:	past, present, future, wishes, constraints
Leisure:	types of, evenings, weekends, wishes for, and constraints
Home life:	clothes, money matters, household chores, wishes, constraints
Community life:	local resources used, friends, best friends, wishes, constraints
Services:	day occupation, service providers, services received, wishes, constraints

Data on these areas (amongst others) were also taken from in-depth interviews with family carers (for those living in a family home) and service providers. In relation to the areas referred to in Table 4.1, the central focus here is on people's community life and friendships.

Basic data on community activities and friendships

The details which follow are rather problematic in that Figures 4.1 and 4.2 include data elicited from family carers and service providers where the person with the learning disability was unable to speak for him/herself. The friends and community contacts listed by the persons themselves were counted from their 'interviews' and, in the absence of such data, were counted from interviews with family carers and service personnel. As such, the quality and meaningfulness of the friendships and contacts with the community are not considered. Rather, the intention of the figures is to get a general sense of the extent and nature of friendships and community contacts for the 54 people in the sample.

Figure 4.1 shows the wide variety of community activities engaged in by individuals. The sample was split into those living independently and those living at home (Figure 4.2). Not surprisingly, those living independently were more likely to be accompanied by service personnel (53%) as opposed to the sample as a whole (40%). For those living at home the service provider input

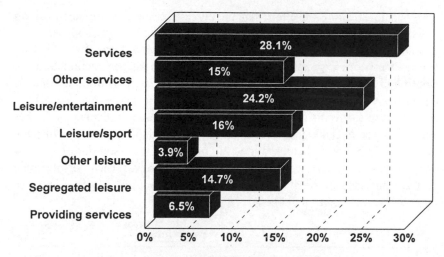

(% adds up to more than 100 due to multiple activities)

Key to Figure 4.1
Services: cafes/town and shops/car boot sales
Other services: library, church, museum, hairdresser
Leisure/entertainment: pub, football, cinema, clubs, parks
Leisure/sport: sports hall, hiking, swimming, sailing, boating,
                                   horse-riding, judo, bowls
Other leisure: caravan, luncheon club, allotment, beach
Segregated leisure facilities: Gateway, Mencap, Mind, Bible supper
Providing services: voluntary work in home for elderly, with children
                                   and babies. Sunday school and Red Cross

Figure 4.1 Type of community activities engaged in

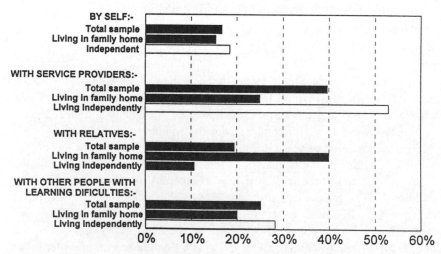

Figure 4.2 With whom respondents engaged in the community

dropped to 25 per cent, whilst family accompaniment was higher at 40 per cent.

The data regarding friends (Figure 4.3) very much mirrors these findings. For the sample as a whole, 40 per cent of friendships were mentioned as being with service providers, 40 per cent with other people with learning disabilities, and only 20 per cent with friends independent of services who were non-disabled. But as the figure shows, 51 per cent of those living independently rated service personnel as friends, the same figure being only 21 per cent for those living in a family home. Moreover, whilst 36 per cent of those living in a family home had independent friends, the same figure was only 14 per cent for those living independently.

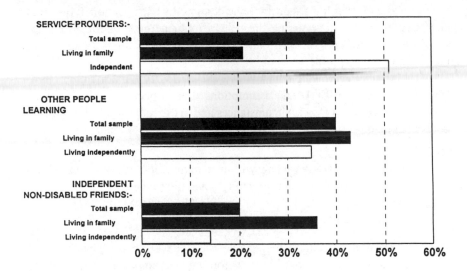

Figure 4.3 Friendship

The data presented so far, although far from perfect, seem to suggest that independent living does not necessarily lead to a greater number of independent friendships, and that there may be an increased degree of dependency on service personnel to fill the vacuum created by the absence of families. It therefore remains vitally important for all people with learning disabilities to extend their independent supportive networks and community contacts. This point assumes that making contact and sustaining relationships with persons in the community is very much at the heart of community care and is a laudable goal. As Flynn and Hirst (1992 p.69) argue: 'Identifying ways of discovering how we might best discern 'the voice of the user'…we find that most young people with learning disabilities aspire to what we recognise as an ordinary life'. Once this is accepted, and given the above data, questions arise as to the constraints which exist on this becoming a reality.

There is a question as to whether the level of independent friendships described above is either low or high, or whether it is 'sufficient'. This touches on the difficult question, mentioned earlier, as to what is sufficient community contact and friendship. In the following analysis an interpretation of 'sufficiency' is made from the point of view of the learning-disabled respondents themselves, being taken, as far as possible, from the 'interview' data. A few further points need to be made in this respect.

As mentioned already, it is exceptionally difficult for the state to legislate at the everyday interactional level. Besides the person with a learning disability, it is the people with whom he/she interacts in their everyday environments who structure his/her life, friendships and community participation. It becomes necessary, therefore, to examine the ways in which these interrelationships structure, support and/or constrain people to achieve their chosen ends. However, there are problems.

Most views of empowerment (Adams 1990; Jack 1995, p.26; Twine 1994; Wistow and Barnes 1993) make assumptions about a person's ability to make choices, take control of their circumstances and act to achieve his/her desired goals and outcomes. In more general texts on empowerment similar assumptions are made:

> Choices are always made within a framework of constraint... Yet human beings...can, in principle, *mould* the frameworks of constraint within which they make their choices. (Twine 1994, pp.1–2)

and:

> If freedom and ability are separate, then we have to ask the neo-liberal what is valuable about liberty, autonomy and empowerment... Surely the answer to the question...is because being free from coercion allows us to *live a life shaped by our own values and ends.* (Plant in Plant and Barry 1990, p.13)

and:

> Citizenship may be defined as that set of practices...which define a person *as a competent member of society*, and which, as a consequence, shape the flow of resources to persons and groups. (Saunders 1993, p.2)

and:

> *Taking control of one's life*...is not only seen as being intimately connected with the formation or reformation of the self as empowered, it is increasingly becoming an ethical obligation of the new citizenry. *Not being in control* of everyday arrangements...suggests there is

something seriously wrong with your ethical constitution (emphasis added). (Baistow 1995, p.37)

But it is precisely this ability to conceptualise choice and then pursue it which remains a central issue for many people with a learning disability. There is a problem here. Jack (1995) has argued that recent community care legislation involves, '…enablement, in the sense of promoting participation and involvement, not empowerment' (p.18). He argues that the role of professionals is therefore peripheral to empowerment, that it is 'enablement', and that the two concepts are quite different. If, however, a person can neither make nor pursue choice then, according to Jack's definition, whether we are talking about professionals, family carers, user movements, friends or others enabling such persons in their choices, we will not be able to achieve empowerment for at least some people with learning disabilities. We are therefore left with the disturbing conclusion that if we accept a model of empowerment based on ability, we are in danger of precluding many forms of empowerment for at least some people with learning disabilities.

In contrast to that, it is argued here that empowerment often requires forms of enablement, or at least advocacy. For a person to have his or her wishes, wants or needs realised, a number of antecedent conditions must be met which are set out in Figure 4.4 (Ramcharan 1995).

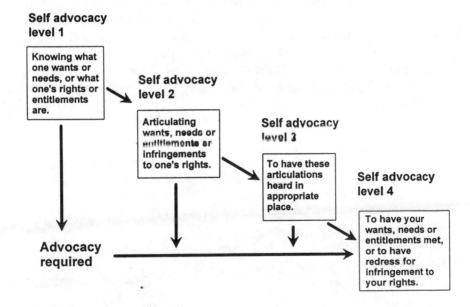

Source: Ramcharan 1995, p.234

Figure 4.4 Basic model identifying needs

This figure represents a simplistic linear model through which an individual secures suitable outcomes and well-being through their own choices and actions. There are problems with the linear and unidirectional nature of the model, but this format works well as a heuristic device for the analysis to follow. In self-advocacy level one the person needs to be able to conceptualise wants and wishes and to recognise rights and entitlements. These need to be articulated in communication or action at self-advocacy level two; these needs and wishes have to be made apparent in relevant forums at self-advocacy level three; and actions pursued to achieve the desired outcome at self-advocacy level four.

Where any of these levels cannot be achieved for one reason or another, others will have to speak and act for, on behalf of, or with the person at that level, that is, advocate on their behalf. (A pre-self-advocacy level which does not appear in Figure 4.4 which relates to profoundly disabled people was included in a previous construction of this model. For such people the issue is more one of substitute decision-making than advocacy. For the sake of brevity this level has been combined with self-advocacy level one for the analysis that follows.) The data were scanned and the following questions asked in relation to each self-advocacy level: at self-advocacy level one, does the 'interview' data indicate that the person can conceptualise, understand and know their wants relating to community life and friendships?; at self-advocacy level two, can this person articulate his/her wishes in relation to the above verbally or non-verbally?; at self-advocacy level three, can this person ask relevant persons for the help necessary to bring his/her wishes at level two to fruition?; and, at self-advocacy level four, can this person actually pursue his/her own wishes without the help of others? On the basis of these questions people with a learning disability were categorised into each of the four self-advocacy levels shown in Table 4.2.

Table 4.2 Self-advocacy level of respondents

	Living independently (n=28)	Living in a family home (n=26)	Totals (%)
Self-advocacy level one	8	12	37
Self-advocacy level two	6	9	28
Self-advocacy level three	5	1	11
Self-advocacy level four	9	4	24
Totals (%)	**52**	**48**	**100**

The important question here is if a person cannot reach any of the levels, *who* makes decisions on his/her behalf? Indeed, more abstractly, *who has the legitimate right* to make decisions on his/her behalf and, most importantly for the analysis which follows, *what decisions are being made and how do they affect people's lives?* It is very much in the domain where advocacy and substitute decision-making are seen to be necessary that the battles of ideology are fought about what is best for people with learning disabilities. It is therefore vital to understand what decisions are being taken by family, service personnel and others in their name.

In the earlier discussion it was suggested that it is necessary to go beyond the notion of 'entitlement' as a purely structural concept. Rather it was proposed that the everyday lives and relationships of people with a learning disability are an important addition in any interpretation of entitlement. What has been missing is a method of linking the two concepts. For an interpretative device, it is intended to draw on the work of Armartya Sen (1981). Sen makes the point that during the Sahel famines in the 1970s there was enough food to go around. That people starved was a reflection of their entitlement to resources, what he terms their Entitlement-mapping, or E-mapping. In a similar vein, the argument being made here is that there are enough resources in our society to provide people with a learning disability with an improved quality of life. However, their entitlement to such resources (their E-mapping) is constrained both by the structural determinants outlined by Rioux (1994), and by the ways in which choice, participation and access to desired outcomes are constrained by others.

The following analysis therefore examines the wishes of people with a learning disability themselves as to whether they wanted more 'community contact' (rated on the basis of a stated wish, or non-verbal communication, or inferred from knowing them well enough to judge if they wanted to participate in any further activities such as those presented in Figure 4.1). Similar ratings were made in relation to 'friendships'. Where the person was unable to express a view in this regard, the nature of the substitute decisions or the advocacy pursued on his/her behalf are examined. In each case the E-mapping constraints at a structural and interactional level are examined and the relationship between the two is laid bare.

For those people who were able to speak for themselves there was a very close fit between their stated wish in relation to friends and in relation to community contacts. Thus, those saying they wanted more friends were also likely to say that they wanted more contact with the community, and *vice versa*. Given the limits of space the 'friendship' and 'community' dimensions can therefore be legitimately collapsed into one category. Five cases are worthy of mention in this regard, however. In one case, data indicated a preference for more friends, whilst there were no data in relation to the wish for community contacts. In another, it was the reverse. Both of these people are included in the category 'wants more friends and community contacts'. In two cases, persons who said they did not want more community contact or friends in general said they wanted a 'special friend' and a 'boyfriend', respectively. These (for the purposes of the present analysis) were rated as 'not wanting more friends and community contacts'. In a third case, a person who was 'too busy' for more friends or community contacts nevertheless wanted somehow to make time to participate in one more community leisure activity (going to see wrestling), and this case too was rated as not wanting more friends and community contacts.

An analysis of the Entitlement-mapping of people with a learning disability in relation to friends and community activities

People with a learning disability living in a family home

Respondents were asked whether they wanted more friends and community contacts. Table 4.3 shows that of those living in a family home 40 per cent wanted more contact with community and more friends, 44 per cent (largely in self-advocacy level one) were unable to verbalise, communicate or did not know their wishes, and 16 per cent did not want more contact with the community, or friends. Since this chapter is about the wishes of people with learning disabilities themselves, these four people have been excluded from the following analysis. Clearly, from their point of view, they did not feel in any way constrained by the actions of others and felt they had the degree of friendships and community contacts they desired. It is noteworthy, however, that three of the four had extensive community networks which took up much of their time whilst the other person simply expressed happiness with her lot. This does raise the very important point about how to raise low expectations without imposing on the person's individual choices. Sometimes, then, the E-mapping may be constrained by the person's own expectations.

Table 4.3 Choices of respondents living in a family home
in relation to friends and community contacts (n=25)

	Wants more	Doesn't know or cannot articulate	Does not want more	Totals (%)
Self-advocacy level one	2	9	1	48
Self-advocacy level two	6	1	1	32
Self-advocacy level three	–	–	2	4
Self-advocacy level four	2	–	2	16
Totals %	**40**	**44**	**16**	**100**

(missing data – 1)

Some comments by respondents in relation to friends and community contacts are shown below. (Text in square brackets summarises questions asked by the interviewer.)

> [Like a friend?] – Yes I would. Spend time with me just like you.

> I wouldn't mind and mum doesn't mind if somebody could come and take me out...I'm handicapped see? I can't go out on my own.

> [See as much of your friends as you'd like?] I don't go out and my friends don't go out so we can't meet. I want to go to the pictures with a friend, but mum won't let me.

> [You look sad (tears were welling up in his eyes)] mm [Something you haven't got?] yes [like to talk to somebody?] L... [lonely?] Listen [you want somebody to listen to you?] yes.

Having examined the responses of the people with a learning disability themselves, the comments of both family and service personnel were examined. The analysis is split into two parts, one relating to families and one to service personnel.

FAMILY EFFECT ON E-MAPPING FOR THOSE LIVING IN A FAMILY HOME

This part of the analysis is made in relation to persons living in a family home who either said they wanted more friends and community contacts or who did not know or could not articulate their wishes (n=21). The interviews with parents yielded a number of categories, shown in Table 4.4, similar to those reported by Seed (1988). The 'home/closed' network orientation refers to families who seldom use community facilities, over and beyond securing basic living requirements such as food, and whose relative seldom does so either. This is represented in the following quote taken from a service provider describing the relationship between an 83-year-old carer and her 74-year-old sister: 'She doesn't go out at all...just for an hour to the pictures or for a meal would be great'.

The 'home/handicap' orientation refers to families who encourage friends and community contacts for their relative with other people with learning disabilities, whilst the 'home/community' dimension relates to families who actively encourage independent friends and community contacts amongst the non-disabled community. There were also a number of families that encouraged contacts with both learning-disabled and other non-disabled people in the community, that is, the 'home/community/handicap' dimension. (There are limits to the data in not explaining these family values and, further, because it is the wishes and values of the learning disabled interviewees which are the centre of attention for this analysis, and not those of family carers or others.)

Table 4.4 also distinguishes between those persons who needed someone to accompany them as a prerequisite to getting out and about in the community (what has been termed an 'accompanier') from those who did not. It is worth

Table 4.4 Family constraints on friendship and community
contacts for those living in a family home (n=20)

Family orientation	Needs accompanier	Does not need accompanier	Totals (%)
Home/closed	7	0	35
Home/handicap	7	0	35
Home/community	1	3	20
Home/community/handicap	2	0	10
Totals %	**85**	**15**	**100**

(Missing data – 1)

noting that those respondents rated in self-advocacy level one were more likely to be closeted at home or to have a decision made for them about staying only in the company of other people with a learning disability. They were also the people who most needed an accompanier. With 70 per cent of cases falling into either the 'home/closed' or 'home/handicap' categories, it can be seen that the entitlement to ordinary friends and community resources is severely constrained by the attitudes and values of family carers. Such carers are highly unlikely to encourage their relative into ordinary friendships and community contacts, as the following quotes from such family members suggest:

JOANNE: I get bored in the house. Joanne's mum – She can't make her needs known. She's a mental age of nine.

MOTHER: She plays up in the shops. I won't take her no more.

ANOTHER MOTHER: I'd like to see her more involved in the community but it must be safe.

SERVICE EFFECT ON E-MAPPING FOR THOSE LIVING IN A FAMILY HOME

A similar categorisation of orientations was deduced from the data in relation to service providers, and two main areas of constraint were found, as shown in Figure 4.5. The first area of constraint concerned the relationship between service personnel and family carers. This was described in terms of the work which service personnel need to do to establish an agenda for services which will enhance community contact and friendships. A typical example came from a key worker who said that, 'I no longer see his case as a priority because of the obstacles in the way [i.e. his mother]. We haven't the time to keep going down there every week'.

In relation to many families the service worker referred to the difficulties of battling against overprotection. For example:

I think we're fighting a losing battle... We tried to get her to be her own person... Then she goes home and she's not.

My opinion is this – they are so protective; they are very, very wary unless there is maximum supervision...I think their need is to be persuaded to allow [him] to go off on his own.

As can be seen from Figure 4.5, 64 per cent of cases fall into these two categories, requiring huge amounts of service worker time and resources in dealing with the family so that community activities and extending friendships can become possible. More will be said about this in the concluding section of this chapter.

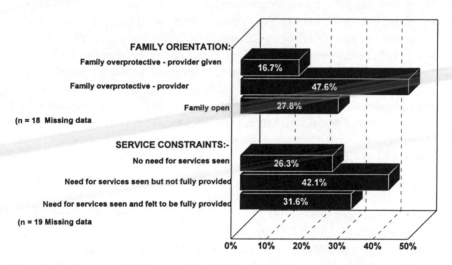

Figure 4.5 Service constraints to community/friendship extension contact for those living in a family home

The second E-mapping constraint in relation to services is shown in the lower half of Figure 4.5. It should be remembered that the persons in the sample either wanted, or could not articulate whether they wanted, more community contacts and friendships. The service providers were asked in each case whether a service was needed and, if so, whether provision was being made. The data show that 26 per cent of service personnel felt that there was no need for services in this area. However, in many cases (42%) service providers saw a need for services but such services were not provided. Some of the reasons given by key workers for not making such provision follow:

Her needs are not ignored, but she's not a priority.

We're hoping to link her in with a volunteer, but the volunteer situation is not that great.

He is not a high priority case. His needs are best met by segregated services.

...his situation would be very much improved if we could influence him on a one to one basis to do more activities [Problem with staffing?] Yes, yes.

It's finding something more than one day a week where she fits in, and the other support to go alongside it.

It is hoped that the data above are beginning to demonstrate that the E-mapping of people with a learning disability in relation to community contact and friendships is severely restricted by the values of family carers, and by the budgetary and other constraints on service personnel. In each case – and even for those who were able to express a preference – the degree of substitute decision-making and advocacy by service providers and parents effectively makes the power over decision-making theirs *despite the person's wishes.*

Before looking at those in independent settings it should be noted that the above constraints were by no means the only ones cited in our interviews. For example, one young woman was embarrassed by scars she had sustained in a car accident, and despite wanting to go swimming, would not do so. The inputs required to overcome E-mapping constraints encompass many types of factors which will be discussed later in this chapter.

People living independently of the family home
The following analysis repeats that made above, but for people (n=28) living independently of the family home. As can be seen from Table 4.5 48 per cent wanted to extend their community networks and friendships whilst 30 per cent were unable to verbalise their wishes. Six of those living independently did not want to extend their community contacts or have more friends, once again raising the important question, for some people at least, of how to raise their low expectations.

Table 4.5 Choices of respondents living independently
in relation to friends and community contacts (n=28)

	Wants more	Doesn't know or can't articulate	Does not want more	Totals (%)
Self-advocacy level one	1	7	0	29.6
Self-advocacy level two	4	0	2	22.2
Self-advocacy level three	4	1	0	18.5
Self-advocacy level four	4	0	4	29.6
Totals %	**48.1**	**29.6**	**22.2**	

(missing data – 1)

SERVICE CONSTRAINTS ON E-MAPPING FOR THOSE LIVING INDEPENDENTLY OF A FAMILY HOME

With individuals in this group living away from the family home, the data on E-mapping constraints are limited to service constraints (Figure 4.6).

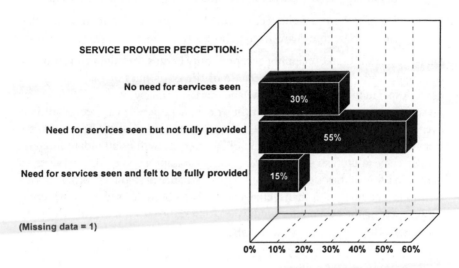

Figure 4.6 Service constraints to community/friendship extension for those living in a family home (n=21)

Figure 4.6 shows that in 55 per cent of cases service personnel saw a need to extend community contacts and friendships but did not provide services to accomplish this. For 30 per cent of the sample (six cases), the providers saw no need for a service, despite the fact that two of these service users specifically mentioned that they would like more friends and community contacts. For those who required an accompanier to move about in the community, the attitude of service personnel tended to be much more liberal than those of family carers and they were more likely to express community contact and more friendships as an entitlement for the person than were families. It is more likely that, in situations such as this, a service shortfall will be recognised. This has clear implications about the setting of agendas for action in extending friendship and community contacts. But this cannot occur where structural constraints do not allow this, as the following comments from service personnel show:

> He could do with a volunteer/befriender, because staff hours are too short.

> To improve things I think we'd need more money...maybe more flexicare or voluntary services.

> We do try to get [him] out but [another resident] needs 24 hour one-to-one support.

> Their lives are ruled by money…how much we can do… In the beginning I could claim for…various things. It's all cut back now.

> She did have a volunteer in the local community to develop that side…these things are always short term.

Hence, constraints on E-mapping occur not only because of values and attitudes, or service organisation, but also because of the economics of care-giving. We need desperately to put back on the agenda the primacy of the cash nexus as one, if not the major, constraint on the entitlement people can secure in their everyday lives. We have been through a very long period of making organisational change the focus of our social policy interests with its attendant interests in efficiency, in professional practice, team organisation and quality services, to name but a few of the factors involved. The imbalance in favour of formal service solutions, economy and managerialism needs to be redressed in considering ways of setting the economic prerequisites for a sufficient equality of well-being for all citizens.

SOME FURTHER E-MAPPING CONSTRAINTS

Before drawing any conclusions from these findings, it is necessary to present some further constraints on E-mapping not yet covered. Many of these are represented in the quotes which follow, taken from members of the sample who did not need an accompanier, but who nevertheless wanted to increase their community contacts and friendships. These demonstrate that, beyond even where the responsibility of family and services ends, there remains a steep hill for people with learning disabilities to climb if they want to integrate into the wider society and communities within which they live.

> Ben (54 years old) lives on his own with a small amount of support from a home support worker. 'I'd like to talk to someone in the evenings. Nobody visits… You hear news about people grabbing people. Say to myself stay at home… I'd like to go to the cinema. Before the bus to the main town was at [times]. Now couldn't get back.'

> Jack (67 years old) lives with his wife. 'Town is too far since we've been living here. If we go from here we'll probably meet new friends.'

> Pete (47 years old) lives in a group home. [why come to live here?] 'I want to go into the community, I don't see my friends no more.' [how feel?] 'Terrible.' [Don't get to go out and meet people enough?] 'No.'

> John (28 years old) lives in a group home with two others. [Go out often?] 'Not much now.' [Want to?] 'Yeah. I wish I went to the pictures. It's the money.'

Jack (48 years old) lives in a flat with a few hours' support a week. '...like to go to the sports centre. I can't afford it... The problem is the neighbours aren't very friendly. I had egg thrown at my window... I would like to see more people drop in. I speak to the bird sometimes. Other people think I'm talking to myself but I'm speaking my problems to the bird.'

The last word in this analysis is left to a young man living independently who did not want more friends and community contact. Although it was implied earlier that low expectations were likely to explain why respondents may not want further community contact and friends, this is not the only reason. Take, for example, this quote from the young man concerned:

I don't think [x] told you this. I'm actually autistic you see. I was told this about over three years ago... I never knew until then... A few days later I looked it up in the dictionary and it meant that I am in a world of my own...and find it difficult to respond... I think that's why...I want to be by myself all the time.

Further questioning within the 'morale' section of this interview established this man's enthusiasm for music, and particularly for The Beatles. However, he went on to say that: 'Out of all the Beatles' songs there is one I don't like...which makes me sad...It's the original version of the song "Fool on the Hill".' The lyrics to this song speak of a man who stands alone; he seldom answers or expresses his feelings to others for seldom is he listened to, no matter how loud he speaks. He looks upon a world of people whom he feels do not like him and reflects that they are the fools, that it is they who are missing the unique gifts he has to offer.

The deep sense of loneliness in this man's personal account of his life very much mirrors that of Stan described by Bayley in Chapter 2 of this volume. So too does it summarise many of the themes in this chapter, highlighting the impotence of people in accomplishing their life aims where others are unwilling to listen, or to hear their voices and choices.

Conclusion and an agenda for the future

It is hoped that the preceding analysis has not been too negative. There were some exceptional cases through which family, staff and friends sought to extend community contact and friendships. The intention of the analysis was to examine ways of establishing the value of 'entitlement' as the basis for providing some equality of well-being for learning-disabled people. Although the sample size was small, it is held, nevertheless, that there is much to be drawn from this type of analysis. But it also suggests the need to start placing people with learning disability on the research agenda, either as our informing subjects, or in commissioning, directing and undertaking research themselves (cf Minkes *et al.* 1995; Oliver 1996, pp.139–144; Ramcharan and Grant 1994).

It has been argued that E-mapping constraint can, at the very least, identify the ways in which equality of well-being is not being met, and the mechanisms, reasons and processes for this shortfall. The notion of constraint is 'constitutionally' comparative, meaning that if there is a constraint it must be against something else and in relation to something else. Given this inherent characteristic the idea of 'constraint' can also allow not only for the identification of the nature, reasons, mechanisms and processes of constraint, but also what needs to be accomplished in order to achieve equality of outcome. However, whilst it might do this it still cannot provide an answer to the ethical question of how much should be provided to ensure that entitlements are met. This will continue to be a matter for personal and public conscience and, ultimately, political will.

In terms of illustrating ideas about equality of well-being, the data have shown that the E-mapping of people with a learning disability is severely restricted at the structural level in terms of the economics of service provision and welfare benefits; at the interactional level in terms of family values such as overprotectiveness and a disability orientation; and by the expectations of individuals themselves. Most importantly it has been argued that for people who are often unable to make choices for themselves and reach desired outcomes, we need to ask who has the *legitimate* right to advocate and make decisions on their behalf. For those who can advocate for themselves in terms of their needs and wishes, it has been demonstrated that others often ignore, fail to hear or strike off the agenda the right to accomplish the chosen outcomes of the learning-disabled person with whom they are associated. The ability to do this rests in the power over people who often know what they want (self-advocacy levels one and two), but are unable to communicate these needs to relevant parties, or to pursue the outcomes for themselves through their own actions (self-advocacy levels three and four). They are therefore in the hands of others in terms of pursuing and accomplishing desired outcomes and, if the values of those who advocate 'on their behalf' differ, they are disempowered and disabled (Lukes 1974). Re-empowerment lies in the obverse of these strategies. We must start by listening to people's wishes and working to their agenda(s). The data used in this chapter have been presented as a partisan account of the wishes of people with learning disabilities themselves, and the constraints they face in making community contact and friendships a reality. However, given that empowerment is a relational concept, that is, that it involves the balance of interests between at least two parties, there will certainly be constraints in the lives of both informal carers and service providers which impinge upon the relationship between these parties. They too require consideration and discussion to seek the structures and conditions for liberating the people with learning disabilities they know, and care about, to achieve citizenship and inclusion.

Earlier in this chapter it was argued that the focus of interest was within the private domain where ordinary everyday actions and choices are made by, for and with people with learning disabilities which the legislative mandate of the state cannot reach. It has been argued that one way of intercepting and examining this area of people's lives is through the notion of 'entitlement to resources' and, in accord with Twine (1994), it has been suggested that 'redistributing resources redistributes power and choice' (p.103). However, Turner has argued that the, '...public/private distinction is equally important and indicates the cultural dimension of definitions of citizenship. When political space is limited, citizenship is passive and private' (1993, p.9). Having considered some aspects of the process of empowerment, it should not be assumed that these can be considered in isolation from the wider structural *conditions* within which they occur. As Lister (1990) says in relation to women, they:

> ...are better represented in weak publics, especially community-based groups and the new social movements. On the whole the weak publics represent a more accessible, fulfilling and enjoyable form of politics... However, if women do not engage directly with the strong publics where political (if not economic) power resides, we will continue to live in man-shaped institutions under man-made laws and policies. (p.69)

Arguments of a similar nature may be made in relation to people with learning disabilities in their acquiescence by default to laws and institutions made and run by non-disabled people. To the extent that systems of institutionalised segregation exist, as within schooling; in terms of a narrow view of work as purely based on economic productivity or paid work as the only means of legitimate economic well-being; in terms of the labelling and separating out of a 'worthy poor' to access the social care system and services (Rioux 1994); to that extent will their carers and advocates be socialised and see the world in terms of these limited options and couch their actions, advocacy and decision-making in terms of the limited options on offer. To this extent too will be the limits of the self-identity of people with a learning disability which are a prerequisite to the formulation of self and self in relation to others be couched in terms of the limited experiences afforded to them in their everyday lives. In short, a process of empowerment in everyday life can only work where the conditions of empowering structures and institutions are in place.

This chapter only begins to present the case for a just and equitable society based on notions of distributive justice and equality of well-being as the foundation of a usable notion of citizenship, and in opposition to systems which label, segregate, and create dependency and disability. But it requires action at a structural level (Rioux 1994) as well as the interactional level. This leads to the central philosophical questions: how much does the state owe its disabled citizens and how much we are all prepared to pay?

References

Adams, R. (1990) *Self-Help, Social Work and Empowerment*. London: Macmillan.

Baistow, K. (1995) 'Liberation and regulation? Some paradoxes of empowerment.' *Critical Social Policy 42*, 34–46.

Flynn, M. and Hirst, M. (1992) *This Year, Next Year, Sometime...? Learning Disability and Adulthood*. London: National Development Team and York: SPRU.

Grant, G., Ramcharan, P. and McGrath, M. (1991) *Appraising Service Packages Initial Findings of a Phase One Questionnaire Survey of 752 Families*. Bangor: CSPRD Report, University of Wales.

Grant, G., McGrath, M. and Ramcharan, P. (1994) 'How family and informal carers appraise service quality.' *International Journal of Disability, Development and Education 41*, 2, 127–141.

Jack, R. (1995) 'Empowerment in community care.' In R. Jack (ed) *Empowerment and Community Care*. London: Chapman and Hall.

Lister, R. (1990) *The Exclusive Society: Citizenship and the Poor*. London: Child Poverty Action Group.

Lukes, S. (1974) *Power: A Radical View*. London: Macmillan.

Marshall, T.H. (1950) *Citizenship and Social Class*. Cambridge: Cambridge University Press.

Minkes, J., Townsley, R., Weston, C. and Williams, C. (1995) 'Having a voice: involving people with learning difficulties in research.' *British Journal of Learning Disabilities 23*, 3, 94–98.

Oliver, M. (1996) *Understanding Disability: From Theory to Practice*. London: Macmillan.

Plant, R. and Barry, N. (1990) *Citizenship and Rights in Thatcher's Britain: Two Views*. London: The IEA Health and Welfare Unit.

Ramcharan, P. (1995) 'Citizen advocacy and people with learning disabilities in Wales.' In R. Jack (ed) *Empowerment in Community Care*. London: Chapman and Hall.

Ramcharan, P. and Grant, G. (1994) 'Setting one agenda for empowering persons with a disadvantage in the research process.' In M. Rioux and M. Bach (eds) *Disability is Not Measles: New Research Paradigms in Disability*. Ontario: The Roeher Institute.

Rioux, M. (1994) 'Towards a concept of equality of well-being: overcoming the social and legal construction of inequality.' In M. Rioux and M. Bach (eds) *Disability is not Measles: New Research Paradigms in Disability*. Ontario: The Roeher Institute.

Saunders, P. (1993) 'Citizenship in a liberal society.' In B.S. Turner (ed) *Citizenship and Social Theory*. London: Sage.

Seed, P. (1988) *Children with Profound Handicaps: Parents' Views and Integration*. Lewes: The Falmer Press, 2nd edition.

Sen, A. (1981) *Poverty and Famines: An Essay on Entitlement and Deprivation*. Oxford: Clarendon Press.

Simons, K., Booth, T. and Booth, W. (1989) 'Speaking out: user studies and people with learning difficulties.' *Research, Policy and Planning 7*, 1, 9–17.

Soder, M. (1993) 'Community integration: on the importance of asking the right questions.' In J.T. Sandvin and A. Frostad Fasting (eds) *Intellectual Disability Research: Nordic Contributions*. Helsinki: Nordlandsforskning.

Turner, B.S. (1993) 'Contemporary problems in the theory of citizenship.' In B.S. Turner (ed) *Citizenship and Social Theory*. London: Sage.

Twine, F. (1994) *Citizenship and Social Rights: The Interdependence of Self and Society*. London: Sage.

Ungerson, C. (1993) 'Caring and citizenship: a complex relationship.' In J. Bornat, C. Pereira, D. Pilgrim and F. Williams (eds) *Community Care: A Reader*. London: Macmillan.

Wistow, G. and Barnes, M. (1993) 'User involvement in community care: origins, purposes and applications.' *Public Administration* Autumn, 71, 279–299.

CHAPTER 5

Families and Empowerment

Marian Barnes

Introduction

Much of the literature concerning people with learning disabilities and their families has two characteristics: first it is concerned with the challenges and stresses which parents of people with learning disabilities face in the day-to-day tasks of caring and seeking support and help from health and social care agencies in providing care and support for their children; and second, the parent roles are occupied by non-disabled people, whilst the child roles (even in the case of adults) are occupied by people with learning disabilities. There are exceptions. Grant and Nolan (1993) have emphasised the satisfactions as well as the stresses which can arise from care-giving; Walmsley (1993) has discussed ways in which people with learning disabilities provide support and care to other members of their families; whilst Tim and Wendy Booth (1993) have written about the experiences of people with learning disabilities who themselves become parents. But such texts are in a minority and there is very little to be found in the literature which considers ways in which family life might be a source of strength and empowerment for people with learning disabilities. Indeed, the service-based focus on the majority of research which has been carried out in the area of learning disabilities has meant that the family lives of people with learning disabilities have been invisible, unless they have been a 'problem'.

The increasingly high profile being given to empowerment within the context of services has caused some commentators to discuss the importance of recognising the different and separate voices of those who may be considered the direct users of services and those who provide care for them in the context of family or friendship relationships (Barnes and Wistow 1992; Ellis 1993; Grant 1992). Carers and those they care for clearly do have different interests and needs, but there is also a danger of assuming a conflictual relationship where one does not exist, or of failing to recognise that conflict may arise from or be exacerbated by the way in which services are provided, or not provided, rather than from within the caring relationship itself. Jenny Morris (1993) has presented evidence of this in the experiences of people with physical impairments and their families.

This area is one in which the dynamics of often complex interdependencies need to be understood if attempts to increase the empowerment of people with learning disabilities are to be successful. Interdependencies define much of ordinary family life, and those which exist within families which have a member who has a learning disability may be better considered as different in intensity and duration, rather than in nature. Interdependencies exist between informal caring relationships and care provided by those paid to give it; and between the individual's need for autonomy and to be cared for. Emphasising the importance of responsiveness to individual needs alone is unlikely to be an appropriate or successful strategy for formal service provision because it does not take account of either the positive or negative aspects of the interdependencies which exist between individuals and their families.

Empowering people within the context of health and social care services is only part of the story. Empowerment within this context is considered to mean enabling people to have a say about the nature of the service which they receive, and it is often seen to imply that those purchasing or providing services have to lose power in order that recipients may become more powerful. This collection is based on the belief that empowerment has to be related to people's lives as a whole – it cannot be understood as simply being concerned with increasing user influence within service systems. Empowerment is thus first a process of personal growth and development which enables people not only to assert their personal needs and to influence the way in which they are met, but also to participate as citizens within a community, influencing the nature of that community and the resources available to it. Second, empowerment implies that processes of social and civic life should be designed to support and enable the participation of those who have previously been excluded from them. This means that change has to take place within social systems as well as within individuals and within services. In this context, families themselves may need to undergo change if family members with a learning disability are to be empowered, both within the family group and beyond. Families may also have the potential to contribute to wider changes supportive of empowerment; and to support their members in their battles to become participants within their communities.

In this chapter I will explore interrelationships within the families of people with learning disabilities and consider their implications for strategies to increase the empowerment of people with learning disabilities, not only in relation to services but within their lives more broadly. The potentially empowering capacity of families is not an area which has provided the focus for research. In this discussion I will draw on research conducted by myself and others which has explored related issues, and on conversations in which I sought to explore some of these issues more directly with people with learning disabilities and, in the case of both adolescents and adults, their parents. The young people I spoke to were members of a Users' Council at an Employment Preparation Unit. I met with the two young women and four young men as a group at the Unit. The ten parents were mainly people I had worked with in a previous project when I had been working with a mixed group of carers. I invited all those whom I knew to be parents of people with learning disabilities to meet with me to discuss the topic. Three parents whom I did not know previously but who were suggested by existing contacts were also invited. I met with two groups on separate occasions in my own home. The informal surroundings and the fact that all were known to each other and/or to me meant that the discussions were wide-ranging and open. I taped the discussions to enable me to participate without having to take detailed notes. This should not be regarded as formal 'research' and what follows is intended to be an exploration of factors relevant to the issue of families and empowerment, rather than a set of firm conclusions.

Before considering the family lives of people with learning disabilities, it is useful to consider the meaning of key concepts relating to the notion of 'empowerment'.

Autonomy, interdependence and empowerment

Doyal and Gough (1991) have identified autonomy as one of two basic human needs of all persons; the other is physical health. They argue that these needs must be met if people are to live within their communities without incurring serious harm. In their conceptualisation autonomy consists, in a minimal sense, of the ability, 'to make informed choices about what should be done and how to go about doing it' (p.53). Since one purpose of their analysis is to explore the type of political, social and economic institutions necessary to ensure basic need satisfaction, they develop their conceptualisation to identify 'intermediate' needs which are capable of indicating the type of services to which people should be entitled if their needs are to be met. Such an analysis could be adapted to consider the role which families might play in providing the basic conditions in which people might become empowered in their daily lives, and how state-provided services and policies should interact with private lives to support this.

Doyal and Gough identify three components of autonomy: the ability of a person to understand herself, her culture and the expectations of herself as an individual within that culture; the psychological capacity to formulate options for herself; and the objective opportunities enabling her to act on those options. Whilst acknowledging that an absence of psychological capacity may be deemed as defining 'mental disability' (their term), they also acknowledge that, with help, people can become less 'handicapped'. Thus, for people with a learning disability, their rights as citizens to have their basic needs for autonomy met in order to participate in social life require the provision of support which enhances understanding, psychological capacity and opportunity to act.

Dependency as a concept guiding decision-making about the provision of services has been substantially challenged by disabled people (for example, Morris 1993). Nevertheless, social services agencies still invest considerable effort in determining assessment procedures which will assign people to a 'dependency category'. At the same time, they espouse individualism to the extent that they assert that every user of services should be treated as a unique individual. Independence is expressed as a desired service outcome:

> In broad terms, there is agreement that people with a learning disability should lead ordinary lives in the community and that statutory and voluntary agencies should help people use everyday facilities and services. All services provided should promote development and independence, treating people with dignity and respect. (Birmingham City Council 1991, p.29)

Developmental psychologists have traditionally emphasised independence as an indicator of maturity. More recently, feminist psychologists (for example, Kaplan and Surrey 1986) have developed what have been termed 'self-in-relation' theories. Such theories challenge the assumption of immaturity assigned to women because of the significance of perceiving their self in relation to others. In contrast they emphasise the high level of psychological development required to experience and respond to the inner worlds of others. Maturity is perhaps better thought of as the achievement of successful interdependence which recognises what people contribute to each other's sense of self and ability to act within the world, rather than independence which asserts the separation of individuals from each other.

Interdependence is a universal feature of human existence. It is at best unhelpful, at worst damaging, to pose dependence and independence as dichotomies with one bad, the other good. It is also both inaccurate and unhelpful to assume that an individual always occupies one position in relation to others within their family or in other relationships. Empowerment needs to be understood as relating to the nature and quality of people's relationships with others, rather than as a feature of an unconnected individualism.

The stresses, strains and supports of family life

'The Family' has been the subject of extensive dispute within both policy and academic circles. Its passing has been mourned and resisted by conservative policy-makers whilst its hegemony has been a central focus of feminist analysis of oppressive gender relations. The assumption that people live in families has profound and wide-ranging impacts within a broad range of policy spheres, sometimes with unremarked but rather surprising results: are we to assume that certain health services are not available to individuals who do not live in families as the term 'Family Health Service Authority' might imply? The multi-cultural nature of contemporary UK society should remind us that models of family structure and relationships are neither fixed nor universal, but also that living in kinship groups is an experience shared by most people in most cultures.

Families may come to the attention of social work agencies if difficulties in family relationships start to generate outcomes which family members feel unable to deal with without help. Sometimes those outcomes are experienced by one member of the family, sometimes they are both experienced and understood as residing in the relationship between two or more family members. Frequently they arise from external pressures caused by poverty, poor housing or unemployment. Often difficulties within family relationships become evident at points of transition: when the birth of a child results in three-way relationships having to be developed where previously negotiation was a two-way process; when children start to develop a level of independence which parents may find threatening or undermining; or when adult children take on the care of their parents in a form of role reversal which neither party may have chosen. In some cases the origin of an apparently individual difficulty may not be seen to lie within family relationships and exploring the problem may expose strains not previously understood by family members. The resolution of an individual problem may itself result in disruption to family life which has been based on interdependencies which have become harmful to one of its members.

Such difficulties occur in families which do not have a member who has a learning disability. But it may be useful to consider more particularly what have been identified as the nature and sources of stress and difficulty within families who do, and which members of the family are most likely to experience such problems. The following have all been identified within the research literature (for example, Ayer and Alaszewski 1984; Booth and Booth 1993; Glendinning 1983; Smyth and Robus 1989) or in discussions I have held with people with learning disabilities and with families who have a member with a learning disability:

1. For parents, coming to terms with having a disabled child.

2. The reduced attention available to siblings and the additional responsibilities which may be placed on them.

3. The social isolation which may be experienced by the family as a whole and the restrictions which may be placed on both employment and recreational opportunities of parents (mothers in particular).

4. The continued support required and provided by mothers in particular beyond the period when they would expect to provide such support to their child.

5. The problems experienced by parents in gaining access to and negotiating appropriate support and respite services.

6. The financial costs of caring.

7. The additional difficulties experienced by people with learning disabilities in trying to develop independent identities, and in initiating new relationships which they have chosen.

8. For parents, the associated uncertainties of enabling their son or daughter to move away and live more independently and their concern about sources of future support and care when they are no longer able to provide this.

9. The challenges and resistances which people with learning difficulties experience when becoming parents themselves.

Whilst it would be wrong to assume that all the difficulties such families may experience are a result of having a member who has a learning disability, it would be naive and inconsiderate not to acknowledge these additional sources of difficulty. I will refer to these in developing my discussion of the relationship between families and empowerment.

In spite of the acknowledged problems of family life, the family is one of the most enduring of all social groupings. Why is the family such a powerful idea and experience? What are the positive aspects of family life which might account for its enduring nature? In considering the perceived strengths of family life I will use an analysis taken from a critique of families, since such a critique opens up the possibility of an analysis of the type of changes which could strengthen families as a source of empowerment for their members.

Barrett and McIntosh (1982), in discussing 'The Anti-Social Family', identify three factors which they consider to account for its lasting appeal. First, families provide emotional security not easily available elsewhere. In particular, whilst relatives may not be particularly liked, they cannot be disposed of and there is a sense that they can always be turned to for support. Related to this is familiarity with the behaviour of family members which identifies them as belonging to the same group. Second, Barrett and McIntosh accept the claim that, within the current social system, a family is the most supportive environment in which to bring up children. This refers both to the material circumstances within which children can be raised and to the perceived advantages of two parents in developing social identities. Finally, they suggest that families are attractive because they are seen to be 'natural'. The enduring nature of families regardless of the type of social system in which they exist is seen to imbue them with a moral superiority, whilst within a capitalist society characterised by *gesellschaft* rather than a *gemeinschaft*, families are seen to provide a haven of pre-capitalist values.

Whilst in practice it is difficult to separate out the reasons why people may experience family life as either supportive or constraining, it is possible to consider how these apparent advantages of family life might contribute to the empowerment of family members who have learning disabilities.

Emotional security, familiarity and acceptance

Barrett and McIntosh's first characteristic would suggest that families are more likely than other social groups to accept the person for her/himself, regardless of their disability or the difficulties to which this may give rise. However, responses from some parents suggest that this is not inevitably the case. The parents I spoke to told me of older siblings finding it very difficult to accept the arrival of a brother or sister with a learning disability and of other relatives (as well as professionals) suggesting that the best thing to do would be to 'put her away'. However, where the child with a learning disability was older than siblings, it appeared that they were more likely to be a taken for granted part of the family into which younger children were born. Moreover, some older siblings do seem to develop an acceptance and an understanding as they grow older. One mother spoke of her elder son saying how he wanted to get to know his brother in a way that he had not found possible when he was younger and that had led to invitations for his brother to come to stay. Thus acceptance may not be unconditional, but families may provide an environment in which such acceptance can grow.

Others have spoken of the difficulty parents can have in coming to terms with knowing that their child has a learning disability:

> When he said abruptly that John was retarded I tended not to believe it at first. I refused to accept it and it took me a long time to bring myself to accept it. (Ayer and Alaszewski 1984, p.112)

> You can justify euthanasia, which morally is still murder, but you can justify it in your own mind. You can think how it would have been far better for Anne and the whole family and the community and everybody if Anne had died at birth, and you'd never have known anything about it. We couldn't bear to lose her now, but you can understand. I think if Anne's done anything, she's done one thing which is very important, she's broadened our outlook, she's made us a lot more sympathetic. (Glendinning 1983, p.39)

Most parents I spoke to felt that they were left on their own to look after their child because of lack of understanding of what was involved, lack of skill in relating to the person with a learning disability, or a feeling on their part that it was their responsibility. They also felt that they should not expect other members of the family to take on the additional responsibilities involved. One result of that was what one father referred to as a 'fiercely protective' response to their children.

Social policies within the UK are based on a belief that families have a natural obligation to care for their own (Finch 1989). Such feelings are largely shared by *parents* of children with learning disabilities, but the sense of obligation may go no wider than this within the family group. Parents are always there because they have to be, for sons or daughters with learning disabilities, for much longer periods of their lives than they would expect with a non-disabled child. They provide an enduring reference point as well as a unique, but not uncritical, source of concern for the well-being of their child.

Parents provided examples of the type of behaviour which could lead to rejection from some social groups, but which will be 'handled' within the security of family relationships. One of the carers with whom I worked arrived late on one occasion because her daughter had thrown a tantrum and thrown crockery around the room. She was very shaken by the experience, but also angry with her daughter and determined to ensure that she learned that this was unacceptable behaviour. Another father described an incident on a family holiday in which his 40-year-old son had thrown both his shoes into the middle of a large room in which 300 people were playing bingo. Parents do not reject their children for behaving badly. Parents of children with learning disabilities may have to deal with behaviour which results from the frustrations of growing up in a society in which many people do not understand learning disability, as well as with the boundary testing that is a normal part of growing up. Thus it may be even more important that families can provide a safe environment in which it is not only possible to behave in a way which could be harmful amongst strangers, but in which it is more possible to learn the cultural expectations concerning behaviour which are a prerequisite for autonomy.

Parents make frequent reference to the significance of the detailed knowledge they have of their sons or daughters. Associated with this is a strong feeling that those who have not experienced having a child with a learning disability do not have any real understanding of what this means, either practically or emotionally. This makes it difficult to accept help from neighbours or relatives who have only infrequent contact and can add to the sense of isolation which many experience. It is also an important reason for wanting to spend time with other parents who have learning-disabled sons or daughters with whom common experiences can be shared.

Parents with daughters or sons with learning disabilities emphasise the importance of the understanding which comes from familiarity with their children's behaviour. A frequent complaint is that their intimate knowledge and the experience and skills which derive from this are ignored or dismissed by the paid workers with whom they come into contact. This makes parents feel devalued and disempowered and can lead to misunderstandings which may leave the person with a learning disability confused or pulled in two directions.

The ability to recognise and interpret feelings which cannot easily be expressed in spoken language, and the development of different forms of communication with those for whom words do not come easily, may be a particular advantage gained from living in close proximity for many years with family members. This may be particularly important where people have no speech. One father spoke of how the only way in which his son could make a decision was to complain at things he did not like. He said: 'You can't present him with a choice, you can only interpret his reaction'. The ability to recognise his son's reaction as a choice, and to interpret the content of that reaction, was seen to depend on a familiarity developed over years of living together.

Whilst there is the potential for this to lead to parents claiming that they can always speak on behalf of their daughter or son and for a confusion between whose wishes and interests are being expressed, this is neither inevitable nor limited to relationships between family members and people with learning disabilities. For example, during interviews conducted with people with learning disabilities as part of a research project exploring developments in day-time opportunities in which I was engaged (Barnes and Wistow 1995), the interventions of a care assistant as well as of a mother made it difficult to find out the views of the people we wanted to hear from.

Material and cultural benefits of family life

Barrett and McIntosh's second identified benefit of family life – the more supportive environment for child-rearing in terms of both material advantages and the 'social, cultural and ideological weight' attached to having two parents – can also be considered to have particular significance for families with a child who has learning disabilities. The well-documented financial, practical and emotional demands of caring for a child with a disability means that lone parents can experience tremendous burdens in the day-to-day responsibilities of child care. For the child, the stimulus provided by having more than one other person to relate to may be of particular importance in assisting the development both of a separate identity and of relationships outside the home. However, evidence from Ayer and Alaszewski's (1984) study of mothers and their mentally handicapped (their term) children caused them to conclude: 'As in other families, the mothers in our study provided the bulk of the care. The extra burden of care did not result in greater support or involvement from other members of the house' (p.150).

This was reinforced by most of the parents I spoke to, who felt that 'families' by and large consisted of parents and their children. Some of the young adults with learning disabilities I spoke to said that their brothers refused to allow them to go to the pub with them and thus a potential opportunity to mix with others of their own age which might have been supported by family members was lost. However, this was not exclusively the case, and some examples were given of ways in which other family members could provide opportunities for people with learning disabilities to fulfil important roles: acting as best man at a brother's wedding, being a bridesmaid and looking after young nieces and nephews were three examples. One mother spoke of the learning opportunities for her son in fulfilling the role of uncle to his young nieces and nephews. She saw this as a way for him to learn patience and responsibility by recognising that he was grown up, but they were only little and not able to do some of the things he could.

In other cases siblings did provide an opportunity for contact with peers of a similar age: one teenage girl attended a youth club with her brother and both a young woman and young man enjoyed shopping with their sisters. As well as providing opportunities to develop separate identities, spending time with other members of the family provided important respite for parents.

None of the young people I spoke to had grandparents living close by so they did not really feature as part of their families. Some of the parents I spoke to identified ways in which their parents had made important contributions to the lives of their sons or daughters, and in at least one instance this relationship was clearly reciprocal. One young woman's grandfather now lives in a residential home and, 'if Grandad's not feeling well it's Elizabeth who can bring a smile to his face'.

The enduring nature of families as 'natural' systems

Barrett and McIntosh's third identified strength of family life related to its 'natural' quality and to the importance of non-materialist values on which family relationships are based. The quality of relationships is hugely important to people with learning disabilities and their parents. Two young men were very critical of their brothers for behaving badly to their parents and, whilst parents came in for criticism for refusing to allow young people to spend money in ways they wanted and for insisting that they were home by a certain time in the evening, the help they gave was recognised and welcomed. For some young people this involved daily personal care, whilst for others it could include help with sorting out difficulties at work or with friends. Most reciprocated by helping around the house and one young man said he would help out financially if his parents were short of money. He said, 'I like my mum and dad in a special way', and became very upset when his parents disagreed with each other. Those disagreements were often about money and he would give his dad money to buy a drink in order to try to prevent disagreements.

Parents emphasised the importance of good quality relationships in the lives of their daughters or sons and they saw the opportunity for them to attend day centres and colleges of the Employment Preparation Unit as important sources of friendships as well as activity. Even those who had profound impairments and were not able to join in work or social activities were considered to enjoy being with other people. Two fathers commented on the fact that meeting and chatting with friends was not considered productive in the increasingly work-oriented day centres. However, they regarded such contact as invaluable.

As well as the practical impact of having a child with a learning disability, this also affected the values held by some parents. One father spoke of his wife, who was both a minister in the church and an academic theologian, whose ideas of theology had been profoundly affected by experiencing the reality of suffering. Another spoke of the importance of relationships rather than 'new cars or position'. All spoke of the satisfaction, love and enjoyment which their children brought to them. But parents also spoke of their other children feeling resentful or deprived as a result of having a brother or sister who required a considerable amount of attention and who might place considerable restrictions on what it was possible for the family as a whole to do. Some parents had taken a deliberate decision that their other children should not be disadvantaged. For example, one father said that the rest of the family went on holiday without their learning-disabled son because they enjoyed very active holidays in which he could not participate because of his additional physical impairments.

It is vital not to romanticise the impact of having a child with a learning disability. Some of the parents I spoke to mused on what their lives would have been like had their child not been born disabled. They wondered how much money they might be earning or where they might be living. All knew their lives had been transformed by the experience and found it hard to imagine life without their sons or daughters. In some cases a lack of understanding had meant the effective fracturing of some relationships within the family. On the other hand, the intensity of relationships between parents and children caused one father to remark that, 'we live his life for him'. Whilst it could be assumed that this is the opposite of empowerment, the profoundly impaired young man concerned had accompanied his parents to Nigeria when they went to live there for a couple of years and had thus had the opportunity for a broader experience of the world than many achieve. Whilst the intense relationship between many young people with learning disabilities and their parents is not usual in contemporary Western families, it may be wrong to assume that it is pathologi-cal or that setting out to achieve independence from parents is necessarily empowering. It may be that the quality of some such relationships provides opportunities for personal growth which others may seek through other means, for example, employment, but which are not inevitably achieved as a result.

Leaving home

'Leaving home' is a critical life event which highlights some of the issues and dilemmas in relation to independence, autonomy and empowerment. Jones and Wallace (1992) describe how processes of transition begin in the family of origin for all young people. But adult status has to be confirmed by institutions outside the family context: 'Until a young adult enters and is accepted by the institutions of the labour market, the state benefit system, the housing market and the consumer market place, their adulthood cannot be socially confirmed' (Jones and Wallace 1992, p.80).

For young adults with learning disabilities the transition is particularly difficult and the help needed to achieve this correspondingly more important. Some of the young people I spoke to were ambivalent about moving away from home. One young man said he would like to leave home because his parents hassled him, but thought he would miss out on some of the support his parents gave him if he did. Some thought that they would like to live with friends, but not on their own, but they also thought they would have to get a job and to sort out money before it would be a possibility. They all thought their parents would help them out in practical ways if they needed this, and one young man said his parents would be very supportive: 'They say, go for it, if you want your own place you go for it'. They also said their parents were supportive of them going to the Employment Preparation Unit, and the one young man who had been actively seeking open employment had had a lot of support from his parents in applying for jobs.

None wanted to get married at this stage. Some were against the idea entirely, whilst one thought he had not met the right girl yet. Again, money was felt to be a significant factor influencing whether or not they should marry. None, at this stage, thought they would want to have children of their own.

Parents' views of their son's or daughter's futures were strongly influenced by the level of care they were seen to need. Some had adult children who required intensive personal care. The parents saw their futures in fully staffed residential accommodation and considered it unrealistic to expect that they might be able to live independently. Others considered a greater degree of independence would be possible, but reflected the young people's concerns that they would need considerable help in dealing with the financial aspects of running a home. One mother spoke of the preparation she sought to give for the future:

> I'm working towards him becoming independent because I don't want him to go into a home, I do want him to live in the community. I don't think he will have a family to call on, I do think he's going to have to do it on his own, so I am trying to give him his freedom. For example, going on taxis, buses, I trained him to do that. I've got that part right, I know I have.

Most of the parents I spoke to could not imagine their sons or daughters having children of their own and some were very opposed to the idea. Some saw sex as frightening in its uncontrollability; others spoke of children creating pressures that their sons or daughters would not be able to cope with. There was more support for the possibility of close loving relationships without a sexual content.

Underpinning much of what parents spoke about in relation to encouraging freedom and independence in their children was the perception of the world as a dangerous place in general, and particularly dangerous to people who were not skilled in verbal communication and who had a tendency to be inappropriately trusting. Fear has been identified as a factor affecting the quality of life of older people (the F Factor) and it was also present in much of what was said by parents of people with learning disabilities. Fear is associated with a lack of trust and that was experienced in relation to services as well as to society more generally. Accordingly attention is now turned to relationships with services.

Services and empowerment: conflict or partnership?

The extent to which families with a member who has a learning disability are involved with welfare services is one highly significant factor separating them from 'normal' families. Hence social policy and its implementation has a much more immediate and profound effect on families where either a child or a parent has a learning disability. If policies and relationships with services are to contribute to supporting empowerment then at least such relationships should not be debilitating and at best they should be designed to promote the potentially positive aspects identified above.

The earliest experiences of parents can lead to a lack of confidence. One mother spoke of following nursing staff around to ensure that her baby was given sufficient food after the hospital matron had said soon after her daughter's birth, 'Forget about her' and a nursing sister had said, 'Children love you and leave you. Buy yourself a dog, a dog will be your best friend'. Others too spoke of unsympathetic responses when they were first finding out what it meant to have a child with a learning disability which left them mistrustful of professional 'helpers'. For some this meant a constant feeling of working in opposition to paid carers, rather than experiencing professional help as supportive of a joint project concerned with maximising their child's capacities.

Whilst the stereotype is of parents as overprotective and doing too much for their children, one father recounted how care staff in a respite care home would use hoists to lift his son into bed because health and safety regulations meant they were not allowed to lift him. Whilst at home, his parents encourage their son to move as much as he is capable of in order to get what physical exercise he can. The parents I spoke to clearly wanted to encourage their sons or daughters to extend themselves, but spoke of the dilemmas of enabling this to happen in a safe way. They spoke of professional encouragement of risk-taking and what that meant for them in terms of sleepless nights whilst their child was away on an Outward Bound course, or hours of worry when their son was sent home on his own from a part of town with which he was unfamiliar, resulting in the young man getting lost. Such concerns are part of the experience of all parents as their children grow up and start moving out into the world on their own. However, both the intensity and the duration of such concerns are different for parents of children with learning disabilities. Another difference is the extent to which professionals occupy a role in which they take on quasi-parental roles for longer periods of their children's lives.

One very practical example was provided by parents of how unhelpful it can be to see the person with a learning disability as an individual, rather than as a member of a family group. A number of the parents I spoke to said their daughters or sons had speech difficulties which meant people often found it hard to understand what they were saying. I too found difficulty understanding the words of some of the young people I spoke to at the Employment Preparation Unit. The parents identified communication problems as an important constraint on the ability of their sons or daughters to become independent. Yet they said it was virtually impossible to obtain speech therapy — one father said the speech therapist spent ten minutes with him with the intention of enabling him to give therapy to his son. Learning sign language was seen as an alternative, but whilst this had obviously been tried in some day centres attended by the people involved, no attempt had been made to teach this to parents. Hence, as one father said, when his son came back using his hands in an attempt to communicate, his father had to guess at what he was trying to say.

None of the parents I spoke to felt that service providers were helping them to plan and prepare for their daughters' and sons' futures. One spoke of an assessment which had led to a decision that his sons were not appropriate for a supported accommodation development, but no suitable alternative had been suggested. There was no sense that a range of options existed which would meet the varying needs of their daughters and sons for support when they were no longer able to live with their parents.

Their current experience of services designed to provide activity on a day to-day basis was of services which expected people with learning disabilities to fit providers' assumptions about holiday periods, and which assumed the preparedness of parents to be there in case the transport was late or the day centre shut because of staff sickness.

All the parents I spoke to were, or had been actively involved in, parents' groups, carers' panels (Barnes and Wistow 1993) or voluntary groups in which they were campaigning for better services for people with learning disabilities, as well as for recognition of their own position as carers. They saw their own involvement in this as one means by which they could contribute to the empowerment of people with learning disabilities through the development of services capable of maximising quality of life and providing long-term security. One focus for criticism was the special school system which segregates people with learning disabilities and can disempower in two ways: first by failing to provide the education necessary for taking on active roles as adults; and second by making learning disabilities invisible to children in general, as they grow up, and hence getting in the way of the development of widespread acceptance of people with learning disabilities.

Some parents were also active supporters of initiatives to empower their sons and daughters in relation to the services they receive, through participation in users' panels and within broader based initiatives designed to increase the influence of users over services (for example, the 'Search Team' within Birmingham City Council, established during the life of the Community Care Special Action project to ensure a continuing focus for user influence over services, see Barnes and Wistow 1992). They were also supportive of initiatives to encourage the development of skills, for example using public transport, whilst also, and inevitably, concerned about safety.

Their willingness to meet with me to discuss the issue of empowerment can be taken as one example of their commitment to developing the debate, even though some admitted that they did not know what they could contribute to this. This view was expressed in particular by parents with sons or daughters with profound impairments who needed extensive personal care. For them the question of living alone, marriage and employment seems entirely unrealistic, and they are looking to ways in which constant support can be secured for their adult children when they are no longer able to provide this. But they are just as concerned with the quality of life of their relatives and to know that the support available will be responsive to their needs and wishes.

Conclusion

Amongst the 'intermediate needs' which Doyal and Gough identify as requiring to be satisfied if the universal needs of physical health and autonomy are to be met are: security in childhood; significant primary relationships; adequate protective housing; and a non-hazardous physical environment. For most people the first three of these needs are met initially within the context of families, whilst the fourth starts within the immediate living environment and extends into the world beyond.

The role of families in increasing self-understanding; in developing the capacity to formulate options; and in providing opportunities to act on options – the components of 'autonomy' – is evident in much of the discussions I have reported here. The cognitive impairments experienced by people with learning disabilities mean that the development of such understandings and the capacity to act on them is a slower process than amongst non-disabled people. Thus the significance of intermediate need-satisfiers is correspondingly greater. Families *are* likely to play a bigger part in enabling their learning-disabled members to achieve a level of autonomy which can enable them to participate within society than is the case with non-disabled children. Opportunities to exercise the capacity to act, for example, to travel to visit a relative or to set up home with a friend, often have to be actively worked for, rather than simply being allowed by non-prevention.

Associated with this is a higher level of interdependence than exists between many adult children and their parents. Both parents and children have challenges to overcome which are not experienced by those who do not have a disabled relative. The relationship between them may comprise levels of intimacy not shared between parents and non-disabled children. At times both may regret or resent this, but it inevitably affects the sense of self of each party. But autonomy and interdependence should not be seen to be in opposition. As Doyal and Gough write: 'An autonomy which pursues individual self-interest at the expense of others hardly constitutes a universalisable human need. In fact, several studies suggest that self-esteem goes hand in hand with pro-social attitudes, altruism and generosity' (1991, p.65).

This has implications for the way in which professional service providers need to approach their relationships with people with learning disabilities and their families. Empowerment is too often viewed as a zero sum – empowering one person is thought to mean removing power from another. Disempowering parents is unlikely to be a helpful strategy in increasing the empowerment of people with learning disabilities. Recognising the skills and understanding which parents bring to the development of their sons or daughters should form the basis of a three-way partnership in those cases where professionals have substantial involvement in people's lives.

Paid care workers should also be prepared to recognise and value the full range of roles which people with learning disabilities may play. Providing care to younger family members; acting as supportive friends and advocates to other people with learning disabilities; or helping out older relatives by cleaning or doing the garden, may be the type of actions which enable people to participate in a capacity consistent with their understanding of themselves and with their formulations of their options. Prioritising paid employment as the only source of valued social roles may serve to devalue the contributions which people can make as members of different social groups. Thus service providers should approach people with learning disabilities not as isolated individuals with the aim of complete independence from others, but as members of social groups which can provide the opportunity for fulfilling a variety of roles.

Many of the difficulties which parents experience in empowering their daughters or sons to take their own decisions and to become autonomous citizens derive from the responses of others. Families become isolated by a lack of understanding which itself comes from the invisibility of learning disability. The world is seen as a dangerous place, in part because it is a world in which their sons or daughters will not receive a ready understanding or welcome. If parents are not to be left on their own and to experience protection as more important than empowerment, then people with learning disabilities need to be integrated within all spheres of social life from the earliest age. Within families both caring and developmental responsibilities should be shared more broadly. Outside the family, early mixing should be facilitated so that communication and understanding between children with learning disabilities and non-disabled children can develop. In social policy terms that means integrated education. The goal is that of participation which avoids the risk of harm.

Perhaps a more general conclusion arising out of this discussion is that we need to broaden our understanding of 'ordinary lives'. Demographic and policy changes mean that an increasing proportion of families will have a member who has a learning disability (or be old, physically impaired or have a mental health problem) living with them during much of their lives. This is part of the ordinary experience of many people and will add to the diversity of that already variable social group: 'the family'. We need to understand much more about the nature of relationships within families with a learning-disabled member if social policy is to be developed in a way which supports the empowering strategies which many parents seek to adopt. At the same time there needs to be a recognition that enabling people with learning disabilities to participate in social life beyond their families is a responsibility which we all share.

Acknowledgement

I would like to thank the young people of the Users' Council at Birmingham's Employment Preparation Unit for talking so openly with me about their families and about their hopes for the future. I would also like to thank the two groups of parents for sharing their experiences and thoughts with me – on this occasion as many other times in the past. Thanks particularly to Bill for helping me set it all up.

References

Ayer, S. and Alaszewski, A. (1984) *Community Care and the Mentally Handicapped: Services for Mothers and their Mentally Handicapped Children.* London: Croom Helm.

Barnes, M. and Wistow, G. (1992) 'Sustaining innovation in community care.' *Local Government Policy Making 18,* 4, 3–10.

Barnes, M. and Wistow, G. (1993) *Gaining Influence, Gaining Support: Working with Carers in Research and Practice.* University of Leeds: Nuffield Institute for Health.

Barnes, M. and Wistow, G. (1995) 'Moving towards employment: corporate responsibilities for community care.' *Social Services Research 1,* 36–47.

Barrett, M. and McIntosh, M. (1982) *The Anti-Social Family.* London: Verso.

Birmingham City Council (1991) *The Birmingham Community Care Plan: Policies, Priorities, Proposals.* Birmingham: Birmingham City Council.

Booth, T. and Booth, W. (1993) 'Learning the hard way: practice issues in supporting parents with learning difficulties.' *Social Work and Social Sciences Review 4,* 2, 148–162.

Doyal, L. and Gough, I. (1991) *A Theory of Human Need.* Basingstoke: Macmillan.

Ellis, K. (1993) *Squaring the Circle. User and Carer Participation in Needs Assessment.* York: Joseph Rowntree Foundation.

Finch, J. (1989) *Family Obligations and Social Change.* Cambridge: Polity Press.

Glendinning, C. (1983) *Unshared Care: Parents and Their Disabled Children.* London: Routledge.

Grant, G. (1992) 'Researching user and carer involvement in mental handicap services.' In M. Barnes and G. Wistow (eds) *Researching User Involvement.* University of Leeds: Nuffield Institute for Health.

Grant, G. and Nolan, M. (1993) 'Informal carers: sources and concomitants of satisfaction.' *Health and Social Care in the Community 1,* 3, 147–160.

Jones, G. and Wallace, C. (1992) *Youth, Family and Citizenship.* Buckingham: Open University Press.

Kaplan, A.G. and Surrey, J.L. (1986) 'The relational self in women: developmental theory and public policy.' In L.E. Walker (ed) *Women and Mental Health Policy.* Beverly Hills and London: Sage.

Morris, J. (1993) *Independent Lives.* Basingstoke: Macmillan.

Smyth, M. and Robus, N. (1989) *The Financial Circumstances of Families with Disabled Children Living in Private Households.* London: HMSO.

Walmsley, J. (1993) 'Contradictions in caring: reciprocity and interdependence.' *Disability, Handicap and Society 8,* 2, 129–141.

Empowerment in Informal Settings
The Themes

John Borland and Paul Ramcharan

Introduction

In this short chapter we seek to disentangle themes that have emerged in Section 1. These themes are used to create an agenda which needs to be addressed within any theory of empowerment relating to people with learning disabilities. This agenda is taken up in a more substantive way in Chapter 13 where the threads are brought together into a more systematic view of empowerment and the everyday lives of people with learning disabilities.

The 'excluded identity' and 'included identity'

The first section of this book has drawn attention to the everyday world of family, friends and community. This world is wholly unremarkable and yet, at the same time, it is the very fabric of each person's lived reality. So what is distinctive about the life experiences of people with learning disabilities which warrants attention?

The notion of 'excluded identities' will be used as an heuristic device to address this question and as a guide through some of the emerging themes. This concept of 'excluded identities' brings together two ideas, namely the importance of inclusion within society, and the development of a self-concept and identity. The two, it is suggested, are inextricably related. If the conditions for experiencing everyday life are those in which the person is excluded, it is likely that a person will be socialised into an excluded self-concept and identity. This applies not just to people with learning disabilities, but to all human beings.

Developmental psychology texts include numerous examples showing the effects of impoverished socialisation processes and exclusion on the formation of self-concept and identity. Some cases, though thankfully rare, of children who are isolated during their early years demonstrate that cognitive, social and other forms of personal development are not achieved if interaction with others is limited or denied. Studies of feral children have shown how learning is primarily a product of interaction within a social group. Some studies even report learned quadriped motion amongst children brought up by animals. Feral children have also shown difficulties in speech development. In one study, 36 of 46 such cases reviewed showed no further development of intelligible speech and difficulties in adjusting to new environments and social interactions (McNeil, Poloway and Smith 1984). These studies clearly demonstrate that socialisation and life experiences from the earliest of ages will greatly affect the development of self-concept, and that prolonged exclusion can lead to irremediable breakdowns in the capacity for reintegration and resocialisation.

Extrapolating from these extreme examples, we may postulate that the self-concept and identity of humans, whether people with learning disabilities or not, will develop in relation to the environment and relationships which they experience. And as Barton tells us: 'Being disabled involves experiencing discrimination, vulnerability and abusive assaults upon your self-identity and esteem' (1996, p.8). People with learning disabilities, with few exceptions, have been consigned to separate development within special schools and largely excluded from the work place within our society, not to say from many leisure and other community facilities. Even at the informal and service levels, there are reasons, as Ramcharan *et al.* illustrate (Chapter 4), why families and service personnel do not provide opportunities for community activities and for friendships to develop. 'Taken in this context, and rather than looking at what is 'broken' about the individual, we can see the individual as telling us what is 'broken' about the community system' (Smull and Burke Harrison 1992, p.6).

Although the contributors in Section 1 use different tones and inflections, they seem to agree that the construction of identity and the empowerment of individuals is a life-long process within which a number of structures and face-to-face relationships are important. From these contributions we also gain insight into some of the complications that attend the process of identity formation: at the individual level the reflexive and introspective awareness of what Stevens describes as, 'the human capacity to be aware of one's self as being a particular person distinct from all others, and to reflect on the experience of being that person, and who that person is' (1985, p.85); and, at the interactional level, the way it is, '...connected with the fateful appraisals made of oneself – by oneself and by others' (Strauss 1977, p.9).

The personal and social identity described above feature strongly in the first chapters of this volume. These categories are dynamic in that, '...the evolution of identity entails the continual and dialectic relationship between personal and social identity. Current social identity is the product of all past personal identities with all past and present social identities' (Breakwell 1983, p.12). Put another way, each person is always in the process of 'becoming'. But these chapters also implicitly infer a third dimension, namely civic identity, which is connected with the political and legal structures of society, defining our rights and duties as citizens. These three aspects of identity are only separable at an analytical level and are inextricably woven together within our everyday lives. In the sense that identity forms and re-forms over time, the three forms of identity may also be viewed in terms of a process of personal growth and development which enables people not only to assert their personal needs and influence the way in which they are met, but also to participate as citizens in the community.

The discourse of personal and familial identity

In families within which learning-disabled members receive care, the non-learning-disabled members are likely to play a bigger part in enabling their disabled relative to be autonomous and independent and to participate in society. Associated with this high degree of involvement is a higher level of interdependence than usually exists between family members. The relationship may continue in this vein long after the 'benchmark' of childhood is passed, and may entail levels of intimacy not experienced between parents and non-disabled children. This, and the physical environment which they share, may affect each party's sense of self and autonomy.

Barnes (Chapter 5) shows that despite these difficulties there remains an overwhelming feeling that families care for, and about, their relatives and would do anything perceived to be in their interests. As she implies, fostering the growth of independence in their relative's autonomy to act for themselves is seldom sufficient, and relatives often have to work actively on behalf of their relatives to achieve such independence. But such action and advocacy by families is a double-edged sword. In Chapter 4, Ramcharan *et al.* show that families, despite always claiming to act in their relative's best interests, can prevent opportunities for community contact and independent friendships from arising, or can take decisions about alternatives which act against autonomy, independence and integration. Where people with learning disabilities cannot act on their own behalf, others will often set the conditions within which they will come to experience the social world. Such conditions are often set in ways which exclude and segregate people with learning disabilities from their communities.

The discussion of constraints on inclusion of many people with learning disabilities presented by Ramcharan *et al.* contrasts with Souza's description of her own life experiences (Chapter 1). In a number of key ways Souza may be seen as a 'border-crosser' (Peters 1996), fighting to move into situations of integration and to be included in the mainstream of society in terms of education and work. Peters argues that:

> If we teach young people with disabilities how to become border crossers at a personal level, the cultural symbols and metaphors prevalent in today's society will begin to disintegrate. Their

> subjectiveness becomes self-evident, rather than the supposed
> objectivity one perceives if one does not take into account the powerful
> human action involved in border crossing. (p.224)

Clearly the self-concept and identity required to pursue such border-crossing
must work on presumptions made by oneself, or one's advocates, about the
right to inclusion, that is, an 'included self-identity'. But the development of
such an identity can only occur where the legal, policy and other structures
within civil society permit.

Souza's account leads us to see that from early childhood her mother treated
her as a potentially valuable member of her community, with the same rights
to education as other children. In one instance Souza's mother went so far as
to seek legal redress to keep Souza in mainstream secondary education. Souza's
sense of self-worth is demonstrable in her writing. The very title of her article
implies that she will tell us everything we want to know about Down's
Syndrome. Yet, apart from recognition that this is a label attached to her by the
medical profession, she otherwise argues that she is the same as anyone else,
with the same sorts of needs and wishes as other members of society. Hers is a
positive account of a person fighting personal battles just like any other person.
Souza, unlike most non-disabled people, has actively had to fight for her right
to be perceived, and to interact with others, as a person first. In this enterprise
the support of her mother and others played a key role in the formation of her
identity. Souza has crossed the symbolic boundary from that of a 'disability
identity' or an 'excluded identity' to one of 'identity as a person' or an 'included
identity' within the wider social world. This progression is extraordinarily
powerful and significant because it is what motivates her life choices and her
interactions with others.

Souza's inclusion within mainstream schooling is in stark contrast to the
experience of the majority of children in Britain labelled as having a learning
disability. The reality, accepted by parents either by default or despite their best
efforts, is that their children go to special schools, and are assessed by
educational psychologists at intervals through the process of statementing. This
process of assessment reaffirms the original decision to exclude them from
mainstream schools on the grounds of their limited conceptual development,
and may lead to these individuals being moved, at a later age, to other
segregated settings. In this way, exclusion is supported by the structural
mechanisms for gaining access to education, the very system which posits
'individual development' as its aim.

But, as Souza says, schooling is not only about academic education; it is also
about finding one's place in society and about the development of civic identity.
Segregated settings cannot contribute to the establishment of an included
self-concept and identity. It is akin to asking a freshwater trout to leave its own
habitat and live with a school of salt-water herring. As Barton has observed:
'Ultimately fundamental questions need to be asked about the current structural

and social conditions and relations of society and how these in often complex and contradictory ways establish and legitimate the creation of barriers' (1996, p.14).

There are implications for family carers and advocates in the above arguments which relate policy and legal constraints to the everyday life experiences of people with learning disabilities. If these policy and legal imperatives were working to promote inclusion, the questions families and advocates might be asking would change. The questions would be about how to find the best possible methods of integration within these inclusive settings, and within education, and about how to get the most out of the system for their relatives or partners. Moreover, it is likely that discussions with and about people with learning disabilities would then be about friendships and relationships with other members of their peer group, whether disabled or not. In summary, the structures within which decisions are made can markedly affect both the choices available to people with learning disabilities, as well as their outcomes. The barriers to inclusion, autonomy and integration which are concomitant with legal and policy imperatives can therefore have a significant effect on the success of personal and/or advocates' strategies for inclusion and integration.

However, some caution is needed in extrapolating from Souza's experience. Bayley's contribution (Chapter 2) shows that, in order to develop friendships and integration, it may not be sufficient simply to provide certain conditions and opportunities. It could be argued that integration from an early age may help non-disabled people to find the gift of friendship amongst their peers with a learning disability. But there are likely to be a number of non-disabled people who, because of their beliefs, values and attitudes, may not want such friendship or contact. As Bayley argues, the sense of loneliness experienced may lead to 'relationship vacuums' which may be filled inappropriately. Where integration and inclusion are to survive in ways which maximise the personal life satisfaction and quality of life of citizens with a learning disability, it becomes vital to examine what further strategies will address the problems that arise in this way.

It has already been argued that with few exceptions family carers will wish to provide solutions which are in the best interests of their relatives. Time and again they mention the need to find a balance between their relative taking risks or being overprotected. Where people with learning disabilities are included in their communities, the tight ties of present systems of disability support within closed and segregated settings is no longer present and this raises vital points about setting up systems of protection. Protective systems can only be informal and non-interventionist if they are to perpetuate and maintain the 'included identity' to which we have referred here.

In summary, it seems that civic identity cannot exist if self-identity and social identity are not geared towards inclusion within civil society, that is, towards inclusion within society's economic, political and social institutions. Others are likely to play a more significant role in actively supporting and advocating the development of such identities by providing opportunities for socialisation in relation to people with learning disabilities. The structures of civil society set the conditions within which at least some choices are made by, for and with people with learning disabilities. These structures may constrain as much as they liberate. Where they constrain individuals, the choices facing people with learning disabilities and their advocates and carers may be exclusionary. It therefore becomes vital to seek to change the structures of civil society in order to reflect the need for inclusion. One route to accomplishing this is through establishing a rights agenda.

The discourse of rights and identity

People coming together to promote their rights has led to significant gains for black and other ethnic minority populations and, at least since the 1960s, for women. More recently such action has been recognised and adopted by disabled people in many areas of the world. Turner suggests that despite many threats to full citizenship and civic identity, 'new social movements have been responsible for citizenship expansion in the post-war period' (1993, p.13). Gooding also argues that:

> Rights discourse promotes the development of a sense of self and a group's collective identity most powerfully through the process in which these rights are asserted. The act of claiming a right is in itself an assertion of moral self-worth. The advocacy process itself, for a group like disabled people who have historically been excluded from public life, combats exclusion. (1994, p.44)

This extract emphasises the importance of the twin concepts of identity and inclusion. Reflecting these ideas, Inclusion International, an organisation working for human rights and social justice for people with learning disabilities, has argued for the need for inclusion, full citizenship, self-determination and family support (Inclusion, 1995). These themes have, in postmodernist terms, been globalised so that globally accepted rights are acted upon at local level. Global statements of rights, such as the UN Charter on Human Rights and the Rights of Disabled People, provide a powerful incentive for people with learning disabilities in their fight for rights. But how can such rights become a reality?

In line with arguments which have already been made, it is suggested that the cutting edge of the rights discourse, and actions by its members, can only develop where there is, first, a sense of personal identity and, on the basis of that identity, a resulting political or group identity with those who share common interests. It is only where such conditions co-exist that the process which Friere (1983) describes as 'conscientisation' can occur. The goal of 'conscientisation' is, '...to develop a self-consciousness as a prerequisite to liberation from an oppression which depersonalises, and therefore dehumanises those who are oppressed' (Peters 1996, p.225). So to what extent has the

self-advocacy movement achieved a common identity as well as 'conscientisation'?

Self-advocacy groups have been burgeoning in Britain for the past decade,
many run as in-house service groups but a growing number working independently. Longhurst (1994) has mapped a similar speedy growth of the
self-advocacy movement in the United States. In 1984, 152 groups with a total
of more than 5000 members were noted in her research; this number had grown
to 380 groups by 1990 and to 505 groups in 1993, involving 11,600 people
(Longhurst, passim 1–11).

Walmsley and Downer (Chapter 3) point to the growing maturity of the
independent self-advocacy movement in Britain. They demonstrate how
women's groups and ethnic minority groups can work together to meet a
common agenda which they may not necessarily share with that of a largely
white advocacy movement which is also largely male-dominated. As they say,
'there was, until recently, a failure by researchers and practitioners to recognise
that people with this label also have identities as men, women, black or white
people, Jewish or Moslem, and hetero- or homosexual, indeed as working,
middle or upper class'. Their article instructs us to see that the construction of
group identity and interests is still in the process of being accomplished within
the self-advocacy movement in Britain today.

Three further issues arise in relation to the development of self-advocacy.
In the first place, can, and indeed should, all people with learning disabilities
participate in such groups? In fact, many people may simply not want to become
involved in groups of this sort. This is not necessarily a question of 'false
consciousness'; it is a question of whether it fits with their perceived self-identity. Indeed, as with other pressure groups and political interest groups, there
will never be a closed shop, nor would we want to require people's participation
against their will. Since not all people with learning disabilities would choose
to be involved in self-advocacy or other groups, the idea of a vanguard group
of leaders or of activists is likely to emerge as a key development in the
continuing fight for rights.

But to imply the need for leaders or activists or a vanguard requires an
understanding of the nature of the rights for which the group is fighting.
Second, to what extent has the self-advocacy movement moved from group
identity formation to one of fighting for rights to an inclusive 'civic identity'
through 'conscientisation'? Whilst Downer and Walmsley report that the
self-advocacy movement has talked to a government minister and that self-advocacy groups have been included in a number of governmental and service
committees, it is by no means clear that a wider statement of rights (addressed
further in Chapter 13), or prolonged action to achieve them, characterises the
movement at present. The focus of self-advocacy groups still seems to be in the
formation of a group identity and within 'weak publics' (Lister 1990), that is,
those in the non-political and informal spheres. The necessary 'conscientisation'

and development of activism within 'strong publics' (i.e. pressure for change of substantive rights within the political sphere and through the political and legal process), still remains to be developed.

This leads to a third point, namely the context within which the self-advocacy movement should activate its rights-based actions. Clearly this remains a choice for the members of the movement to make for themselves, but it has been suggested that: 'User groups such as Survivors Speak Out (mental health) and People First (learning disabilities) need to feed into the broad disability movement which in turn can join other oppressed and marginalised groups in challenging the existing political system' (Means and Smith 1994, p.75). The extent to which the aims and actions of the disability movement reflects those of people with learning disabilities in ways which allow for concerted common action is a point taken up in the concluding chapter.

Summary and continuing themes

In the Preface to this text it was suggested that empowerment should be viewed as a system of interdependencies between people, institutions and structures. The chapters in Section 1 have described some aspects of the mundane lives of people with learning disabilities, providing a base from which to make links with the larger structural influences in their lives, such as the legal system and services, in ways which reflect their everyday interests and concerns. A number of themes characterise the discussion above.

Systems and structures are needed which ensure the maximum opportunity for people with learning disabilities to be included in mainstream society. Segregated service settings provide close supervision and formalised service responses and there is a need to move to a more informal system of support in familial and community settings. Also necessary is the positive action of others in providing informal facilitative mechanisms which promote inclusionary practices. At the point at which these mechanisms become closed and institutionalised their liberating potential evaporates, and we are drawn into those formal systems which smother personal identity, development and growth.

Personal and social identities emerge over time in relation to the types of socialisation processes experienced by the individual. Inclusionary socialisation processes are necessary for inclusion, and are antecedents to an inclusive identity with other groups and individuals. Included identities are therefore likely to be multiple identities reflecting the person's interests and connections within the spheres of their families, friends, communities and with other parties with whom they may share 'civic interests'. As Peters says: 'These notions of multiple identities, their interdependence and the dynamics of border crossing involved in creating identities might serve as the focus for sociological studies on disability' (1996, p.232). Both personal and group identities are therefore antecedent prerequisites to civic identity, 'conscientisation' and the fight for rights.

Not everyone may wish to fight for these rights because they may have personal identities which are centred in other concerns. In theory it is the ultimate objective of the rights movement to work itself out of existence when the accomplishment of its interests is attained. But how such rights can be achieved must be a central debate for the future and one which is tied to the way in which the civic structures of society in terms of services and legislation constrain or liberate the individual. Some aspects of the nature of present structures are considered in Section 2 and further proposals for change are outlined in Section 3.

We end, however, on a cautionary note. In this chapter we have examined how self-identity is formed, and have argued that certain conditions are required in order to avoid an 'excluded identity'. Abberley has warned (in the context of paid employment) that theories of inclusion, '…imply the progressive abolition of impairment as restrictive on the development of people's full human capacities. But as a total achievement of this aim is impossible, some non-oppressive disadvantage still remains for some impaired people in such utopias' (1996, p.61). In this chapter we have assumed 'nurture' to be the major predetermining factor in the formation of both 'excluded' and 'included' identities. Whilst Abberley rightly has reservations in relation to the extent to which nurture can overcome the impairments of nature, there is still a strong sense that the will and the resources of human creativeness can overcome the barriers to inclusion. This opens up the issue of what actually constitutes 'inclusion', what constitutes a sufficient inclusion and, indeed, whether 'inclusion' is a universal concept. Some of these issues are developed further in the chapters which follow.

References

Abberley, P. (1996) 'Work, utopia and impairment.' In L. Barton (ed) *Disability and Society: Emerging Issues and Insights*, 61–82. Harlow: Addison Wesley Longman.

Barton, L. (1996) 'Sociology and disability: some emerging issues.' In L. Barton (ed) *Disability and Society: Emerging Issues and Insights*, 3–18. Harlow: Addison Wesley Longman.

Breakwell, G.M. (1983) *Threatened Identities*. Chichester: John Wiley.

Friere, P. (1983) *Pedagogy of the Opressed*. New York: The Continuum Publishing Corporation.

Gooding, C. (1994) *Disabling Laws, Enabling Acts: Disability Rights in Britain and America*. London: Pluto Press.

Inclusion International (1995) *Inclusion (ILSMH News)* May, No.17.

Lister, R. (1990) 'Women, economic dependency and citizenship.' *Journal of Social Policy 19*, 4, 445–467.

Longhurst, N.A. (1994) *The Self-Advocacy Movement by People with Developmental Disabilities: A Demographic Study and Directory of Self-Advocacy Groups in the United States.* Washington: American Association on Mental Retardation.

McNeil, M.C., Poloway, E.A. and Smith, J.D. (1984) 'Feral and isolated children: review and analysis.' *Education and Training of the Mentally Retarded 19*, 1, 70–79.

Means, R. and Smith, R. (1994) *Community Care: Practice and Policy.* London: Macmillan.

Peters, S. (1996) 'The politics of disability identity.' In L. Barton (ed) *Disability and Society: Emerging Issues and Insights*, 215–234. Harlow: Addison Wesley Longman.

Smull, M.W. and Burke Harrison, S. (1992) *Supporting People with Severe Reputations in the Community.* Alexandria, Virginia: National Association of State Directors of Developmental Disabilities Services, Inc.

Stevens, R. (1985) 'Personal worlds.' *Social Psychology: Development, Experience and Behaviour in the Social World.* Block 4, No.D307. Milton Keynes: Open University.

Strauss, A.L. (1977) *Mirrors and Masks.* London: Martin Robertson.

Turner, B.S. (1993) 'Contemporary problems in the theory of citizenship.' In B.S. Turner (ed) *Citizenship and Social Theory*, 1–18. London: Sage.

Further Reading

Beyer, S. (1996) 'Real jobs and supported employment.' In T. Philpot and L. Ward (eds) *Values and Visions: Changing Ideas in Services for People with Learning Difficulties.* London: Butterworth-Heinemann.

PART 2

Empowerment in Formal Settings

CHAPTER 6

Empowerment Within Services
A Comfortable Delusion

Steve Dowson

Introduction

In social care, good ideas lose their glister when they become accepted, everyday realities. They cease to be the cause of enthusiastic professional debate and career-enhancing innovation. Between the conception and the creation, one might say, falls the fashion. Thus it may safely be assumed that 'user empowerment', one of the hottest topics in the industry, is not yet a commonplace reality. On the other hand, one might suppose that so much attention on the subject is at least a sign of a genuine professional commitment to hand over power, and of real progress being made.

This chapter offers an alternative explanation in relation to the empowerment of people with learning difficulties: that the level of professional interest is not so much a sign of progress as a substitute for action. The volume of discussion supports the comfortable delusion of change, whilst allowing professionals to keep their power in all the ways that matter.

It may be that this conclusion is drawn from a particular perspective: not the perspective of an academic, nor that, in recent years, of a practitioner. As the Director of a national advocacy group, and as a trainer and researcher, I have heard the conference rhetoric and read the literature, but I have also worked with staff and service users who have told me – sometimes in anxious, unattributable whispers – about a very different reality. It is also, it should be admitted, a values-based viewpoint. The values may be dressed up in the clothing of normalisation or social role valorisation, but they are rooted in the straightforward belief that people with learning difficulties are fundamentally the same as other people. They have the same basic needs, wishes and rights.

It may be difficult to see how those needs and wishes can be met, those rights honoured; but that is a challenge which we must face, not a reason to force on people with learning difficulties an identity which would allow us to set less demanding objectives. It is difficult to strip away the misconceptions of the past, to see people with learning difficulties as people like ourselves, and to identify the implications for services. The health and social care industry deserves credit for the progress it has made in recent years in that task. However, whereas our ability to see the ultimate goal may still be evolving, the goal itself does not move. Once we accept that people with learning difficulties are entitled to the same respect, dignity, basic rights and opportunities which we expect for ourselves, we have established an absolute standard. Against that standard, as I argue in this chapter, the industry still fails miserably.

If it is true that the prospect of user empowerment within the whole sphere of services is a delusion, it is particularly unfortunate for people with learning difficulties, for whom ordinary life usually means a life dominated by, and enveloped in, social services. Ordinary life, in the sense of ordinary activities carried out in the community and in the company of ordinary people, is something that most people with learning difficulties rarely experience. They witness it, but are usually excluded from it.

That exclusion has become less obvious, though hardly less real, in recent years. Twenty years ago the mental handicap hospitals had a major and almost universally accepted role in the provision of 'mental handicap' services. Each one was a total institution which combined residential, occupational, leisure and most health care services for their inmates, on an enclosed campus. For anyone who looked beyond the high walls and fences that surrounded them, the hospitals were a very visible demonstration of society's assumption that people with learning difficulties should be kept away from ordinary life.

With more than 10,000 people in England still resident in mental handicap hospitals,[1] these institutions are not yet history. Nevertheless, the general pattern of services has changed. Most people with learning difficulties now go to different places for the various kinds of service they need, and most of those places are geographically located within ordinary communities. This pattern is the extent to which community care has been achieved for most people with learning difficulties. Community care is happening, to the extent that people are receiving care in services located in the community. They remain, however, almost as much confined within services, and excluded from ordinary life, as they were in the old hospitals. People with learning difficulties may travel on their special bus from their group home to the day centre, and then on for an evening of leisure, probably with the same companions, at the Gateway Club. The new pattern of services may be regarded as the dispersed institution. The campus has been broken up, but not the institution itself. The main difference

---

1   In a written reply to a Parliamentary Question (PQ 1357, submitted 20/01/95) the Junior Minister for Health, John Bowis, stated that the estimated number of long-stay residents of mental handicap hospitals in England at 31/3/94 was 11,500. When compared with the previous year, this suggests that the long-stay resident population is contracting by about 2000 residents per annum.

now is that people with learning difficulties can look out of the windows and see what they are missing.

This is, of course, a generalisation. There are many service agencies which are trying hard to introduce the people they support to ordinary community opportunities and activities, and there are enough success stories to prove that it can be done. A conception of community care as a way of supporting people which will lead to citizenship for people with learning difficulties is by no means an impossible dream. But even the better service agencies are finding it difficult to leap the gap between community presence and community partici-pation. Good services can now offer many stories of service users who go to community leisure activities and college classes or have jobs in mainstream employment. On closer examination it usually becomes clear that people are spending time in the same places – often the same rooms – as ordinary citizens, but *alongside* them rather than engaged *with* them. The staff who proudly tell these stories are usually stumped when asked to cite an occasion when another student or employee from these community activities has been known to pay a social call to the service user's home.

Good news arrives from those services which not only espouse the goals of dignity, choice and community participation for their service users, but are based in community locations and designed in a way which puts those goals within reach. It has to be balanced against the continuing existence of the large hospitals, hostels and residential homes where indignity and oppression are inherent, abuses all too common. We may find comfort in the fact that hospital scandals on the scale of Ely and Normansfield have not occurred – or at least have not entered the public domain – for some years. But even if deliberate, systematic cruelty no longer occurs inside institutional provision, everyday indignities and deprivations undoubtedly remain features of life for many of their inmates. In some cases they are the inevitable consequence of a service located far from ordinary community resources, and designed on a scale which makes block treatment unavoidable. In others they result from the perversion of values which all too easily occurs inside a total institution (Goffman 1961).

An example at the relatively trivial end of the scale would be the hostel where 25 residents share the same hairbrush. More alarming is the instance of the man who, after many years in hospital, was resettled in a community service where he frightened the staff by his violent language and intimidating manner. Eventually it was realised that this behaviour had been learned from the staff on the hospital ward, who communicated with him, even in the way they woke him up in the morning, entirely by verbal abuse. This same, middle-aged man had to be taught by his new support staff that on his birthday he should keep the gifts, throw away the wrapping paper, and display the cards. His birthday had never before been celebrated. I receive other accounts of life in hospital which leave me in no doubt that the loss of ordinary standards of decency in these 'total institutions' sometimes has consequences which are even more appalling. They include an instance of a male resident who systematically raped the female residents. What made this account particularly horrifying was that hospital staff did not see any urgent need to make sure that the rapes were stopped.

Progress needs to be acknowledged and celebrated, but should not lead us to deny the continuing inadequacy of many services, or distract us from the more general truth that, for people with learning difficulties as a group, the struggle for power must take place on territory securely under the control of the social care professionals and their service agencies. Furthermore, the domination of services not only covers the breadth of activities and needs of people with learning difficulties, but also the length of their lifetimes. Indeed, pre-natal screening now means that the process of labelling and discrimination often precedes birth. A few disabled people manage to escape from the 'system', or re-define themselves in a way which makes the given label insignificant, but most will carry their devalued status for life. Amongst the many groups of people who use social services – and are therefore subjected to devaluing labels – people with learning difficulties are uniquely disadvantaged in their ability to challenge the identity forced upon them. Unlike people who are elderly, or going through a time of emotional distress, they cannot support their claim to humanity by reference to the lives they used to lead. They can rarely offer other socially valued skills to compensate for their disability, unlike people with physical impairments. The image of the disabled hero is, to say the least, a mixed blessing; but a wheelchair-using astrophysicist who writes impenetrable best-sellers and provides synthesised voice-overs for airline commercials is quite helpful in nudging the public to accept that people may be real human beings 'in spite of' their disability. People with learning difficulties can offer extremely few examples of this sort.

Service agency staff often claim that their ability to improve the lives of service users is limited by public attitudes. To some extent this is fair comment, particularly in the sense that government spending levels on welfare reflect the priorities and perceptions of the electorate. In many other ways, however, it is passing the buck. Social services are the executors of state policy, the primary manifestation of the way in which the people they serve are identified within society. If people are labelled as sick they will be housed in hospitals. If, as in Nazi Germany, they are deemed non-human, they may go to the death camp. There is a vicious circle at work here: in the process of performing its service, the industry supports a public perception of service users which justifies the actions of those services. The social care services not only have enormous influence over the quality of life of people who are labelled as having learning difficulties. They also, by the images they present to the wider society, largely determine the significance of the label itself.

Moreover, the staff within services are all too easily drawn into the vicious circle. Immersed in the culture of the service, they adopt the prevailing perception of the people they serve, and as a result accept — and even enthusiastically carry out — practices which by other standards would be considered abusive. The best, and most dreadful, example is the doctors, nurses and secretaries at Haddemar hospital in Germany who, in 1941, held a party to celebrate the fact that they had just achieved a total of 10,000 deaths in their systematic killing of disabled people (Wertham 1966,1978). The likely explanation is not that Haddemar recruited staff who were inherently evil. They were probably averagely good people, but were caught in a culture which convinced them that they were doing the right thing. Many lesser but still appalling abuses in UK health and social services must have been similarly rooted in a pathological culture.

If, then, we are to consider how people with learning difficulties might achieve more control over their lives, we need to begin by confronting the very disadvantaged position from which they start. It is a struggle which not only has to take place mainly inside territory securely under the control of professionals. To extend the military analogy, it is up against an extremely effective propaganda machine one so effective that even the people who operate it believe the message it broadcasts. This has important implications for the nature of the struggle.

The first implication is that action to shift the balance of power has had to await an initiative from the social care professionals, and as a result it is the professionals who have defined the goals, means and language of empowerment. The term 'empowerment' is, in itself, revealing. To empower — to 'give or delegate power to, to authorise' (*Collins' English Dictionary*) — is an action taken by those who hold the power. The recipients of the power (the object of the verb) are passive. The very grammar of the word indicates that the powerful will exercise their power even in the very act of empowerment.

There is an obvious contrast between the idea of user *empowerment* and the idea of users *taking power*. Taking power implies action by the discmpowered on their own initiative to wrest power from the powerful. When people take power within a formal system (for example, a political or managerial system), they usually take it completely and unconditionally. The boundaries of their power are explicitly defined, and so any bid to encroach on those boundaries, to re-capture power, must also be made explicitly, perhaps violently, or by a prescribed process such as an election. In contrast, those who are *empowered* may well find that the power has not been given but merely loaned, as in the gift of the parent who allows a teenager to exercise choice — but only if the parent judges that the choices are sensible.

A second implication concerns the location and availability of power. In some areas of life, particularly the mundane activities (see Chapters 3 and 4) of informal private life, we have the option to make choices that do not impinge on the freedoms of other people. The choice is there, free to be taken; and in the act of taking it we empower ourselves. The position is more complicated when one person's choice conflicts with another's – but in a private relationship between equals (between friends, for example) power is not pre-assigned to one person or the other: it still waits to be claimed, though it may then need to be negotiated.

The conditions inside services are very different. Here, power has already been fully assigned. Empowerment must operate by the rules of a 'constant sum game' in which the gains of one party can only be at the expense of another. This game begins with the power allocated almost entirely to service professionals. The assessment of the needs of the user is controlled by professionals through the care management process or through Individual Programme Planning (or similar procedures) within the service setting. The allocation of funds is done without their participation. In most residential services they have no recognised tenants' rights, and hence no security of tenure. Most people with learning difficulties who rely on daily support in the place where they live have few guarantees of privacy, choices of routine or choice of living companions which are not dependent on the goodwill of staff. The definition of consent in relation to people with learning difficulties remains sufficiently vague that, notwithstanding many good practice guidelines, people frequently have little control over medical treatment and are denied sexual relationships.

Most who need support during the day have little choice but to go to the local day centre where they have no direct control over the policies or activities of the centre. Those centres which pay people a few pounds a week as a 'wage' do not treat them as employees; and the increasing number of centres which make a charge for attendance have not noticeably adopted the service values of consumerism.

It is plainly to the advantage of the professionals and their agencies to maintain this gross imbalance of power. Services can be operated to suit the professionals, whether in the choice of food served at the group home, the working hours of staff, or the way in which individual needs are identified to ensure that spending is kept within budget and used to buy services from preferred agencies. By restricting the privacy and freedom of service users, staff reduce not only the inconveniences created by service users acting unseen and on their own initiative, but also the threat of official or public proscription for risk-taking which goes wrong. There also remains in the culture of most services a pervasive – and therefore largely unremarked – presumption that staff have higher status than users. Service agencies are almost always hierarchical organisations structured in the familiar form of a tree with downward-pointing branches. Direct care staff are positioned at the lowest level of the tree. However, decisions which users might want to make about their lives are also passed to care staff and thence upwards to the appropriate management level. By implication and – to judge from many conversations with staff and users – by common recognition, the users are also attached to the tree, as the lowest, least empowered tier of all. Many professionals whole-heartedly reject the charitable model of welfare services, and scoff at the common public perception that they are 'wonderful people looking after the poor handicapped'. Yet they still want to be seen as more than mere service-givers. Workers in provider agencies are learning to live with the new reality that their employment is dependent on the policies of purchasers. To be hired and fired by service users would be another matter entirely.

When the initiative for user empowerment rests with people who would best serve their own interests by holding on to the power they already enjoy, there is good reason to be sceptical about the prospects for real change. History, in every context, suggests that privileged groups of people very rarely give away their power freely. They have it removed from them, or hand it over only when it becomes too costly to keep. The oppressed are not empowered: they take power.

The preceding section has offered arguments to support the view that the social care agencies and their representatives can be expected to hold on to their power, and as a result maintain the severe disempowerment of people with learning difficulties which, it has been suggested, exists at present. If one accepts these arguments, one is still left to ask what may be made of the many, apparently sincere, attempts being made within services to promote user empowerment. The following section considers the strategies that may be used to increase user empowerment, and argues that they are all too easily obstructed or diverted, even when they are employed by professionals whose commitment to the goal is entirely genuine.

Strategies for empowerment: the construction of the delusion

There are three broad strategies for the empowerment of people with learning difficulties within services:

The first is to remove them from the service sphere, or at least to marginalise the role of specialist services in their lives. They would then be able to have the same protection of their rights available to other citizens, and the wider freedoms which, though not enshrined in law, are generally presumed to exist for citizens in ordinary life. This strategy is part of the rationale of de-institutionalisation and, by some interpretations, of care in the community. The second strategy is to import 'ordinary life', usually in the form of ordinary citizens, into the service sphere, in order to strengthen the position of the service user. Initiatives which mainly rely on this strategy include citizen advocacy (Wolfensberger and Zauha 1973) and circles of support (Beeman, Ducharme and Mount 1988; Snow and Forest 1986). The third strategy is to change the operation of the service system itself. It may involve adding new ingredients, such as user consultation or participation forums, to the existing structure; or more fundamental changes to the components of the service industry and their interrelations. According to the rhetoric of its promoters, the recent reform of community care amounts to the most potent example of this strategy.

The three strategies are not incompatible, and a policy or practice initiative may combine more than one strategy. For example, if services are to continue to provide people with support in ways which allow them to become citizens, services will need to change the way they operate. The emphasis usually given to citizen advocacy is its intention to support the service user in dealings with services (strategy two), but the underlying aim is to bring the person into membership of the community (strategy one). The import of advocates may also help to change the way in which services operate (strategy three) just as, conversely, changes inside services might better support the role of advocates. Nevertheless, the three kinds of strategy offer a framework to examine initiatives in user empowerment and the obstacles they are likely to encounter.

Removal from the service sphere

The transition of provision from the institutional model of the mental handicap hospital to smaller-scale services in community locations has taken people with learning difficulties a very important first step closer to an ordinary life in the community. When it began, the language of empowerment, participation and self-advocacy had not been invented. Indeed, there was no recognition that people with learning difficulties had opinions which might have any relevance to planning their own futures, let alone planning services. It cannot be demonstrated that the changing pattern of services produced the recognition that people with learning difficulties have feelings, views and rights, any more than changing attitudes produced change in services. Each supported the other, by the circular process outlined earlier. The monolithic culture of the institution was challenged and fragmented. In the smaller residential units it became easier to identify people as individuals, and to create environments which suggested that they were at least human beings, if not ordinary people.

This process has been extended by the further shift from large hostels and residential homes to small group homes, staffed and unstaffed. A parallel change has taken place in day services with the development of small day centres and outreach programmes which enable people to spend at least some of their time in ordinary community settings. The point has now been reached where the next major step needs to be taken: to release people from the confines of services, and hence, by the logic of the first strategy identified above, to give them access to the rights and safeguards enjoyed by other citizens. At this point progress has, by and large, been halted. In some cases the reasons are obvious, and the motives transparent. Throughout the changes of the last two decades, the reactionary tendencies of both staff and parents have hinged on the existence of the bricks and mortar, of the buildings in which services were provided. For protective parents, they were the symbol of security and permanence; for professionals, the locus of their power base. This preoccupation is now shared by a third group of people, the product of the split between purchasers and providers. In the social care market-place, managers of provider agencies tend to acquire entrepreneurial values, in particular the assumption that a successful business is an expanding business. And expansion is most easily defined by the number of properties or bed spaces managed or, better still, owned.

The trend is most marked amongst the NHS trusts which inherited the old mental handicap hospitals. A few trusts measure their success by the number of people served, and by the quality of life which those people enjoy. Many others develop their new 'community based' services in a way which keeps users firmly inside the boundaries of the service (Collins 1992, 1993, 1994). Some of these trusts purchase large properties to develop community units, staffed by nurses redeployed from the hospital. Others have entered into agreements with housing associations for the provision of accommodation, on the basis that support to residents will be provided by hospital staff seconded to the housing association. The trust is likely to have enormous influence over the housing association, not least because the survival of the association may depend on the patronage of the trust. The nursing staff are likely to retain their old culture and allegiances. Thus, below the plausible surface of small-scale community provision, elements of the institution live on.

The result is a lost opportunity to increase the empowerment and autonomy of service users. Even if they are in housing association property, they are very rarely acknowledged to have tenants' rights. They can be moved between the residential units, or returned to the hospital campus, at the whim of the centralised management. They may still be designated as hospital patients, which will have various adverse effects on their rights, including the fundamental right to vote. It is very likely that elements of the old institutional culture will transfer to the new services, and many minor aspects of life 'in the community' will continue to follow the old pattern. In one trust it was found that jam was being distributed in 5lb tins by the central catering service to community units which each had four residents (Collins 1992).

In other cases the circumstances contrive to confound the best intentions of service agencies to release their control over the service users. For example, one social services department recently saw an opportunity to dispose of one of its hostels for people with learning difficulties. Money became available to build four bungalows on the extensive land around the hostel. With the addition of one nearby house, already owned by the department, these could accommodate all 25 hostel residents. It was recognised from the outset that the weakness of the plan was that it would perpetuate the congregation of people with learning difficulties in one neighbourhood, especially as there was also a day centre for people with learning difficulties nearby, but it seemed that in all other respects the residents of the new bungalows would be able to enjoy an ordinary life in the community. Yet, even as the bricks were being laid, other shortcomings became apparent:

- Because the bungalows would be owned by the social services department, rather than the housing department, the residents would not be tenants, and would not be included in the normal services or entitlements available to council housing tenants.

- Because the bungalows would be identified as a social services resource, which had to be used effectively, residents would be expected to move on after two to three years, to make way for other people requiring the 'service'.

- Because all the hostel residents had to be moved into the new properties, and to make full use of the resource, residents would not have control over how many people they lived with, or with whom they would live.

- Because the local authority had a responsibility to monitor the quality of services provided, councillors (as well as various inspectors) would be entitled to carry out visits of inspection to the bungalows.

- Because the staff were accountable for the welfare of the bungalow residents, they would need to have guaranteed access to the bungalows, and would have to be issued with keys.

- Because the bungalows would be identified as the locations of residential services, the buildings and their occupants would have to conform to fire regulations, and to food hygiene practices which include such things as prohibitions on pets in the kitchen, a separate sink for handling fish products, and a series of requirements which make it impractical to have a barbecue in the garden.

These constraints substantially reduce the prospects of providing an ordinary life in the community for the bungalow residents, and interfere in their lives in ways that most citizens would regard as outrageous infringements of their rights. And it is important to note that these problems occurred solely as the result of regulatory constraints imposed from outside on a staff team committed to progressive ideals. The full list of threats to the rights of users would also include inadequate resources resulting, for example, in staffing patterns and levels which did not match the needs and choices of residents. In many residential support services, users cannot choose to take a day off from the day centre, because there are no staff available to supervise them at home. In some services, users who return to 'their' home early at the end of the working day may have to wait on the doorstep until staff come on duty.

Nor does the list take account of the more insidious ways in which a service may presume to claim ownership of the space in which their users live. In another service – an extremely careful, values-driven, not-for-profit agency – the senior managers were concerned to avoid a centralised management approach which would restrict the autonomy of the residents in the various forms of small-scale residential service which were being developed. Their response was to minimise the role of management. Head office accepted the lead role in finding accommodation suited to each new group of service users, and appointed staff groups specifically to serve each group in their accommodation. Each set of residents and staff was then launched into semi-autonomy, backed up by administrative support, supervision of support staff team-leaders, and a methodical but gentle style of quality monitoring from senior managers.

Control did move away from senior management, but not to the service users. It was picked up by the stable groups of staff identified with the group homes. Almost unconsciously, they came to see the home as their home. As a stable, closely knit group, their values and preferences began to obliterate those of the residents. The staff group (like those of many agencies with less noble intentions) determined the decor, the routines, the choice of food and the destinations of social outings.

Letting go of control does not necessarily mean that it will come to rest with the service users. Perversely, an equitable distribution of power may actually require leadership – the kind of leadership which symbolises power, though in truth it may be almost impotent, the obvious parallel being the role of the monarchy in the British Constitution.

More generally, the lesson would appear to be that a strategy for user empowerment which relies on helping people to escape from services is likely to be ineffective. The structures, methods and culture of the service system will cling on, even within the community. If they are to be prised off, it can only be achieved by making fundamental changes to the service system itself – in other words, by using the third strategy outlined earlier.

Importing ordinary life through ordinary citizens
The second of the three strategies is to bring the community inside the service system to strengthen the position of the service user. Most initiatives of this sort are described as advocacy, but not all forms of advocacy bring in community resources or values. Professional advocacy, when carried out by a social worker or welfare rights officer from within the social services department, is a device created by, and operating within, the service system itself. On the other hand, a solicitor who includes people with learning difficulties as part of an ordinary legal practice may serve to import the perspective of the community.

Citizen Advocacy (CA), as it was originally conceived (Wolfensberger and Zauha 1973), explicitly draws its strength from the advocate as someone from outside services. The essential logic of CA is clear and, at first sight, uncontroversial. People who are devalued tend to be segregated from mainstream society – which, for people with learning difficulties, means inside specialist services – and lose their individuality within a monolithic system. They become isolated from 'valued' citizens and separated from the positive images, resources and safeguards which surround people in the community. The CA response is to re-establish the links between the devalued person and the community, through long-term relationships based on mutual choice and personal commitment. Unfortunately, the logic of CA – if applied rigorously – actually leads to a number of uncomfortable issues of principle and major practical difficulties:

- If CA schemes are not to become part of the service system, they must not be linked to services by lines of accountability or funding.

- If the citizen advocate is to have a relationship with their partner which is based on personal commitment, they should not be given inducements or rewards which might corrupt the relationship. Even the payment of expenses might have a corrupting effect.

- If CA is to assist devalued people by helping them to find relationships with people who are socially valued and secure in their position as citizens, the role of advocate cannot be taken on by people who are themselves devalued, or at risk of devaluation. To put it bluntly within the context of this book, people with learning difficulties cannot be citizen advocates.

There are also practical problems facing CA schemes in the UK. It is extremely difficult to find long-term funding which is not linked to services. And it is extremely difficult to find people who have the motivation, personal skills and detachment from services to make effective citizen advocates.

Not surprisingly, Citizen Advocacy in this country is in poor shape. In a paper presented in 1990, Sally Carr – who has been closely involved in the British CA movement – quoted an evaluation of the flagship Sheffield CA project which found that the project still had only 40 advocates, a third of whom are just good befriending relationships, and that the scheme's only source of funding was from the providers of their local services. 'Today there are roughly 20 programmes around the country which are either practising CA or striving to develop initiatives into CA. Virtually all are experiencing difficulties with long-term funding, many have less than 20 advocates.'[2]

As a result of these difficulties, some CA schemes have chosen to move away from Wolfensberger's principles – joining those other projects which have found it convenient to use the language of CA, but never felt the need to discover its meaning. This has been to the accompaniment of a heated and divisive debate about whether such schemes are a corruption or a legitimate adaptation of CA to the UK context. The net result is that CA in the UK has not so far been

---

2   From a paper, 'The Development of CA in the UK', presented by Sally Carr in 1990 to the Citizen Advocacy World Congress in Lincoln, Nebraska; quoted in Brandon (1995).

significant as a force for the empowerment of people with learning difficulties, and is unlikely to become one.

That is not to suggest that CA has no value. For those marginalised people who now enjoy the committed and able support of a citizen advocate, it is plainly very important. But it would be a mistake to incorporate it as a key element in policy where, in any case, it does not fit comfortably. If CA is to remain independent from services, it cannot be called into being by the service sector. Nor can citizen advocates be recruited to order. Within the last few years, one large mental handicap hospital proposed to make it policy not to discharge any resident without the involvement of a citizen advocate. It sounded like an earnest commitment to user choice and empowerment. It would have served only to keep residents inside, and firmly under the control of, the hospital.

One weakness of the CA model is that it incorporates the naive assumption that CA schemes which are independent in funding and accountability are adequately defended against the influence of the service sector. This leaves schemes wide open to infection by the culture of services – a culture which prizes rational decision-making and strong hierarchical systems of control, and persistently believes (in spite of the lessons of history) that formal procedures have the potential to eradicate failure (Dowson 1991). Citizen Advocacy has no difficulty with these values. CA projects typically follow traditional com-mittee and management structures, have set procedures for vetting prospective advocates, and make use of elaborate formal evaluation systems, notably the Citizen Advocacy and Program Evaluation (CAPE) system (O'Brien and Wolfensberger 1979). This acceptance of the service culture has the benefit that social care professionals feel comfortable with the concept of a CA project, even if they do not enjoy the intervention of advocates. However, it also makes it easy for schemes to be drawn into complicity with services. In one instance, a local authority informed a CA scheme that a prospective advocate was unsuit-able because she had a professional connection with the social services depart-ment. This was in fact untrue, as the aspiring advocate explained to the CA coordinator: she was a former social services employee, and would therefore have had the knowledge to be a very effective advocate. Nevertheless the CA scheme unquestioningly endorsed the local authority's position, and declined to approve the advocate.

A different approach (Beeman et al. 1988, 1989), also first developed in North America, takes a much more knowing attitude to the social care industry and its culture. More a movement than a model (and deliberately, since fixed 'models' are conceptions which belong to service culture), it works by such means as 'bridge building', 'daring to dream' and 'circles of support'. The movement carefully avoids the language and methods of services, prefers telling stories to writing reports, and emphasises trust and cooperation. The tone is radical, visionary and mostly celebratory. The goal is to strengthen communities so that they will welcome people with learning difficulties and others who have been excluded from the mainstream. To that extent it belongs within the first of the three strategies for empowerment. Although the movement reckons to 'push back' the service system, and to break down the barriers of the system in order to reach people trapped inside, it remains to be seen how effective it will be. These bridges to people inside services have to be secured at both ends, and the bridge builders need to address the mentality and the interests of those who hold the territory on the far side. The unfamiliar language and methods of the movement may catch the vested interest groups off guard. Alternatively, it may leave them completely untouched. At one conference, a UK exponent of this movement illustrated her point with a 'dream catcher' – an artefact of the tribal culture of North American Indians, made from wood and feathers. For some of the conference participants this may have been inspirational, and perhaps hastened them along the road to enlightened change inside services. The majority of the audience, however, appeared to find it whimsical or baffling, and certainly not threatening to their professional positions.

The contrasting methods of Citizen Advocacy and 'bridge building' illustrate at a collective level the dilemma which continually faces the individual advocate working inside services. An advocate who is too radical in her or his views, or too assertive in expressing them, will be excluded. An advocate who accepts the ways and, very often, the timescale of services, is unlikely to be effective. Whilst the rights of the advocate are not protected within the service system, the role of advocate is based on nothing more than a pretence of authority, which services may indulge or expose.

Values Into Action, as a national campaigning organisation, is often contacted by advocates – official and unofficial – with stories of obstinate service organisations. The pattern of these anecdotes has changed as health and social services have separated into purchasers and providers. Before the changes, advocates were usually able to get and hold the attention of services. Public service traditions meant that service managers felt an obligation to deal respectfully with someone labelled as 'advocate'. There was not, of course, any guarantee that the advocate would win the argument; but it was at least possible for the argument to take place.

That sense of public service and accountability is now much less evident, particularly amongst the large service providers. Executives are noticeably less impressed by the label of advocate. It is no longer unusual for the response to be abrupt and bluntly dismissive. A minor but telling example concerns a woman who was being unjustly treated by the service which supported her. A friend was so incensed that he wrote on her behalf – and with her agreement – to the service provider. In order to identify himself, and perhaps to add weight to his arguments, he described himself as an advocate. The chief executive replied that he was not willing to discuss the complaints, because the friend was not known to the agency as a person authorised by an approved advocacy scheme to speak on the woman's behalf.

Changing the operation of the service system

If the public service tradition has been lost, perhaps it has been replaced by 'customer orientation'. That, according to the government, was the rationale for the community care changes arising from the NHS and Community Care Act 1990 which were fully implemented in April 1993. If these changes were intended to improve user choice, they would be the most substantial effort that the social care industry has made in recent years to promote user empowerment by the third strategy – by changing the operation of services themselves.

The origins of the changes provide cause for scepticism. User choice was, at best, a secondary objective of the reforms. The government's decision to bring in Sir Roy Griffiths to recommend change (Griffiths 1988) was motivated by a desire to stem the flow of public funds into private residential care. At that time, residential charges could be met by payments from the social security system. Claims for these payments were filtered by eligibility criteria, and there were ceilings imposed on the level of charges which would be met; but it was essentially a system based on the principle of *entitlement*. If an individual met the criteria, they could expect to receive the payments, regardless of the level of national or local demand for the same sort of state assistance.

The new community care arrangements re-directed these funds to local authority social services departments, in the form of fixed annual budgets. This capped the level of expenditure, and obliged social services departments to make decisions about whether, and how much, help should be given in each individual case. The principle of entitlement vanished. By this one change, the empowerment of service users has been substantially diminished.

Social services continue to provide support services themselves, but their main role now is that of purchaser: they ration the funding available, using a system based on government guidelines, and purchase services from independent social care agencies. These activities have been given a positive, consumerist gloss. They are performed by care managers who carry out assessments of need, with consumer participation, and they supposedly support greater consumer choice.

There are some benefits in the new system. As a greater variety of independent provider agencies develops, there will be more choice for consumers. There is no longer the 'tilted playing field' which favoured residential services, paid through social security, over more flexible, but local authority-funded, community care. The paternalism of public welfare has been undermined by consumer ideology – though the increasingly organised and militant disability lobby has probably had greater impact. The functional separation of purchasers and providers has opened up the system, highlighting the opportunities for innovation which support user empowerment. These opportunities may have existed previously, but social services departments now seem more interested in them. For Dave Morris of Choice, an advocacy and consultancy agency closely associated with the disability movement, the improvements in user empowerment have resulted more from culture than structure: 'Things have improved. I think the rhetoric of the Community Care Act, more than its practice, has enabled people to do things they have probably wanted to do for a long time' (Whitely 1994, p.5).

Jenny Morris, from a similar perspective, sees the new structures and new attitudes as complementary forces in achieving improvements:

> The development of needs-led assessment and care management systems will help to promote user-led services, as will the division of social services into separate purchasing and providing functions. Increasingly, social services organisations, in both the statutory and voluntary sectors, are placing user involvement at the centre of their purchasing and providing functions. (Morris 1994, p.28)

Some social service departments, in their purchasing role, are increasingly willing to fund self-help groups and services controlled by service users. They are also funding independent living schemes, which provide a route for money to be paid directly to disabled people, so that they can purchase their own services or hire their own personal assistants. These developments, and recent indications from government that they are to be more strongly supported in national policy, are very welcome. Direct payments, which enable people to hire their own personal assistants, put users in complete charge of the services they receive. But these initiatives are not necessarily early signs of a general shift in attitudes and power. They rely on users who are able and willing to organise them, and although they are very likely to empower the people who use them (where there is a distinction between users and organisers), the systems at the core of social services may be untouched. Independent living schemes, for example, may have to accept that the normal local authority care management procedures are used to determine how much money will be allocated to an individual (Dowson 1995). Unless these initiatives are adequately structured and safeguarded, they will be vulnerable to the same corrupting and compromising influences which have, as described earlier, damaged the effectiveness of Citizen Advocacy. People with learning difficulties, who present obvious, though not insuperable, problems in the operation of user control, are likely to be the last to benefit. Thus, rather than being signs of a developing general commitment to user empowerment, these service initiatives may prove to be no more than occasional gestures, crumbs thrown from the table of the power-holders.

Certainly there are several flaws in the support that the new community care system gives to empowerment. Whatever the language of the reforms might suggest, the new system is not true consumerism. In the context of the ordinary, commercial market-place, consumerism puts the money – and thereby the power – into the hands of the consumer. Thus the range of goods and services available is determined by the pattern of individual purchasing decisions. But in community care, spending decisions are made by care managers. Except in a very few cases (notably independent living schemes), the money goes straight from the local authority to the service providers. Service users consume, but they do not purchase.

The consumer model might still apply if the local authority care managers truly reflected the wishes of users, and so made the users the purchasers by proxy. But this is unlikely to be the case. Care managers are employees of the local authority, and it is wildly naive to suppose that they will – or can – set aside their professional culture and their awareness of the inadequacy of the funds available whilst they carry out an assessment of need. According to Department of Health guidance (Social Services Inspectorate 1991), assessment should be an exercise which focuses carefully on the needs and strengths of the individual in the context of their everyday life, and values their own ability to assess their needs and solutions. A more typical picture of assessment in practice would be an overworked officer struggling to fill in the boxes on a sheaf of forms. The picture may improve as the new system settles down, but assessment is set to remain very clearly in the ownership of professionals, a process which is done *to* users, not *with* them.

Social workers have never enjoyed a very high reputation as advocates for their clients, and social services staff themselves acknowledge that their divided loyalties weaken their potential as advocates. On the other hand, and for all their faults, social workers in the old system were free to argue their client's need for services with their line manager. The conflict between departmental budgets and individual needs was played out inside the area office, albeit in the absence of the individual concerned. Now, the conflict has been internalised in the person of the care manager (much as, in the parallel context of health care, it has been internalised in the fund-holding GP). There is no one left inside the purchasing agency to argue for the user.

There *are* ways in which the fundamental processes of social services could be changed to give real power to users. The key principle of all the changes would be for the social care industry to return to its core mission, which is to provide people with the support they need to access the ordinary resources and opportunities of community life. This would require a retreat from the ownership of the properties in which service users live, and from cosy relationships with housing agencies which blur the proper boundaries (Collins forthcoming). It would mean abandoning special provision, such as day centres, where people with learning difficulties (and others) pretend at being workers or students, with none of the rights or other benefits of the real thing. Yet more radically, it should mean that purchasers cease to be involved in deciding the needs of people who want services.

Methods consistent with this principle have been developed and tested. For some years there have been services which avoid links with housing agencies, instead providing community support for people with learning difficulties in whatever circumstances it is required (Simons 1995). Only lately has this approach been 'discovered' and made fashionable under the title of 'supported living' (Kinsella 1993). Supported employment, though hampered by the benefits trap, has offered the equivalent radical alternative to day services. And the service brokerage model, as first developed in Canada, has shown a way to separate purchasers from the assessment of need. The service broker is independent of both purchasers and providers but – unlike an adviser or advocate – has a functional role alongside them (Dowson 1995). The broker is chosen, if necessary with the assistance of family and friends, by the service user, and works solely for the user. The broker then supports the user in negotiating the money required with the agency which rations funds. Under this system, the inevitable tension between individual need and limited public funding is externalised in a process which involves the user.

Drawing the strategies together: A conclusion

None of these models has made any real impact on the pattern of UK services for people with learning difficulties. Why not? Common professional explanations are the lack of funding, the concerns of carers and the prejudices of the public. These are genuine difficulties, but not impassable obstructions, as those successful innovative services are demonstrating. The obvious explanation is that these changes would allow service users to take control, and that is not something which social care professionals, collectively, or the government, would countenance. If people with learning difficulties were legal tenants in their own homes they might refuse to move out when it suited the service agency, and purchasers might then find themselves obliged to pay for services which they no longer judged cost-effective. It would be the staff who would have to wait on the doorstep until the user came home. The comfortable, institutionalised world of day centres would be broken up. Users allowed to define their own needs might confront the industry, and the government, with the inadequacy of welfare funding and services. The status and security of professional careers would be jeopardised.

When asked for evidence that they are committed to user empowerment, professionals will offer the very long list of participation projects, consultation exercises, and self-advocacy and user groups which have sprung up in the last few years. These allow people to 'have a voice'. They are 'involved'. This is undoubtedly better than being excluded and ignored; but it does not, by the standards of most citizens, come anywhere close to having power. How many of us – those enjoying an ordinary life – would be satisfied that our rights as tenants, employees or consumers were secure if they were safeguarded by nothing more than a promise that we would be 'consulted'?

It is when these soft options are compared with the rights and safeguards which ordinary citizens (including the social care professionals) expect for themselves, that the belief that they represent major progress towards user empowerment is most tellingly revealed as a delusion. And people with learning difficulties are in no position to make unkind comments about the emperor's new clothes. Their national voice, in the form of People First, has begun to talk in terms of rights – to jobs, housing, adequate benefits – but the most specific and insistent demand of the last few years has been for acceptance of the term 'learning difficulties'. It was a demand with minimal cost implications, and yet it was only met half way, and belatedly, by the government's adoption of 'learning disabilities'. At the local and individual level the 'demands' of people with learning difficulties are more likely to be whispered requests for small mercies. Whilst the professionals talk about user empowerment, there are people like Pearl, encountered by Andrew Holman (in press) during a study of the views of residents in an English mental handicap hospital:

> Pearl wanted to be allowed to make a pot of tea. She was capable of making tea, but not allowed to because she had not passed the necessary exams and health and safety requirements. We speculated on what changes would need to be made to allow this to happen and I stated that if these changes occurred she would then be able to have a cup of tea when she wanted to. Pearl insisted she would only have tea at morning and afternoon break times and could not conceptualise any possibility of wanting tea at any other time. (p.14)

At the risk of being unduly bleak, and unfair to the minority of services where real progress is being made, this chapter has attempted to resist the comforts of the delusion. Innovative services have shown, at least in outline, the kind of changes in social care which would allow people with learning difficulties to take power. Certainly there would be some difficulties. For some people with learning difficulties, a high level of autonomy would be impossible or very dangerous, and the limits to power might have to be fixed. These problems could be addressed, if those with the power were serious about handing it over. Not surprisingly, there is little evidence that they are. Unless people with learning difficulties, perhaps in alliance with other disabled people, can find a way to *take* the power, there is little prospect of change.

References

Beeman, P., Ducharme, G. and Mount, B. (1988) *What are we Learning about Circles of Support: A Collection of Tools, Ideas and Reflections on Facilitating Circles and Support.* Manchester, CT: Communitas Inc.

Beeman, P., Ducharme, G. and Mount, B. (1989) *One Candle Power: Building Bridges into Community Life for People with Disabilities.* Manchester, CT: Communitas Inc.

Brandon, D. (1995) *Advocacy: Power to the People.* Birmingham, UK: Venture Press.

Collins, J. (1992) *When the Eagles Fly: A Report on the Resettlement of People with Learning Difficulties from Long-Stay Institutions.* London: Values Into Action.

Collins, J. (1993) *The Resettlement Game: Policy and Procrastination in the Closure of Mental Handicap Hospitals.* London: Values Into Action.

Collins, J. (1994) *Still to be Settled: Strategies for the Resettlement of People from Mental Handicap Hospitals.* London: Values Into Action.

Collins, J. (forthcoming) *The Relationship between Housing and Support Services for People with Learning Difficulties and its Impact on the Rights of Service Users.* London: Values Into Action.

Dowson, S. (1991) *Moving to the Dance-or-Service Culture and Community Care.* London: Values Into Action.

Dowson, S. (1995) *Means to Control: A Review of the Service Brokerage Model in Community Care.* London: Values Into Action.

Goffman, C.E. (1961) *Asylums: Essays on the Social Situation of Mental Patients and Other Inmates.* London: Anchor Books.

Griffiths, R. (1988) *Community Care: Agenda for Action – A Report to the Secretary of State for Social Services.* London: HMSO.

Holman, A. (in press) *Do They Still Have Trams?* London: Values into Action.

Kinsella, P. (1993) *Supported Living: A New Paradigm?* Manchester: National Development Team.

Morris, J. (1994) *The Shape of Things to Come? User-Led Services.* London: National Institute for Social Work.

O'Brien, J. and Wolfensberger, W. (1979) *Standards for Citizen Advocacy Program Evaluation.* Toronto: Canadian Association for the Mentally Retarded.

Simons, K. (1995) *My Home, My Life: Innovative Approaches to Housing and Support for People with Learning Difficulties.* London: Values Into Action.

Snow, J. and Forest, M. (1986) *Support Circles – Building a Vision.* Downsview, Ontario: The Roeher Institute.

Social Services Inspectorate (1991) *Getting the Message Across.* London: HMSO.

Wertham, F. (1966) *A Sign for Cain: An Exploration of Human Violence.* New York: Macmillan.

Wertham, F. (1978) *The German Euthanasia Program: Excerpts from a 'A Sign for Cain'.* Cincinnati, OH: Hayes Publishing.

Whitely, P. (1994) 'Power to the people.' *Community Care Journal,* 1 September, 5.

Wolfensberger, W. and Zauha, H. (1973) *Citizen Advocacy and Protective Services for the Handicapped.* Toronto: National Institute on Mental Retardation.

CHAPTER 7

Consulting to Involve
or Consulting to Empower?

Gordon Grant

Background and assumptions

Despite being a signatory to the UN Declaration on the Rights of Disabled People over 20 years ago, the British government has been extremely coy about according people with disabilities the means to express their civil or citizenship rights. Oliver (1996) draws attention to well-known illustrations: the less than full implementation of the Disabled Persons Act 1986, a refusal to implement anti-discrimination legislation, charters for public services which remain devoid of adequate user control, short-term or chronic underfunding of organisations controlled by disabled people, and the refusal to allow direct payments to be made to disabled people to purchase personal assistance services. To these we might add a dependency on judicial review processes for key decisions about users' rights, and a care management system which reinforces professional hegemony in decision-making. Against the background of this culture of dependency it is little wonder that increasing numbers of disabled people are seeking means of collective empowerment to further their interests and concerns.

Important though these structural problems are in their range, significance and effects, this chapter deals with only one of the dimensions involved, namely how people are consulted. It will be argued that, as an idea, consultation has not been sufficiently well problematised, that people have adopted everyday or common-sense assumptions about what it means, and that those assumptions have carried forward into the experience of consultation itself. In what follows, the All Wales Strategy for the Development of Services for Mentally Handicapped People (Welsh Office 1983) is used as a case study precisely because it set out to consult with users and families in key aspects of service planning, design and delivery. Attention is focused on two mechanisms for involving citizens: individual planning and local planning.

It will be suggested that there seems to be a natural progression in thinking about the 'ingredients' of involvement and consultation. New structures to involve users and families are established; multidisciplinary planning forums for all the relevant stakeholders are designed; mechanisms to link individual, local and county strategic planning are put in place. All this seems entirely rational. It is assumed that all those so involved have the appetite, capacity and knowledge necessary to turn involvement, through effective consultation, into meaningful participation. It is also assumed that the involvement of users and families will somehow ensure that grass-roots ideas based upon an appreciation of individual needs will inevitably lead to strategic plans which help to empower people. But is this the reality? It will be argued that the rules for engagement in these processes are yet to be fully worked out. Hence, although many structures for involvement are in place, the dynamics, definitions, and even the goals, have remained rather problematic.

In none of the policy guidance about learning disability or community care services has consultation ever been defined, nor have its necessary qualities been enunciated. Its meaning appears to have been taken for granted. Dictionary definitions do not help very much, suggesting a process of 'taking counsel with', 'seeking information or advice from' or 'taking into consideration' (*Oxford Dictionary* 1981). Each of these definitions implies a process of interaction and involvement with others in which information and advice is traded but little else is made explicit. This creates the prospect of a whole range of positions which are difficult to reconcile being taken up, for example about consultation as meaningful participation, power and accountability, and anticipated outcomes.

Consultation by empowering people, it is suggested, has the potential to strengthen disadvantaged or disempowered groups at the grass roots and give individuals the confidence to speak out. Being based on the strengthening of interpersonal ties and natural networks, consultation allows change to be pressed for over time, and is a realistic option which can link 'what is' with 'what should be'. Since services constitute only a small part of the life experience of most users, empowerment is far from being the sole preserve of services. Rather it can be seen as an essential underpinning of moves towards enhancing the status of those who have been oppressed towards full citizenship, with all the rights and responsibilities that entails (see, for example, the Report of the Committee on Citizenship 1990).

However, there have been two competing discourses about participation which help to illustrate different assumptions about what is involved. Croft and Beresford (1995) argue that the discourses of politicians, policy-makers and service providers are concerned more with services, how to make them more efficient, cost-effective and responsive. The discourses of disabled people and other service users, they contend, are primarily concerned with their lives, rights, choices and opportunities. Not only are there differences in the primary concerns about involvement or participation, there are differences in definitions, language and ideology.

Such discourses seem to have parallels in debates about the nature of empowerment in community care. Jack (1995) suggests that there is a 'professional' approach which is linked with ideas about personal empowerment, people taking increased responsibility for managing their affairs, living in conformity with prevailing values, and changing in accordance with professionally set goals and norms. Redressing the balance of power between service providers and service users is seen as the best guarantee of improving the quality of a service in this context (Social Services Inspectorate 1991a,b). This would seem to be a central tenet of the new assessment and care management arrangements within the terms of the NHS and Community Care Act 1990. In contrast the 'liberationist' approach, more closely associated with the disability movement, is concerned with changing people's position within society by seeking to ensure that they have the means to achieve not only personal change but social change (Croft and Beresford 1995).

Straddling the middle ground between these two extremes and drawing on other work (Freire 1972; Rose and Black 1985; Rosenfeld 1989), Rees (1991) seeks to make a connection between the personal and the political in outlining some steps towards empowerment in professional practice:

> The maintenance of trust, an awareness of exercising power in different contexts and a sensitivity to the use of language are features of all exchanges concerned with empowerment… Enabling people to make connections between their lives and political and economic trends in other contexts contributes to political literacy. This externalising, making connections between one context and another, is not only a means of focusing on the distribution of power and its consequences, it is also a guard against that easy tendency to privatise or localise problems – as though no one else shares them, as though they are only the product of individual shortcomings. (p.87)

In stressing the relational context of power and empowerment, Rees places a strong emphasis on the use of biography and storytelling:

> The unravelling of bits of biography is a way of beginning the process of empowerment with those who have felt powerless for a long time. In that process, a marking of small victories can combat a history of defeats. Some of the small victories will include the replacement of ignorance with information, and fear with a willingness to challenge authority. (p.28)

Fisher's (1994) discussion of partnership practice and empowerment in social work is also relevant here. He suggests that partnership assumes that in each interaction where inequality is recognised and a more egalitarian approach adopted, society is itself gradually transformed. Though focusing on local policy and individual cases, partnership practice is not ignorant of the wider causes of inequality and disadvantage, but it is strategically directed at those processes it can realistically affect. By contrast, empowerment assumes that people should be assisted to free themselves from oppression in order to change society. According to Fisher the link between partnership and empowerment can be articulated partly in terms of local policy-making where involvement and consultation can be seen as a right, and partly in terms of individual cases where the right to participate must be translated into effective preparation and support. As he says, a right to participate remains mere ideology unless matched by the means of making it a genuine experience of shared decision-making.

All the foregoing ideas can be applied to helping vulnerable or oppressed individuals to take more control of their own lives, to shape and utilise the resources and institutions in the community, and thereby to lead more fulfilling lives. It is important to reiterate that formal services represent only one resource in this context. Hence, concentrating efforts on changing services in relation to how people want to use them will only solve part of the problem. Nevertheless, services themselves need to be creative in how they involve both users and families. Barnes and Wistow (1992) identify two broad categories of purpose associated with 'user involvement' strategies in relation to services:

- to improve the quality of services by making them more sensitive or responsive to the needs and preferences of individuals who use them

- to extend the capacity of users to participate in decisions about the design, management and review of services.

They suggest that these objectives should not however be too rigidly demarcated. This is because the cumulative effects of activities which have the initial purpose of sensitising service delivery to user needs and preferences may have lasting consequences in increasing user empowerment with involvement and influence evolving in unanticipated ways. Hence they are not dismissive of initiatives which appear modest in scope when set against the apparently more fundamental objectives of user empowerment. The assumption is that the sum of a series of feasible incremental changes may be greater than a more radical initiative which fails through over-ambition.

It has been suggested that shifting the balance of power towards users implies a number of preconditions: having the right of access to participatory forums, the ability to exercise choices, the availability of information, redress, means of representation, power-sharing and accountability (Grant 1992; Potter 1988). As Barnes and Wistow (1992) have argued, each of these preconditions seems to acknowledge three key underlying traits: viewing users as fellow citizens rather than as recipients of devalued services; perceiving involvement as a mechanism for personal growth, thereby helping people to extend the degree of control that other citizens take for granted; and finally, looking upon power-sharing and accountability marking an alternative to market-place consumerism as the route to service responsiveness and service quality. These questions are revisited at various stages in this chapter.

In the steadily emerging mixed economy of welfare, key questions therefore become: How are local agencies making it possible for people to participate in local and individual planning? Do people want to be involved? Is there evidence of people feeling empowered, and if so what factors are associated with this? These form the central concerns of this chapter.

The Welsh Strategy: expectations for involvement and consultation

The Strategy (Welsh Office 1983) placed an emphasis on the involvement and cooperation of service users and families in the *preparation, implementation and monitoring of individual plans*. These plans were to take account of user and family judgements about their own needs and preferences and were not to be the product of professional assessment alone. Moreover they were to provide individuals, 'with opportunities for choice and development of independence'. In this sense they can be seen as reflecting the type of partnership practice described earlier by Fisher (1994).

The *day-to-day monitoring of the quality and development of services* was seen as a responsibility shared between individual service providers, service users and families. Named professional workers were to be the main point of contact for individuals to obtain the help they required at any time.

Social services departments, having been given lead responsibility for planning, were expected to *consult fully with other statutory and voluntary bodies and with representatives of service users and families in the development of county plans*. Formal and informal arrangements were to involve representatives of people with a learning disability and their families in this process, but the methods involved were left for local determination. Similar assumptions were made about *district service planning*. No clear criteria have ever been published about how judgements would be made about the extent or adequacy of consultation.

Voluntary organisations were given a *customer representative role in the planning and management of services*, as well as being expected to assist in developing information systems, independent advocacy, encouragement of mutual support groups and the development of more accountable services.

The Strategy's participatory intent was designed to reduce the historical distinction between 'givers and takers' of services described almost 30 years ago in the Seebohm Report (1968). It aimed to create a more level playing field for users and providers of services in that decision-making about the meeting of needs had to be open, subject to consultation, and based on the specification and review of clearly stated goals. Moreover, the opportunities for service users and their families to participate in the planning and management of services were made specific. Plans submitted to the Welsh Office for funding could be, and were, vetoed, especially where consultative arrangements remained unclear. The right of users and families to be consulted was therefore very real.

Data and methods

The observations that follow are based on evidence collected by the author and others about the Welsh Strategy over a ten year period. The core of the author's own evidence comes from a survey of 190 families in North Wales, interviews with members of local and county planning groups, and participation in both local planning groups and voluntary sector forums over a number of years. Additional use was made of research carried out by others into different aspects of planning and service delivery in Wales over the same period. Where relevant, experience is compared with that in other parts of Britain and other countries.

Early reactions

Q. Do you think parents should be involved?

A. I think some parents but not me personally. I think you need someone
   outgoing. Parents do need to be involved because the experts can't
   be experts unless they've had a handicapped child. They need to
   learn from parents really, but then again you need a parent who is
   able to express themselves and someone who has the time.

This parent neatly captured the sense of many initial reactions to the lure of the consultative process. 'Good idea but don't ask me; it requires people with particular qualities – people who can speak out, people with time, people whose expertise as parents is acknowledged.' These were typical sentiments when it came to pondering the pros and cons of their inclusion in consultation regarding services. Immediately the field of people likely to participate began to narrow. More is said of this later.

The participatory principles set out in the Strategy were nevertheless greeted with enthusiasm on all sides. No one had a blueprint for designing new community services, and in any case there were no databases anywhere giving an overview of local needs. The logic of consulting users and families to find this out became overwhelming.

It soon became clear that 'involvement' in the planning process could mean anything from manipulation and degrees of tokenism to forms of partnership, delegated power and citizen control (Douglas 1985). Consequently, ambiguities and tensions about what was supposed to be taking place emerged very quickly (Grant 1985).

A survey of the newly established county planning structures in Wales during 1985 showed that parental influence was more marked in respect of the selection of priorities in plans than in their content (Beyer et al. 1986). The involvement of parents helped to change the tone of planning meetings, with greater emphasis apparently being given to discussion of individual needs. At the same time the majority of respondents were described as being dissatisfied with the level of consultation that had been achieved to date. Families in particular were concerned about having insufficient influence over the passage of events.

The Welsh Strategy provided considerable impetus for voluntary organisations to become more actively involved in the design and delivery of new services, one report indicating that voluntary organisations accounted for one-third of newly funded projects in one area (McGrath and Grant 1992). However, questions are still being asked about whether or not it is legitimate for voluntary organisations to play a part in consumer involvement, whether they can avoid conflicts of interest between their (consumer) representative roles and those in which they act as partners with the statutory sector, and what the risks are of the consumer voice being substituted or submerged in the process (Drake and Owens 1992). Similar concerns about the roles and identity of the voluntary sector have been raised in relation to the demands of the mixed economy of care (Lewis 1993).

Whilst this early experience illustrated an enthusiasm for participation, it also demonstrated that attention to putting the structures of participation in place had overshadowed the processes of consultation. The new planning structures suited people with high commitment but the conventions adopted kept people with a learning disability largely on the outside (SCOVO 1986; Welsh Office 1987). Questions were already being raised by families about the timing and the level of consultation allowed for, and whether the personal investment expected of them was realistic in relation to their likely influence. The real issue here was whether enough was being done to shift the balance of power to secure the needs, preferences and interests of users and families.

This is now examined more closely in relation to individual planning and local planning.

Individual planning

In its most recent policy guidance the Welsh Office stated unequivocally that, 'everyone who wants one should have an 'individual plan' coordinating care throughout their life and properly reflecting their needs and preferences' (Welsh Office 1994). But what does this involve? And is it achievable?

Individual planning can be seen historically as an attempt to overcome the inherited problems of fragmented services, service-led provision and ill-defined systems of accountability. The basic idea of an individual plan (IP) is to, 'assist people who deliver services to focus on the unique needs of the individual receiving those services and to ensure that he or she has a major say in planning his or her life and determining the help he or she requires' (Blunden, Evans and Humphreys 1987). The principles underlying individual planning are similar to those of shared action planning and appear to have had a widespread influence (Brechin and Swain 1987).

The claims and achievements of individual planning are various. Research evidence suggests that IPs are seen as a useful forum for service users, families, key workers and other practitioners to share information regularly and to plan for the future (Humphreys 1987b). Compared with traditional case conference methods which generally exclude service users and families, IPs were reported to provide better coordination of services and improved access of services to individuals. Better targeting of resources to needs was evident, as was the improved awareness of families about the needs, rights and achievements of their disabled relatives. The structured approach to the monitoring of progress was mentioned as a particular advantage.

A review of community mental handicap teams in Wales (McGrath 1991) provided further endorsement of the value of four IP characteristics: they were *client-centred*, with service users being involved in the planning; they were *goal-oriented*, making progress easier to evaluate; they did appear to facilitate *coordination of services*; and they offered a *planning base*, reflecting the needs of individuals. However, four years into the Strategy, only a minority of people had had IPs. Five teams reported having undertaken IPs for 25 per cent or more persons, 13 teams for less than 10 per cent and eight teams had not completed any.

Reasons for the apparent slow rate of progress were not difficult to discern. The workload demands on front-line workers were overbearing. A considerable amount of direct work was often necessary with service users and people in their social networks prior to an IP taking place, and this seems to have been underestimated. Lack of integrated record systems added to the complications. Staff shortages impeded progress in some localities. Effecting the transition from a crisis-led to a more pro-active system involved dealing with a backlog of work with people who had not been seen for a long time. Finally, resource shortfalls were another reason commonly reported for a reluctance to move forward with IPs. Given these circumstances the system was not viable. Active participation of users within IPs is reportedly low (Humphreys and Blunden 1987) and in some localities users and their families can find themselves excluded (Laws, Bolt and Gibbs 1988). It is difficult to avoid the conclusion that a universalist system of individual planning depends upon a finely tuned planning infrastructure and conditions of resource sufficiency, neither of which were in place at the time.

Despite these difficulties a widespread belief in the value of IPs remains and adaptations have followed. Some community teams started to publish their own target group priorities based on local knowledge. Others attempted to simplify the original IP model by reserving larger meetings for times of major life change. Another modification involved creating flexibility by allowing users to decide the type of meetings they would like. Finally, there were moves in some places to draw support workers into IP coordinating roles.

So what has been the net effect of trying to involve people in their own life planning?

One set of indicators is provided by a Social Services Inspectorate survey (Welsh Office 1991) which looked at the extent to which 755 service users were involved in making day-to-day choices which affected their lives in each of 98 different settings, including hospitals, hostels and ordinary housing schemes. Autonomy and the exercise of control in everyday affairs were more in evidence amongst residents in ordinary housing schemes. They were more likely to have more control over their daily lives, some say in who lived with them or worked with them, and choice about where they ate and about what they did in their free time, suggesting that new service models based on progressive policy paradigms provided a context in which key improvements in the self-esteem of individuals could flourish.

Consulting with individuals about what they would like to do, where they would like to live, or who they want to be with, involves questions which most people take for granted. Carrying this out, especially with people who have very severe or complex disabilities, is much less easy than the rhetoric suggests. National practice guidance provides few pointers about how such service users can be meaningfully and effectively involved in assessment and decision processes that affect them (Social Services Inspectorate 1991a,b). Consequently much is left to the individual creativity or ingenuity of people with learning disabilities themselves, their families or support workers. There is an urgent need therefore to consolidate knowledge and understanding of techniques and technologies for helping people to express their needs and views.

But here too there are problems. The validity, reliability, effectiveness and ethical underpinnings of facilitated communication technologies are the subject of dispute (Felce 1994; Goode 1994). It is also claimed that decision-making theories deriving from research on the general population have been assumed rather than tested and validated in day-to-day work with people with learning disabilities (Jenkinson 1993).

Meanwhile there is mounting evidence of different ways of helping people to participate actively in everyday matters. How the views of people with learning disability can be solicited through more sensitive research approaches (Flynn 1986; Lowe, de Paiva and Humphreys 1986), and through enabling people to take ownership of the research process itself (Ramcharan and Grant 1994; Townsley 1995; Ward and Flynn 1994), is becoming increasingly evident. Professional interventions, for example psychotherapeutic approaches (Lloyd and Todd 1995), are claimed as empowering for users. Self- and citizen advocacy projects (Bourlet, Sims and Whittaker 1988; Butler, Carr and Sullivan 1988; Ramcharan 1995; Simons 1993), and quality assurance systems (Ash, Ritchie and Scott 1989) represent further means of securing the involvement of users in efforts to maintain a drive towards a user orientation in service designs. There are also good examples of what services can do to involve users more directly in day-to-day management, with empowering consequences for individuals (All Wales Advisory Panel 1991).

Case studies of younger disabled people illustrate the challenges for user involvement in terms of needs assessment (Day 1994). These mirror many of the difficulties and concerns expressed above, for example in relation to: proven methods of interaction for people with speech disorders or autistic tendencies; inhibitions about needs assessment itself; lack of experience and low expectations of parental carers; and the perpetuation of a resource-driven, 'forms-led' approach to assessment.

In the author's experience of the Welsh Strategy, five developmental challenges emerge in particular here:

1. *Time and strategies to develop empathetic relationships.* How family carers, and in their opinion their disabled relatives, evaluated the quality of support from services was tied inextricably to the perceived empathetic relationship with key workers (Grant, McGrath and Ramcharan 1994). Continuity in professional–user/family relationships was often a crucial underpinning here, as it was only in this way that professionals could begin to draw upon the special knowledge of family members and to use this to work with individuals in more effective ways. Empathy was a crucial underpinning in Simons' (1993) study which suggested that users took a more favourable view of IPs when they were being listened to and when decisions reflected their aims and concerns.

2. *Theoretically rooted, empirically tested assessment systems.* Some assessment models overlook the interlocking relationships and mutual dependencies between the individual, the informal support system and the community. This can lead to siblings and friends being overlooked as significant contributors to the support of individuals. As noted elsewhere (Ellis 1993), assessment can too easily reflect the values of professional workers. However, social systems theory appears to show promise as an integrating framework in this context as a backcloth to family-centred case management involving people with learning disabilities and their families (Dunst *et al.* 1993a,b).

3. *Power relations.* Individual planning was often at its best when service users and families were enabled not only to contribute to decision-making but also to take ownership of what was to be done. Examples included users assuming responsibility for the chairing of IP meetings or in being able to link up with self-advocacy groups. Independent advocacy, particularly citizen advocacy, was not always available. Its absence became particularly conspicuous when users and

families appeared to take up different value positions on issues whose resolution became unduly protracted. However, the empowerment of individuals was too often undermined by the simple fact that key workers reported having insufficient authority to problem-solve and to broker, particularly across agency boundaries, on behalf of users.

4. *Sharing of written case information.* Written details about the processes and outcomes of IP meetings were not always passed on to service users and their families or representatives. This made it difficult to question, in an organised way, how decisions had been reached, the actions that were to follow and who was to carry them out. In these respects it weakened any intent to make systems more accountable to service users and families.

5. *Recognising the discontinuous nature of assessment and service provision.* As 'care managers', key workers were in the front line as supporters and brokers, but unlike care managers they could also be very much tied in to service provision. Indeed, given the long-term work which was usually involved, effective work with individuals and families appeared to work best when assessment and service provision were 'seamless'. It was frequently said that assessment never stops, that it cannot be artificially separated from service provision, and that it is hence a feature of good practice within this particular field. This leaves an obvious rift between individual planning as described above and the preferred care management model espoused by the community care White Paper.

Although these findings serve as indicators of what can be done to consolidate individual planning, they also lend support to Day's (1994) conclusion that front-line workers may have little or no influence on the outcome of completed assessments and they are not necessarily in a strong position to negotiate for the provision of even very basic services. Future planning tends to be based on the availability of resources rather than the user's wishes. In fact the community care policy guidance leaves the dice loaded very much in favour of the assessor and purchasing authority in this respect (Secretaries of State for Health and Social Services, England, Wales and Scotland 1989, 1990).

Involvement of service users in local planning

It's the needs of the person with a learning disability that are important and the needs of the parents may be quite different. The Strategy is really providing for something the parents don't want. It's going to take a long time...

This comment from a parent early in the life-cycle of the Welsh Strategy turned out to be prophetic. Forums to involve people with learning disabilities in planning took a long time to take root, often because of a reluctance to accept that users had just the same right as families to discuss matters on their own terms.

Although some successes have been reported in bringing service users on to local planning groups, little is known about how this may help to change the culture of meetings in making them more sensitive to service user needs and expectations. In some counties the presence of service users appears to reflect no more than a permissive policy which, whilst condoning involvement, does little to enhance representation and empowerment of the user constituency. It has been noticeable in many of the local forums that service users seem merely to be there to accompany parents or informal carers.

Users appear to come on to local planning groups in a variety of ways, including election by other service users, personal recommendation, direct invitation, local newsletters and word of mouth. By 1989 four of the eight counties were providing this kind of involvement (All Wales Advisory Panel 1991). However, the report also tells us that in one planning group, service users comprised one-quarter of the membership but they made only 2 of the 78 contributions identified in the minutes of the meeting.

This picture has moved on, helped by the appointment of participation officers and by the emergence of citizen advocacy and self-advocacy projects. These developments have helped to develop more opportunities for the involvement of individuals in local planning. What is more at issue now is the question of influence. On the one hand county plans, services and service designs are increasingly being influenced by a better appreciation of individual user needs. At the same time there have been contrasting value positions about three closely connected issues: first, the belief that representation of service user views can be maintained effectively through families; second, the belief that the interests of parents and their sons and daughters are synonymous and, third, equivocation about the possibilities of direct representation by service users in the planning, management, delivery and review of services on the grounds that people with learning disabilities cannot speak for themselves.

This last point is being contested strongly by voices within the user constituency itself. As the experience of community care planning increases, users are increasingly laying claim to the right to debate key issues in their own forums, separate from family carers, and for their forums to be seen as an integral part of the local planning infrastructure. This can be seen as part of the movement to rid services of oppressive or paternalistic practices and to render those who plan, purchase or provide services more accountable for their actions. An increasing range of initiatives which enable service users to work alongside or separately from other interest groups are now in evidence (Beresford and Harding 1993).

For service users the story has been one of courage, persistence and continuing struggle. Winning arguments about participatory rights is one thing; being able to justify claims on resources for an infrastructure to support those rights is another. It is not easy to prove in advance what participatory mechanisms will work. With participatory stratagems being exceptionally difficult to evaluate (Richardson 1983), it is perhaps also convenient for officialdom to adopt a cynical view of their likely effects.

Families and local planning

What's the point of consulting if it's left to experts to decide?

Certainly there are sometimes confidential and tricky problems. I think parents should have a say and that professionals should note in all seriousness what parents are wanting because very often, as professionals, they might not have the deep personal insight into the problems of handicaps that parents have. As long as note is taken of parents' wishes and opinions I would be quite happy with that. And as long as we have evidence that our suggestions are taken seriously.

These two comments from parents in North Wales give a sense of different stances about involvement in local planning. During the early stages of the Welsh Strategy, parents were in the vanguard of pressures for change but they also showed themselves as wanting to work in strategically different ways from one another. One account showed that three broad categories of participant could be discerned: 'pragmatists', 'democratic radicals' and 'endurers' (Humphreys 1987a), each with their own agendas and strategic intent, as summarised in Table 7.1.

The three groups described each gave predictably different answers to the question 'has participation in local planning been worthwhile?', with only the 'endurers' likely to offer an affirmative response. These illustrations also highlight concerns about stability and instability in involvement over time, varied expectations for involvement and consultation, and how best to ensure a fair means of representation.

However, there was a considerable silent majority of families unable or unwilling to participate in planning. A survey of 190 families in one area (McGrath 1989) showed that 64 per cent had never attended any of the local planning meetings, despite vigorous attempts at advertising and invitations being mailed to everyone. Family members who had not attended local planning meetings or who had stopped attending at an early stage fell into four overlapping groups (Table 7.2).

Table 7.1 Some characteristics of parent participants

'Pragmatists'	'Democratic radicals'	'Endurers'
• take a simplistic view of involvement	• involvement seen as a means to an end and an end in itself	• high commitment to involvement, and greatest exposure to administrators
• main aim: securing of immediate, tangible benefits in terms of services	• involvement a platform to energise a latent political force and challenge the status quo	• ability to empathise with other constituencies of interest
• realisation of above benefits seen as prerequisite to continued involvement	• not prepared to accept paternalism or tokenism	• preparedness to negotiate, or compromise, with administrators
• failure to appreciate planning complexities coupled with a perception of slow progress in realising new services leads to early withdrawal from planning	• not afraid of waging 'moral crusades' in the mould of pressure groups, often using the media to good effect	• on the whole, non-confrontational
	• influence out of proportion to their numbers	• trading position both with other parents and with administrators requires considerable skill but could lead to adoption of a conservative stance

Table 7.2 Categories of non-attenders at local planning meetings

Reason for non-attendance	Comment
Lack of essential knowledge	Only 13% had awareness of purpose of local planning groups, of how proposals were processed. Fifty per cent disclaimed any knowledge of local planning groups.
Little interest in contributing to plans	Confined mostly to those who rarely went out, families who saw little to be gained from attending because they felt their needs were already met.
Constraints on attendance	*Psychological*: lack of confidence, fears about discussing private concerns in public, fears re personal experience being devalued.
	Practical: Lack of personal or public transport, shiftwork patterns, personal ill health or chronic illness, unmet baby sitting or respite needs.
Experiences leading to withdrawal	Perceived delays in moving from plans to provision of services, inappropriate scheduling of meetings, over-use of professional jargon, lack of guidelines or structure for consultation.

Orlowska (1995) has similarly described a wide range of stances taken up by parents in relation to services and how these are shaped in particular by available information, attitudes to service philosophy, expectations for their son or daughter, and levels of parent and professional responsibility. The complexities and contradictions faced by parents led her to conclude that they may be damned if they participate and damned if they do not. Others have called for a much more comprehensive and coordinated approach to the involvement of family carers in the design and delivery of services based on a clearer enunciation of their participatory rights (Richardson, Unell and Aston 1989).

The 'paradigmatic battle' (Heifetz 1980) suggested by these descriptions once again indicates that issues about power relations and due process underlie people's central concerns. Before bringing this section to a close, a final word is in order about representation:

> I personally find it extremely difficult to maintain, one could almost say, my integrity because if you're outside the system and a member of the voluntary organisation, you can, as it were, keep to very pure principles and say, 'this is what we want and we will not accept anything less than that', but as soon as you're involved in any kind of planning process with professionals, you have to be aware of the constraints, the machinery, the money, the structure, the personalities,

etc., etc. – all that mass of things that professionals have to do. It's extremely difficult to work positively in a group like that, bearing all these things in mind and yet, at the same time, keeping as much objectivity as you can, keeping your principles...I've had to compromise my independence to some degree. I think I'm inhabiting a very uneasy middle ground...

This eloquent comment from a parent neatly captures one of the central dilemmas for individuals acting in representative roles (McGrath 1989). Should a person be expected to work to a mandate from their constituency of interest, thereby 'representing' or acting as a spokesperson for that constituency, or should they be free to speak and act according to their own conscience, unfettered by demands from an outside body?

The issue at stake here remains open to debate. People acting to a constituency mandate can face conflicts of role identity in which their independent-mindedness has to be traded for the sake of their continued participation within planning forums against the roles and duties of professionals and administrators. Those acting without a mandate, on the other hand, can find themselves out of touch with sentiments within their constituency of interest. Fulfilling the expectations of either kind of representative role can be onerous, yet the machinery for supporting people in these roles was frequently found wanting. This quickly gave rise to feelings amongst local planning groups that their primary mission was to generate new ideas for services based on identified local needs rather than to have any direct influence on decision-making and priority-setting.

The existence of participatory structures and mechanisms, itself an achievement, is not in dispute, but the questions raised at the beginning of the chapter now need to be revisited in the light of the evidence reported.

Consultation as involvement or empowerment?

Do people want to be involved?

This can be addressed on two levels. Involvement in decision-making at the case level was widely accepted as the norm. There was considerable enthusiasm from service users and families for individual planning, with everything it entails about decisions prompted by a primary concern for the individual's needs and preferences. It is therefore of concern that policy imperatives about the coverage of IPs seem to be largely unfulfilled. The reasons for this have to do less with the enthusiasm and commitment of families, users and care managers or key workers and much more to do with mismatches between resources and demand, as well as with basic infrastructure problems. There are major obstacles yet to be overcome with assessment technologies, in the establishment of empathetic relationships with users and families, and with enabling people to take more control of decision-making.

By contrast, attitudes to involvement in local planning proved to be very varied. Only a minority of family carers demonstrated an interest in prolonged involvement at this level and a majority appear to have no interest in contributing at all. For such individuals any apparent incremental changes they may have noticed as a result of involvement (Barnes and Wistow 1992) were insufficient to sustain their involvement. Whilst there seems little doubt that preconditions about shifting the balance of power towards users and families (Barnes and Wistow 1992; Grant 1992; Potter 1988) were far from being in place, the quality and organisation of the consultative experience also left something to be desired.

However, there appear to be quite large numbers of people who remain unaware of local planning arrangements and of their right to participate, despite the best efforts of the local publicity machine. Practical and psychological barriers were reported to have prevented others from participation. The involvement of people with learning disabilities in local planning has taken longer to take root. Where service users have joined forces with families in local planning groups there are indications that their voice is not heard. As more and more participatory initiatives emerge it becomes vital to assess what helps involvement the most.

At the inception of the Welsh Strategy in 1983 there was widespread enthusiasm for involvement, prompted as much by the knowledge that there was significant new funding available for investment in community services. The appeal of being able to shape the new pattern of services through participation in planning was accordingly very strong.

The sustainability of such a commitment from service users and families is perhaps more questionable under circumstances of severe resource constraint where the realisation of tangible services is far less assured. Wistow and Barnes (1993), on the other hand, suggest that dissatisfaction with services is significant in motivating involvement. Whilst this may be true it is important to be able to understand how users and families frame their judgements about satisfaction. A person may well be dissatisfied with services but if the prospect of realising improvements is perceived to be small their desire for involvement may be more likely to wane.

Do people feel empowered?

There is no simple answer to this question. Parents identified as 'pragmatists' (Table 7.1) seemed to be looking for quick, tangible gains in terms of services and if these were not achieved they withdrew from the consultative arena. Those labelled as 'democratic radicals' assumed a more crusading role and were most likely to challenge establishment methods. For them the opportunity to consult and to influence planning priorities and decision-making served to energise a very considerable latent force expressed in the form of pressure for change. They more than the other groups were seeking a shift in the balance of power and accountability. Those referred to as the 'endurers', straddling a more middle position, strove to identify with all the interest groups, persevered with the consultative arrangements, but more often than not adopted a position of compromise when faced with good organisational reasons for proceeding in a particular way. However, for all service users and parents, their feelings about empowerment were very much tied to the structure and process of consultation itself.

Terms which kept on cropping up in this regard were things such as: 'being heard and listened to', 'empathy', 'having a common purpose', 'mutual respect', 'influence', 'control' and 'consensus', as if people were striving to create consultation which was egalitarian both in form and essence. These were closely connected to ideas about partnership practice (Fisher 1994) or what would now be recognised as anti-discriminatory, anti-oppressive practice (Braye and Preston-Shoot 1995) which seeks not only to remove barriers to services but also to achieve a shift in the power structure itself. Despite the challenges, it was as if people were striving to bring their own ideas about consultation, largely hitherto uncharted, into an arena more used to bureaucratic processes. If consultation as an empowering force in people's lives is to be given a chance it is important that these ideas are brought into the open.

The process of consulting in this context seemed to imply a number of things about the qualities of interpersonal relationships of those consulting. As a problem-solving, goal-setting device, consultation seemed to involve a search for consensus, wherever possible, about the reality of a given situation and the wisest choice of action amongst the options available at any moment in time. This assumes, however, that people should be free to express, with candour and courtesy, and without prejudice, their views and experiences. Where power relations were felt to be unbalanced or the parameters of consultation left uncharted this was less likely to be achieved, with the result that people often failed to speak up or, worse, left the stage.

However, in the more egalitarian model of consultation to which many people aspired, ideas which arise can be viewed less as belonging to the individual and more to the group as a whole to take up, discard or revise as seems fit (Kolstoe 1985). Here, consultation is not about scoring points or asserting a position, but about seeking the best decision in the light of all contributions to consultation. It not only seeks to ensure that everyone's expertise is used, it also aims to help the group to work with unity of purpose. It is a model that holds no quarter for egotism and the maintenance of personal self-image above all else. It recognises the balancing required by the need to incorporate conflict as well as consensus into the consultative arena, demanding much of the skill and maturity of participants. The expression of different or contradictory views is a necessary part of the experience, otherwise uniformity and stagnation are the likely end result. Training programmes are required to help people practise their skills in this regard.

Another characteristic of this type of consultative model is the improved prospect of group solidarity. With each and all participants contributing to consultation, the opportunities for mutual learning are increased. This in turn helps to maintain a unity of purpose and commitment which each and all are likely to find empowering. Hence, in this model consultation as empowerment is not about the transfer of power *from* professionals or administrators *to* users or families, as if some kind of zero sum game. Neither has it anything to do with historical bases of authority such as formal position, status, charisma or tradition. Rather it concerns the sharing of life experience, knowledge, information and insight between all members of the group, users, families, professionals and planners alike. The exchanges, reciprocities and building of relationships between individuals help not only to empower the individual but the group as a whole, supporting ideas about the wider transformational potential of partnership practice and empowerment (Barnes and Wistow 1992; Fisher 1994) in terms of promoting not only personal growth but improvements in service responsiveness and quality.

Central to the spirit of a more egalitarian model of consultation is the assumption that each individual should enjoy the freedom of thought and action conducive to his or her personal growth. This is likely to require an acceptance that there are both metaphysical or spiritual pathways (for example inner reflection, meditation, inspiration, intuition) and material pathways (reason, tradition, sense perception) reflecting different cultural and religious traditions which individuals can use to explore the realities they face. Used as complements these represent routes for individuals to enter the consultative process. These seem likely to become increasingly important as more people from different ethnic and cultural backgrounds enter consultative arenas (Blakemore and Boneham 1994; Yee 1995).

In most of the aforementioned respects the NHS and Community Care Act 1990 does little to provide a new sense of direction. Indeed, through its emphasis on market principles, competition, means of redress and so forth, it could be claimed that it perpetuates forms of dialogue based on the adversarial model, conflict, even protest, and an apparatus of partisanship. In an environment which loads decision-making power into the hands of enabling authorities; control and influence are wrested from users and families. The agencies concerned are thus sanctioned to continue this style of working which seems inimical to a model which sees consultation as the operating expression of justice in human affairs. In this regard the 'new' community care can be construed as a lost opportunity to consolidate key lessons from the participatory principles of the All Wales Strategy.

What is being called for is therefore a deconstruction and reconstruction of consultation itself, but in the context of a continuing dialogue between users, families, providers and purchasers of services. This will not satisfy those who view collective empowerment strategies as the only effective or pre-eminent route to achieving user control. However, as the oppressed or disadvantaged the world over seek to assert their position and to have the rest of the world acknowledge their difference and their worth, as other chapters in this volume suggest is their wish, we must at least learn how not to disempower them through how we relate. In the writer's view the struggle for identity and claims on citizenship rights must somehow work hand in hand with the development of models of consultation that are capable of empowering all who participate. It is hoped that the experience in Wales demonstrates something of the problems and prospects involved.

References

All Wales Advisory Panel (1991) *Consumer Involvement and the All Wales Strategy*. Cardiff: Welsh Office.

Ash, A., Ritchie, P. and Scott, S. (1989) *Quality Action Project Update 3, December 1989*. Bristol: Norah Fry Research Centre, University of Bristol.

Barnes, M. and Wistow, G. (1992) *Researching User Involvement*. Leeds: Nuffield Institute for Health Services Studies, University of Leeds.

Beresford, P. and Harding, T. (1993) *A Challenge to Change: Practical Experiences of Building User-Led Services*. London: National Institute for Social Work.

Beyer, S., Evans, G., Todd, S. and Blunden, R. (1986) *Planning for the All Wales Strategy: A Review of Issues Arising in Welsh Counties*. Research Report No. 19. Cardiff: Mental Handicap in Wales Applied Research Unit.

Blakemore, K. and Boneham, M. (1994) *Age, Race and Ethnicity: A Comparative Approach*. Buckingham: Open University Press.

Blunden, R., Evans, G. and Humphreys, S. (1987) *Planning with Individuals: An Outline Guide*. Cardiff: Mental Handicap in Wales Applied Research Unit.

Bourlet, G., Sims, J. and Whittaker, A. (1988) People First presentation at the BIMH Annual Conference at which the initial results of the national survey of self-advocacy projects were reported. Keele: Keele University.

Braye, S. and Preston-Shoot, M. (1995) *Empowering Practice in Social Care*. Buckingham: Open University.

Brechin, A. and Swain, J. (1987) *Changing Relationships: Shared Action Planning With People With a Mental Handicap*. London: Harper and Row.

Butler, K., Carr, S. and Sullivan, F. (1988) *Citizen Advocacy: A Powerful Partnership*. London: National Citizen Advocacy.

Croft, S. and Beresford, P. (1995) 'Whose empowerment? Equalizing the competing discourses in community care.' In R. Jack (ed) *Empowerment in Community Care*. London: Chapman and Hall.

Day, P.R. (1994) 'Ambiguity and user involvement: issues arising in assessments for young people and their carers.' *British Journal of Social Work 24*, 577–596.

Douglas, T. (1985) 'Change: the implementation of the All Wales Strategy.' *Mental Handicap 13*, 1, 14–16.

Drake, R.F. and Owens, D.J. (1992) 'Consumer involvement and the voluntary sector in Wales: breakthrough or bandwagon?' *Critical Social Policy 33*, 11, 76–86.

Dunst, C.J., Trivette, C.M., Starnes, A.L., Hamby, D.W. and Gordon, N.J. (1993a) *Building and Evaluating Family Support Initiatives.* Baltimore: Paul H. Brookes.

Dunst, C.J., Trivette, C.M., Gordon, N.J. and Starnes, A.L. (1993b) 'Family-centred case management practices: characteristics and consequences.' In G.H.S. Singer and L.E. Powers (eds) *Families, Disability and Empowerment: Active Coping Skills and Strategies for Family Interventions.* Baltimore: Paul H. Brookes.

Ellis, K. (1993) *Squaring the Circle: User and Carer Participation in Needs Assessment.* York: Joseph Rowntree Foundation in Association/Community Care.

Felce, D. (1994) 'Facilitated communication: results from a number of recently published evaluations.' *British Journal of Learning Disabilities 22,* 4, 122–126.

Fisher, M. (1994) 'Partnership practice and empowerment.' In P. Nurius and L. Gutierriez (eds) *Education and Research for Empowerment Practice.* Washington: University of Washington.

Flynn, M.C. (1986) 'Adults who are mentally handicapped as consumers: issues and guidelines for interviewing.' *Journal of Mental Deficiency Research 30,* 369–377.

Freire, P. (1972) *Pedagogy of the Oppressed.* London: Penguin.

Goode, D. (1994) 'Defining facilitated communication in and out of existence, role of science in the facilitated communication controversy.' *Mental Retardation 32,* 4, 307–311.

Grant, G. (1985) 'Towards participation in the All Wales Strategy: issues and processes.' *Mental Handicap 13,* 2, 51–54.

Grant, G. (1992) 'Researching user and carer involvement in mental handicap services.' In M. Barnes and G. Wistow (eds) *Researching User Involvement.* Leeds: Nuffield Institute for Health Services Studies, University of Leeds.

Grant, G., McGrath, M. and Ramcharan, P. (1994) 'How family and informal carers appraise service quality.' *International Journal of Disability, Development and Education 41,* 2, 127–141.

Heifetz, L. (1980) 'From consumer to middleman: emerging roles for parents in the network of services for retarded children.' In R. Abidin (ed) *Parent Education and Intervention Handbook.* Springfield, ILL: Charles C. Thomas.

Humphreys, S. (1987a) 'Participation in practice.' *Social Policy and Administration 21,* 1, 28–39.

Humphreys, S. (1987b) 'Individual planning in Nimrod: results of an evaluation of the system four years on.' In G. Grant, S. Humphreys and M. McGrath (eds) *Community Mental Handicap Teams: Theory and Practice.* Kidderminster: BIMH Conference Series.

Humphreys, S. and Blunden, R. (1987) 'A collaborative evaluation of an individual plan system.' *British Journal of Mental Subnormality 33,* 1, 19–30.

Jack, R. (ed) (1995) *Empowerment in Community Care.* London: Chapman and Hall.

Jenkinson, J.C. (1993) 'Who shall decide? The relevance of theory and research to decision-making by people with an intellectual disability.' *Disability, Handicap and Society 8,* 4, 361–375.

Kolstoe, J.E. (1985) *Consultation: A Universal Lamp of Guidance.* Oxford: George Ronald.

Laws, M., Bolt, L. and Gibbs, V. (1988) 'Implementing change in a mental handicap hospital using an individual plan system.' *Mental Handicap* 16 June, 74–76.

Lewis, J. (1993) 'Developing the mixed economy of care: emerging issues for voluntary organisations.' *Journal of Social Policy 22*, 2, 173–192.

Lloyd, J. and Todd, M. (1995) 'Psychotherapeutic interventions.' In M. Todd and T. Gilbert (eds) *Learning Disabilities: Practice Issues in Health Settings.* London: Routledge.

Lowe, K., de Paiva, S. and Humphreys, S. (1986) *Clients' Views.* Cardiff: Mental Handicap in Wales Applied Research Unit.

McGrath, M. (1989) 'Consumer participation in service planning: the AWS experience.' *Journal of Social Policy 18*, 1, 67–89.

McGrath, M. (1991) *Multidisciplinary Teamwork.* Aldershot: Avebury.

McGrath, M. and Grant, G. (1992) 'Supporting needs-led services: implications for planning and management systems.' *Journal of Social Policy 21*, 1, 71–97.

Oliver, M. (1996) *Understanding Disability: From Theory to Practice.* London: Macmillan.

Orlowska, D. (1995) 'Parental participation in issues concerning their sons and daughters with learning disabilities.' *Disability and Handicap 10*, 4, 437–456.

Potter, J. (1988) 'Consumerism and the public sector: how well does the coat fit?' *Public Administration 66*, 149–164.

Ramcharan, P. (1995) 'Advocacy and people with learning disabilities.' In R. Jack (ed) *Empowerment in Community Care.* London: Chapman and Hall.

Ramcharan, P. and Grant, G. (1994) 'Setting one agenda for empowering persons with a disadvantage within the research process.' In M. Rioux and M. Bach (eds) *Disability Is Not Measles: New Research Paradigms in Disability*, 227–244. Canada: Roeher Institute.

Rees, S. (1991) *Achieving Power: Practice and Policy in Social Welfare.* London: Allen and Unwin.

Report of the Committee on Citizenship (1990) *Encouraging Citizenship.* London: HMSO.

Richardson, A. (1983) *Participation.* London: Routledge.

Richardson, A., Unell, J. and Aston, B. (1989) *A New Deal for Carers.* London: Kings Fund.

Rose, S.M. and Black, B.L. (1985) *Advocacy and Empowerment.* London: Routledge.

Rosenfeld, J.M. (1989) *Emergence from Extreme Poverty.* Paris: Science and Service Fourth World Publications.

SCOVO (1986) *Evidence from Welsh Voluntary Organisations for the Welsh Office AWS Three Year Review.* Cardiff: Standing Conference of Voluntary Organisations.

Secretaries of State for Health and Social Services, England, Wales and Scotland (1989) *Caring for People: Community Care in the Next Decade and Beyond.* Cm.849. London: HMSO.

Secretaries of State for Health and Social Services, England, Wales and Scotland (1990) *Caring for People: Community Care in the Next Decade and Beyond. Policy Guidance.* London: HMSO.

Seebohm Report (1968) *Report of the Committee on Local Authority and Allied Personal Social Services.* Cm. 3703. London: HMSO.

Simons, K. (1993) *Sticking Up For Yourself.* York: Joseph Rowntree Foundation in association with Community Care.

Social Services Inspectorate (1991a) *Care Management and Assessment: Practitioners' Guide.* London: HMSO.

Social Services Inspectorate (1991b) *Care Management and Assessment: Managers' Guide.* London: HMSO.

Townsley, R. (1995) 'Avon calling.' *Community Care* 12–18 January, 26–27.

Ward, L. and Flynn, M. (1994) 'What matters most: disability, research and empowerment.' In M. Rioux and M. Bach (eds) *Disability Is Not Measles: New Research Paradigms in Disability.* Canada: Roeher Institute.

Welsh Office (1983) *All Wales Strategy for the Development of Services for Mentally Handicapped People.* Cardiff.

Welsh Office (1987) *All Wales Strategy for the Development of Services for Mentally Handicapped People: Review of Progress Since March 1983.* Cardiff.

Welsh Office (1991) *Still a Small Voice: Consumer Involvement in the All Wales Strategy.* Cardiff.

Welsh Office (1994) *The Welsh Mental Handicap Strategy – Guidance.* Cardiff.

Wistow, G. and Barnes, M. (1993) 'User involvement in community care: origins, purposes and applications.' *Public Administration* 71, 279–299.

Yee, L. (1995) *Improving Support for Black Carers. A Sourcebook of Information, Ideas and Service Initiatives.* London: Kings Fund.

CHAPTER 8

'I'm Stuck Here with my Poxy Star Chart'
Listening to Mentally Disordered Offenders with Learning Disabilities

Margaret Flynn, Sian Griffiths, Liz Byrne and Kevin Hynes

Introduction

Adults with learning disabilities who commit crimes are a very small population. In spite of their minority position, they cause disproportionate concerns to the range of services which endeavour to support them. These services operate mostly in isolation and are prone to high public and media profiles when they waver or fail. Until recently the experiences of adults with learning disabilities who commit crimes, and all that results from these, have had limited recognition, not least because service and judicial responses have resulted in arbitrary outcomes for some offenders, including, for example, imprisonment, detention in special hospitals or Secure Units or long-stay hospital wards for undetermined periods.

This chapter draws from a National Development Team project funded by the Department of Health (1994–1996) entitled, 'Listening to Mentally Disordered Offenders with Learning Disabilities'. The twin aims of this project are:

- to ascertain from 20, self-selected people with learning disabilities who have committed offences, their experiences and their version of events without recourse to anyone else
- to host workshops for the purchasers and providers of services for adults with learning disabilities who offend.

The project had its genesis in the Reed (1992a,b) and Mansell (1993) reports. Although these offer health authorities, local authorities and criminal justice agencies specific guidance regarding the development of service provision for people with learning disabilities, challenging behaviours and mental health needs, they make no reference to people's first-person experiences. Thus this project can be viewed as a codicil or natural progression from their recommendations. It owes a particular debt of gratitude to six men and women with learning disabilities who live in a Medium Secure Unit. They met with Sian Griffiths, the project worker, twice a month and provided a wealth of background information, numerous suggestions about the course of the project, and ideas about how service responses to the minority of adults with learning disabilities who offend might be more effective.

The chapter provides two narratives and one case study about two men and a woman. It is perhaps problematic that in a book about empowerment, we have chosen to highlight the lives and circumstances of three people whose lives have pivoted on acute disadvantage and abuse, neither of which sit comfortably with images of empowerment. It is significant that none of the three adults are co-authors. This is to avoid their identification. Accordingly we have anonymised these three people and altered some potentially identifying details.

The three accounts led us to the view that it is empowering to believe that people with learning disabilities who commit offences can change. Services which tolerate or ignore sexual abuses and offending behaviours cannot confer empowerment. Their want of initiative in checking and challenging offending and criminal behaviours speaks of an ungenerous view of people with learning disabilities. Such services leave their mark, not least in the form of centralised, inward-looking provision which excludes people; the absence of local expertise; and damaged expectations about the capacity of services to keep people safe.

We have found the ideas and approach of Smull and Burke Harrison (1992) influential in writing this chapter. They challenge conventional approaches to supporting adults with learning disabilities by underlining the critical tasks of identifying and honouring the *non-negotiables* in people's lives, that is, the:

> ...lifestyle choices which are essential to a reasonable quality of life for the individual...essential for a person's life to be tolerable and pleasant...essential to the individual's well being... Negative non-negotiables make life so unpleasant and intolerable that their presence will make people act out or withdraw. Examples of non-negotiables...are: not living with smokers...living where I grew up...not living in the city. (pp.13–14)

In the narratives which follow, Tony and Eva's language is unedited. Readers may find Tony's language particularly shocking. However unwarranted it may appear, it illuminates the ever-present membrane of continuing abuse that connects many narratives gathered during the course of this work. Tony's life experiences are appalling, not least as his invariably modest non-negotiables were folded into punishing experiences. It would be quite wrong to suggest that the weight and intention of his language is shallow. Tony's narrative, along with that of other interviewees, is highly charged with anger.

Tony's narrative

Tony is 36 years old. He is a Londoner. His mother is white and his father Afro-Caribbean. He has never known his father. Tony has experienced many years of racial abuse from his mother and from people in the service settings in which he has lived. Although he has lived in many different homes and hospitals, he cannot remember how many or for how long he lived away from his mother. He has spent many years in prison and in Medium Secure Units. Tony has been in trouble since he was 'about 18'. He has epilepsy which is poorly controlled. He loves Elvis Presley songs and 'to be outside'. He is vegan. These are Tony's own words:

> *People think I'm queer. I was raped when I was seven. I told a friend when I was grown up and she reported it to the police. I wanted the bastard locked up but they couldn't trace him. I want to fight my way through it until he's locked up.*

> *I was shopping for me mum, next minute I found I was in the cell in the police station. I made a lot of phone calls and no one came for me so I called the Guv'ner and said 'You'd better get me out of here'. He said 'Next time, leave him alone. He's just had a fit'. I weren't even in drink. I only had a fucking seizure and they picked me up in the van and took me down the cells didn't they? They thought I was pissed. I got my mate [the sergeant] to let me out.*

> *I was out cold and no one looked after me. It happened to me again. I had me head in the gutter moaning and groaning. The police throw me in the meat wagon and I wake up in the cells because they think I'm drunk. They should think and see a doctor to check me out. They're only fit for picking up drunkards. They need training. They should learn about medical stuff instead of locking people up. Should learn about psychology, people's minds and that. I nearly died because I had a bad fit. When I'm fitting they just fucking leave me. They don't give a shit. When I have a fit I get abusive all the time because I'm frightened. They ignore me. They think I'm faking it. They pinch me here and there. They laughed at me when I have a fit. At the [Secure Unit] I nearly died because I had a bad fit. They gave me suppositories, steroids, epilim intravenous, valium intravenous, valium rectal and they brought me round with valium intravenous and it took a long time. They even gave me oxygen and these bastards here have got the cheek to leave me when I'm fitting. They don't give a shit. I've got an identity card from the Epilepsy Association now. Saw a programme on epilepsy on TV so I ring the number. It's a free call. I carry it around so nobody knows I'm pissed when I get arrested. [Now] every time I get my Depo I get side effects. My eyes are rolling but they don't give me nothing for it. I was on Largactil. It fucked me speech something chronic. I was stutterin' and stammerin'. All these staff thought I was fucking about. A nurse took me pulse then the doctor took me off it just like that. My [step] dad died. He drank didn't he? His kidneys were fucked. They even medicated me the staff. I said 'I don't need fucking medication. You don't need to*

medicate some fucker sat in the hospital'. If you was outside and somebody died, a friend of yours, they wouldn't medicate you then, would they?

[A while ago] *I thought I'd get a job with a fairground, travel around. Every time the rides went off I used to go hunting 'round with a metal detector. Got a load of money. They said I mugged a pensioner. I never did. I said to police I did it just to fuck them off. They were pressurising me. I had to say something just to get them to take the piss off my back. I told them what they wanted to know and said 'Now leave me alone'. [In court] I felt like a fucking lunatic. I thought, what am I doing here? This is all wrong.*

They used to kick the living shit out of me. Everyone. Ever since, I've been kicking fuck out of them too because my mum told me to. She said, 'If anyone starts on you, kick fuck out of them' or she wouldn't let me in the house unless I did it. I said 'It's not the right thing to do'. Look where it's got me.

When I went into the Secure Unit I hit 'the priterior', the manager. She went deaf. She got the police in. The first time I got to know Pete [a support worker]. He used to get me food I liked so I could be vegan, I respected him for that. Two years later when I went back the new manager was there. As soon as she saw me she said 'You'd better fucking behave yourself for me'. They made me eat things I didn't like. I had to eat steak and kidney pie. It was disgusting. 'Cos I didn't eat me dinner I couldn't get me pudding so I threw it at her. The manager and staff jumped on me. I got away and hit her and she went deaf. They made me eat something I didn't like. I went to prison.

[Tony was once on remand in a prison hospital wing]

It was horrible. I didn't even get my Depo. I spewed up in my cell with withdrawal symptoms. I even had a fit in my cell and no fucker ever came to me. I could die, swallow my tongue. What could I do? They don't give a shit. I were in a hospital wing but there were no one there.

[Since a conviction for assault, Tony has been detained in three hospitals. He did not like the first.]

They're like babies in there. They're grown up but they're like babies in the head. They masturbate on the floor, shit the bed, piss the bed. I had to sleep with that lot all the time in the same dormitory. I said I'm not putting up with this. I tried to talk to them. [Now, here] some days it's all right. I liked Don, Baz, Mick, Sean and Dave but they're gone now. I'm stuck here with my poxy Star Chart [cf. Williams 1986] all the time. Every time I lose my temper I get restrained and lose my parole. It takes me a month to get it back. Every time I give verbal abuse to staff they write it down. I don't even get a chance and it says in that folder I should get two verbal prompts but they just write it down.

The best time was when I was on parole. I used to be out all the time enjoying fresh air. That's what I liked. Now I only get half an hour. It's no good. My key worker is Jenny. I don't like her. She's too bitchy with me. I'm glad to get rid of Brian though. He used to treat me like dirt. I said 'Can I get me T-shirts off the radiator?' and he goes 'five, ten, fifteen, twenty...' and it means Quiet Room. If I keep arguing he just slams me down and restrains me. He's no shit respect for any fucker. He never gives me respect. I don't even get a session out of the social worker, psychologist or Dr Ryan. We can't even paint about our feelings like we did at the last Unit. What was it called now? Let me think. 'Creative Workshop' they called it. They told us to paint how we feel and things we like doing. If you can't draw you can just draw shapes like black dots when you're sad and blue for the sky when you're happy.

You can't have your own opinions here. They don't listen to you. Social workers and [Mental Health Act] Commissioners don't visit often. They don't know what it's like. Gary is good. He's my solicitor. He listens to you. So is Aled, my advocate. He comes to your reviews. He talks to you and that. [Also Bob.] He was good to me Bob was. I always respect his truth and honour. He tells you straight. He's different from the other staff because he understands me more. He knows how I feel. He just treats me right, fair, square. He's got patience with me. Staff haven't on this ward. They don't understand me problems. You see how I work with people. I get to know them first then I respect them because they understand me. If I know people from before they know what I'm like so I respect them.

[To make Medium Secure Units better...] I'd try and talk to them, residents. Find out what the problem is and if they [staff] have got an attitude, I'd say 'Get out. We don't want you'. I'd put things straight. I don't believe in bank staff. They're not trained properly. They don't know nothing. All they do is train C and R [Control and Restraint]. That's what they use, techniques and put locks on you. If staff want to become qualified I'd let them. I'd give them more money. I'd make sure they get a good wage. I'd take the cameras down.

[For the future] I want to go somewhere where no fucker knows me. For a community nurse I'd have Bob 'cos he's understanding. He listens to me...I'll never get a chance to get out of here. I've no chance.

Eva's narrative

Eva is 58 years old. She is from the North East. She cannot remember how long she has lived in a Medium Secure Unit.

My dad abused me and hit me and I jumped out of a bedroom window and I broke my leg. He used to beat me something awful and my dad, he used to do it on all of us. I used to be terrified. To make matters worse, he used to go for my mum. I had a social worker, Miss Starfield, but she used to stick up for my parents, not me. I couldn't even go nowhere on my own. He [dad] used to make me mad saying that I was mentally disordered, mentally retarded and everything. My other social worker Bernie used to tell my mum and dad to let me walk down to the town centre so I can get more used to walk[ing] on my own. I thought one way of doing it if I walked down to see her. I was anxious and depressed and she said 'What for?' so I didn't say much. I walked past my own doctor's surgery. It was a different doctor. I wasn't over keen on him so I broke his aerial, his windscreen wipers and goodness knows what. They put me in hospital. I was about in my early thirties.

From hospital I came here. I didn't know I was coming here or nothing. I came in 1990 or 1991. Social services sent me to one hostel and I didn't like it so they put me in another one. I didn't like that either. You see they're very strict. You see my dad was strict with us and I don't like it like that. They should say 'You can stay out until 12 o'clock' or something. I went to another resident in the hostel with a knife and I was cautioned by another copper so the boss of the hostel put me in here. I done another incident when I was in here. I was in trouble with the police. They took me to the police station and I was in there overnight and that until the next day when they questioned me. Eric [nurse manager] was with me and then they asked me at the police station, 'Do I want a solicitor?' and he was flipping brilliant. Then I went to a Magistrates Court.

[At the police station] I felt shaky and on edge. They put me in a cell. There wasn't a light. They just used to give me a light. He was coming to see how I am. I was all right but I wasn't over keen on it. Honestly they were really nice and friendly. They used to say to me 'Do you want a brew?' and 'Do you want a smoke?'. The policeman's telling me 'You're in here and you got to go to the Magistrate's Court tomorrow and everything. We got to keep you in here until you go'.' [In court] the solicitor said 'Don't worry. You won't have to say anything if you don't want to in court. We will stick up for you'. Then I had to go to prison.

Prison wasn't very nice. Your brews was nice and warm and hot but your meals was freezing cold. You used to scrub on your hands and knees, scrub the hallway. First time they put me in a room on my own. I didn't like it so they put me in a room with somebody and it was all right 'cos I was talking to someone.

[In the Crown Court] my stomach was like nobody's business because I was worried that I'd go down to prison or something like that... A policewoman had to stand with me when I was in the thingy in Crown Court. She said 'Don't worry. Stop worrying about it. You'll be all right'. They sent me here. I can't go anywhere. Today I'd be sitting on the ward bored to tears. You see this is what happens. You're bored like this and you've got nothing to do. That's when things happen. One of the residents goes for people and he used to try and bite me and he picked up the telly and tried to smash it.

I couldn't go out with fellas when I was with my parents but now I've got a boyfriend and he asked me to marry him when I get into the community. We go down the fields at the back. The only time we have to have sex is down there. Some of them do it behind the garages. It's not safe 'cos round here, if one of the staff saw you having it they can report you to a member of staff. You'd be in trouble then. I think it's all wrong. A person shouldn't have to have sex like that if they want to have sex. Should have a place for people who want to have sex with their boyfriends and that.

I wouldn't mind living in a house, two or three residents, staff all the time to protect us. One of the residents might go for us for instance. I want to go out more on my own. It would be hard for me to look for a job 'cos I'm nearly 60 and there's not much jobs to help people my age. I want more outings. We should have little flats where one staff is with us all the time, say one resident and two staff. Not all the time but they could keep an eye on us to see if we're coping all right. When we need our medication come and see us. Your consultant could come with a member of staff to see if you're doing better on your own instead of with the rest of the residents. If he says you're more better on your own than where you were last time, that proves he knows you're ready to go out in the community.

They should be helping us to get back to the community but they're not doing much for you. You see last time I was in here I was in four years and I was still waiting for a place out in the community. I was Informal then, not on a Section so I discharged myself. That's why I went into this hostel because you see while you're in these sorts of places, you're missing your brothers and sisters. I would rather go to prison because when you go to prison a judge says you got to do such and such a time in prison. But you see with this place, I know it's open grounds, but some of these residents have been here since 1904. They haven't been out in the community or nothing. That really is upsetting. There's one resident here and she's 100. I don't want to be here when I'm 100.

When I've got a complaint I go to see the boss. First time I was in here I did. One of the staff, he shouldn't have done it in the first place. He threw me up in the air. He picked me up like that and threw me down twice on my back and I made a complaint. Person who did it went to see the manager and went on nights. But the trouble is, that same staff's come back on days. He's in another unit.

When I were with me mum and dad, if I had a row with them when I was outside I would have got battered. In here, I'm protected by a member of staff. It's twice now that I've been in here that he's threatened me. Me social worker had to help me write the statement about me dad. This is what I can't understand. When they are due to come and see me I smoke more.

Instead of having everyone in the same place, they should have different sorts of people in different places. I think they should have some parts like open prison for people like us who can walk about and that.

Some initial reflections

There is a level at which Tony and Eva's narratives can be read as an exposé of inept, inadequate and sometimes abusive service responses. At another level, it is clear that adults with learning disabilities who offend place extraordinary requirements on a wide range of services and pose significant difficulties and challenges for the criminal justice system. Further, the narratives can also be viewed as the expert testimony of a man and woman whose voices would otherwise be unheard. They describe shameful abuses which did not end when they ceased to live with their parents. They have both been subject to brute force and there is little that is enviable about their lives.

Had Tony's vegan diet been cast as non-negotiable it could not have been used as a means to diminish and then punish him. Tony was distressed by the physically abusive treatment he did not expect from police and service personnel. Although Eva had more benign contact with the police, necessarily she is attuned to the brutality she witnesses in the Unit. She was and remains frightened of her father's violence. Initial social work contact was aligned with the needs of Eva's parents. Eva's voice was unheard. The administration of Tony's essential anti-convulsant and other medication has not been routinely honoured. Similarly his expressed non-negotiable *to be outside* does not feature in any service response. In contrast, Eva's non-negotiables of being believed, requiring reassurance and having company were largely acknowledged and honoured when she was in police custody and subsequently in prison.

Tony and Eva's lives and circumstances are broadly familiar to professionals working with adults with learning disabilities who offend. In fact when we described Tony and Eva in workshops for service purchasers and providers, some discreetly but erroneously suggested that they knew them. The identifying hints of these professionals only confirm the typicality of these demeaning experiences and dislocations which we have learned to be the lot of the 'mentally disordered offenders' known to us.

A case study

Tom is 46 years old. He lives in the south east of England where most of his seven brothers and sisters still live. As children they were all subject to persistent physical and, it is now believed, sexual assaults from their father. They all sought to protect their mother from their father's violence. When Tom's father died his mother became ill. He looked after her until she died. Then Tom moved in with his brother. He briefly attempted living alone but it did not work out. Now Tom lives with Kate who is described by a professional as '*much less able than Tom*'.

Tom was arrested after sexually assaulting two young relatives of Kate's. Staff in Tom's Adult Training Centre contacted a local specialist support team for their help. Preliminary discussions suggested that in the past, Tom's sexually inappropriate behaviours towards some of the women at the Adult Training Centre had been tolerated or ignored. The team accepted the referral and informed Tom that they would support him through the courts and begin to work with him on his offending behaviours and his behaviours towards women. The team's psychologist determined from cognitive functioning tests Tom's level of understanding, his learning style and how best to teach him things given the areas of comprehension with which he had particular difficulties. This information was conveyed to the police and the Magistrates Court.

Tom was remanded to a probation hostel before his court appearance. The team took on the responsibility of ensuring that he kept in touch with Kate. The same member of the team accompanied Tom to police interviews, meetings with his solicitors and court. Following the leads from the psychologist's work, this team member emphasised to all the professionals who came into contact with Tom the importance of using easy words and short sentences and the merits of using pictures to assist his understanding.

The psychologist's report was instrumental in the court deciding that Tom should return home. A two year probation order was imposed. The experience of members of the public shouting abuse and spitting at him outside the court left Tom visibly shaken and to this day he recalls their anger. A condition of the probation order was that he attended weekly sessions with his probation officer and the member of the support team who had worked with Tom throughout. As the local probation service had not previously worked with a person with a learning disability they sought more involvement from the support team than the court had envisaged, namely supervision from the team psychologist and the line manager of Tom's support worker. This matched the support team's policy of joint working to effect better outcomes for people.

The joint work has several strands, all of which are premised on the importance of making sense to Tom. A key strand is that of sanction. Tom understands that the probation officer is powerful and her contact with his family has underlined the importance of Tom not having unsupervised contact with children, for example. She has also stipulated that Tom must be occupied during the day, and accordingly a work placement was found for him. The placement insists on Tom's attendance and the specialist support team are informed if he is absent. In contrast to the Adult Training Centre, the work placement involves physically strenuous work with a new peer group. The importance of these factors lies in an occupation which is more like Tom's own picture of *real work* than that which the Adult Training Centre could offer, regular contact with role models he values, and Tom's growing sense of positive achievement. A further strand of work focuses on the seriousness of Tom's crimes. The joint sessions are helping Tom to look back and track the build-up to his offending. The objectives include helping Tom to understand how his history has influenced his life and exploring with him ways in which he can control his behaviours and respond differently to children, to women and to situations that make him feel humiliated and distressed. Importantly as well, Tom's work with the specialist support team draws from his own experiences as a child to assist him to understand the impact of his behaviour on children. To make more tangible the work that Tom does with team personnel, the sessions are informed by information supplied by the psychologist and a pictorial diary has been devised for him. This permits him to describe what he does and the contact he has with children and women. Tom has commented on how useful he finds this. Further, the diary provides focus to the weekly discussions with team personnel and the probation officer about how he might avoid inappropriate and abusive contacts in the future.

Some concluding comments

Criticism of services provided to adults with learning disabilities is hardly new or unusual, most particularly with regard to their capacity to disempower and damage individuals and groups. In contrast, Tom's contact with the probation service and the specialist support team comprising both health and social care personnel, contains an array of instructive experiences and gives starring roles to: joint working; having a good picture of people's level of understanding and what would help enhance this; structured days; and consistent messages delivered in understandable ways.

As we suggested earlier, Tony and Eva's narratives and Tom's case study render them equivocal residents in the territory of empowerment. It seems to us that the bewildering mix of service practices visited upon Tony and Eva speak of rivalries within and between professional disciplines, fundamental uncertainty about how to respond and enduring assumptions about their incapacity to change. Our discussions with and about Tony, Eva and Tom lead us to believe that: even though there is no helpful, one-dimensional stereotype to describe adults with learning disabilities who offend, conditions of detention without time limit are typical service responses; failing to identify and assist abused children with learning disabilities can yield extraordinary and long-term loads for criminal justice and associated services; and, in contrast to Tom, service responses to Tony and Eva are not suggestive of competent, experienced or knowledgeable services which have the will to effect positive change.

To reconnect with empowerment, we would argue that knowing and honouring people's non-negotiables lean towards more humane service responses – surely a necessary precondition of empowerment. Standing back and looking at Tom's circumstances, it appears that known non-negotiables also characterise his services, namely, his relationship with Kate and having work mates. It would be incorrect to suggest that Tom is entirely in control of his life. He is not. His probation order and required contact with the specialist support team side-stepped the Secure Unit or prison options which would have drawn a decisive line under his sexual offending against children. Given Tony and Eva's narratives, it seems unlikely that the coercive mechanisms embedded in such settings would have been as attuned to his particular galaxy of needs and circumstances. Of necessity Tom's service is controlling and a critical non-negotiable is *no unsupervised contact with children*. Only time and Tom can say whether this control is more than a transitional, if powerful influence.

To sharpen the applicability of Smull and Burke Harrison's work, we identify some shifts in service responses which would be favoured by the 20 adults who have been interviewed during the course of this work:

- a renewal of detention and secure settings which would ensure the elimination of physical brutalities and which would open them up to external scrutiny

- accessible and illustrated information which includes the words and descriptions of adults with learning disabilities who are current and former service users

- more competent and effective assistance in changing their offending behaviours from individuals with whom they can develop positive and enduring bonds

- improved skill and knowledge base for all professionals working with adults with learning disabilities who offend

- a commitment to giving them worthwhile skills which they can value and may render them employable and/or more equal to realising their aspirations

- sentencing options which have a rationale, are understandable and do not hinge on their unlimited detention

- local joint working and skill-sharing between criminal justice and associated services to extend the range of possibilities for sentencing options

- greater accountability of professionals working in detention and secure settings.

Some items in this compelling wish-list have their origins in secure service monopolies which have resisted giving some people a confidence that they are citizens with rights. If this list exerts any influence on other people's views, then the authors, not us, have played an important part in shaping those changes.

Finally, adults with learning disabilities who have committed offences are a marginal and oppressed group. The glimpses into their worlds afforded by our work, speak of abuses, powerlessness, despair and bewilderment. Even though much is stacked against them, something of their outlook, experiences and views has to contribute to changing service responses, not least as the best solutions emerge from involved parties. We end with the reproachful imperative of one woman known to this project: '*You can't just leave us. You've got to help us stop doing this*'.

References

Mansell, J.L. (1993) *Services for People with Learning Disabilities and Challenging Behaviour or Mental Health Needs: Report of a Project Group*. London: HMSO.

Reed, J. (1992a) *Review of Health and Social Services for Mentally Disordered Offenders and Others Requiring Similar Services*. Final Summary Report. London: HMSO, Department of Health, Home Office.

Reed, J. (1992b) *Review of Health and Social Services for Mentally Disordered Offenders and Others Requiring Similar Services* Vol 5. *Special Issues and Differing Needs*. The report of the official working group on services for people with special needs. London: HMSO, Department of Health, Home Office.

Smull, M.W. and Burke Harrison, S. (1992) *Supporting People with Severe Reputations in the Community*. Alexandria, Virginia: National Association of State Directors of Developmental Disabilities Services Inc.

Williams, C. (1996) *The Star Profile. Annual Training Achievement Record*. Kidderminster: BIMH.

CHAPTER 9

Empowerment and Community Care
Some of the Legal Issues

Gwyneth Roberts

Introduction

In Britain, the aim of the new system of community care, introduced by the
NHS and Community Care Act 1990, was to enable people, 'to live as
independently as possible in their own homes or in "homely" settings in the
community', and to achieve their full potential by providing them with the
right amount of care and support (Department of Health 1989, p.3). Individuals
were to be given, 'a greater...say in how they live their lives and the services
they need to help them to do so' (*ibid.*, p.4).

To what extent have recent changes achieved these objectives? Despite the
rhetoric of the White Paper, and subsequent policy guidance, such as *Community
Care in the Next Decade and Beyond* (Department of Health 1990a),[1] the evidence
suggests that the new community care system has contributed little, if at all, to
empowering people with learning disabilities in their everyday lives. In this
chapter, it will be argued that although a number of additional duties are placed
on local authorities by the NHS and Community Care Act, these have created
few, if any, legal rights for service users. Indeed, in stark contrast to the emphasis
on customer care and quality assurance which, supposedly, were the priority
issues for social services authorities in the 1990s, and despite the aims of reform
being to enable users and carers to, 'exercise the same power as consumers of
other services' (SSI/SWSG 1991a, p.11), many of those providing help and
support for people with learning disabilities have become increasingly alarmed

---

1   A considerable body of policy guidance has been issued by the Secretary of State
    under the provisions of s.7 of the Local Social Services Act 1970. Although such
    documents, 'are not themselves law in the way that regulations are law, [they] are
    likely to be quoted or used in court proceedings as well as in local authority policy
    and practice papers. They could provide the basis for a legal challenge of an
    authority's action or inaction...' (Department of Health 1990b, p.2).

at the erosion and/or complete withdrawal of many services over the last few years.

Two aspects of the current system are of particular significance in relation to the empowerment of service users. These are, first, the better opportunities which the legislation should offer in terms of participation in the process of planning community care services, and better access to information; and, second, the extent to which the new community care provisions enable service users to obtain the services they need.

Consultation and participation

One of the aims of the community care reforms was to provide a mechanism for joint consultation, collaboration and better provision of information for service users and their carers. Section 46 of the NHS and Community Care Act places a duty on every social services authority to prepare and publish an annual community care plan. The Act also states that these must be up-dated, and replaced, on a regular basis.

In preparing a community care plan for its aims, a social services authority must consult with a number of bodies, including any voluntary bodies which appear to represent the interests of users or potential users, locally. It seems, however, that although there was widespread publicity and considerable consultation in relation to the first set of community care plans, in many areas the process now consists of a local authority appointing 'representatives' from amongst users and voluntary organisations who will then sit on planning groups and working parties. As a result, it is not necessarily evident whose views are being 'represented', nor what responsibilities these 'representatives' have to consult their constituencies (Bewley and Glendinning 1994). For consultation to be effective, and for people with disabilities to be properly involved in planning services, they are likely to need a considerable amount of background information on such matters as the structure, funding and organisation of services, as well as information about the planning process itself. Certain groups – especially those from ethnic minorities and those living in rural areas – may need support by way of community development to bring them together in the first place, before they are able to take part in consultations of this kind (Bewley and Glendinning 1994). A recent Department of Health circular advises local authorities that groups which represent users and carers, as well as agency representatives, should be more fully engaged in drawing up community care plans. The plans themselves should be a better reflection of the input made by groups of this kind (LAC(95)19).

In addition to improving consultation, and increasing the degree of participation in the planning process by users and their representatives, another aim of the new statutory provision was to ensure that information about community care services is easily available. To ensure better dissemination of information, policy guidance sets out the kinds of information which a community care plan should contain. It should contain the authority's criteria for determining priorities, and identify the client groups for whom the authority intends to arrange community care services. It should demonstrate that balanced consideration has been given to the needs of certain groups within its area, such as people with learning disabilities. It should also state how practical help, such as respite care, will be offered to carers; and how the authority intends to develop domiciliary care services. The plan should also state how the local authority intends to carry out an assessment of need under s.47 of the 1990 Act, and how it intends to ensure wider choice for service users. It should contain information about the nature and amount of resources, such as residential care homes, nursing homes and community care facilities, which are available in the public and independent sectors. It should explain how the local authority intends to inform service users and their carers about the services which are available, as well as how individuals can make representations and complaints about the delivery of community care services.

A community care plan should also contain information about the authority's assessment of the care needs of the population in its area, after taking such factors as age distribution into account. It should include an estimate of the number of homeless or transient people who are likely to be in need of care in its area. Local authorities in inner city areas should include information in their community care plan about the problems which are likely to be associated with such areas, and should also refer to the special needs of ethnic minority communities. Rural authorities should refer to the special problems facing those living in rural areas.

So that the information reaches those for whom it is intended, community care plans should be made available in a form which is readily understandable. Apparently, however, some local authorities are uncertain about the audience for whom a community care plan is intended. According to a recent circular, community care plans have a dual purpose: one purpose is to aid in the authority's own collaborative business planning, and the second is providing the public with information. According to the circular, accessibility for both audiences should be the watchword, and concise jargon-free community care plans should aid accessibility for all readers (LAC(95)19). In practice, however, the way in which most community care plans are prepared and issued makes the information contained in them barely accessible to the general population, let alone people with learning disabilities. This applies especially to those for whom a written document presents particular difficulties. In practice, it is rare for community care plans to be available other than in writing, and in any language other than English. Even in the Welsh local authority which was included in Bewley and Glendinning's survey of local authority community care plans, the plan was available only in English. It is also rare for a plan to be available in Braille, or on video or audio tape, or in pictures (Bewley and

Glendinning 1994). Ironically, therefore, many groups, such as people with learning disabilities, for whom the information should be available, are likely to be barred from proper access to it (Allen 1995).

From this evidence, it does not seem that in relation to the duty to consult users and potential users, and encourage participation, nor in relation to the duty to provide access to information, that the new community care system is achieving the major objectives set out in policy guidance. It seems highly unlikely that requiring local authorities to prepare and publish a community care plan has made any significant contribution towards empowering people with learning disabilities in their everyday lives. As a result, even in relation to such apparently non-contentious procedural rights as these, there is a considerable way to go in empowering service users. Indeed, many anecdotal examples are given of misinformation being communicated to individuals and carers, as in the case of one group of parents of people with learning disabilities who were told that their daughters and sons could not have a place in a Special Care Unit because 'they hadn't got social workers'.[2]

If service users are not consulted in accordance with s. 16, or if they, or those who care and support them, are given incorrect or partial information of the kind referred to above, they should always consider making a complaint or using any of the other procedures for redress set out on pp.168–169.

Community care and individual rights

An important aspect of the NHS and Community Care Act 1990 which, in theory, should empower people with learning disabilities in their everyday lives, is the duty, placed on social service authorities by s.47, to carry out an assessment of need. Assessment is, therefore, a key part of the process of translating the general duty to provide or arrange community care services within a particular area into a specific service or package of services for a particular individual.

The duty to assess arises, 'where it appears to a local authority that a person for whom they may provide or arrange for the provision of *community care services* may be in need of any such services...' (NHS and Community Care Act 1990) (emphasis added). The introduction of the 1990 Act provided a golden opportunity to consolidate and simplify this area of the law. Unfortunately, that opportunity was missed. As a result, current provisions in the field of community care are still based, 'on a rag-bag of legislation passed at intervals over half a century, some of it rooted in the Poor Law, much of it reinforcing outdated stereotypes of user groups and discriminating irrationally between them' (Harding 1992, p.4). If consumer rights are to have any meaning, the statutory

---

2   Evidence provided by personal communication with the National Development Team.

provisions must be made much more accessible and user-friendly for those who depend upon this area of the law for many of their basic service needs.

'Community care services' are defined by s.46(3) of the NHS and Community Care Act 1990 as services which a local authority may provide or arrange to be provided under Part III of the National Assistance Act 1948; s.45 of the Health Services and Public Health Act 1968;[3] s.21 of, and Schedule 8 to, the National Health Service Act 1977; and s.117 of the Mental Health Act 1983. A characteristic of most of these statutory provisions is that they are couched in very general terms which are then converted into specific powers and duties by means of ministerial directions and approvals which are set out in the relevant circulars, in particular Circular LAC(93)10.

As a result of ministerial directions, a local authority must arrange for accommodation to be provided for those in need of care and attention because of age, illness, disability or any other circumstances, who are resident in its area; and for any person who has urgent need for such care and attention. Specific arrangements must also be made for those who suffer, or have suffered from, mental disorder, as well as arrangements for the temporary accommodation of any person who is in urgent need as a result of circumstances which could not reasonably have been foreseen. A local authority may also arrange accommodation for those without settled residence, who need care and attention because of age, illness, disability or any other circumstances, as well as those who are, or have been, suffering from mental disorder, and who have become resident in its area following discharge from hospital; and those who are specifically alcohol- or drug-dependent. It may also arrange accommodation for the prevention of illness, and the care and after-care of those who are, or have been, ill; and, with the other authority's consent, and to the extent it considers desirable, for those who are ordinarily resident in another authority's area (National Assistance Act 1948, s.21; LAC(93)10).

An authority must also make arrangements for a social work service, as well as domiciliary advice and support, to be available for disabled people in its area. It must also arrange facilities for social rehabilitation and adjustment to disability, including assistance in overcoming limitations on mobility or communication; and for occupational, social, cultural and recreational activities, and, where appropriate, payment for work done. It must make arrangements for payments to be made for specialist advice in determining whether or not a person is disabled for this purpose. A local authority may also arrange for holiday homes to be provided; for free or subsidised travel for those not receiving concessionary travel from another source; for assistance in finding suitable supportive lodgings; for contributing towards the cost of employing a

---

3 Since the provisions of s.45 of the Health Services and Public Health Act 1968 are concerned with the welfare of 'old people', as such, they are not discussed in this chapter.

warden to carry out welfare functions in a warden-assisted housing scheme; for providing warden assistance for occupiers of private housing; for a service to be provided by another local authority or voluntary organisation; for instructing people in their own homes, or elsewhere, on how to overcome their disabilities; for providing workshops which are suitable for disabled people and hostels where they may live; for providing suitable work for disabled people in their own homes, or elsewhere; and for compiling and maintaining classified registers of those who are disabled (National Assistance Act 1948, s.29; LAC(93)(10).

A local authority must also arrange for facilities, including occupation centres, training centres, day centres and domiciliary facilities, for the prevention of mental disorder, and in relation to those who suffer, or have suffered, from mental disorder. It must also appoint a sufficient number of social workers to act as approved social workers, and must arrange for the exercise of guardianship functions under the Mental Health Act 1983. It must also arrange for the provision of social work and related services to help to identify, diagnose, assess and provide social treatment for mental disorder, as well as social work support and other domiciliary and care services for those living in their homes or elsewhere. It must also provide, or arrange, on a scale which is adequate for the needs of its area, a home help service for households where help is required because, amongst other reasons, of the presence of a person who is suffering from illness, or who is handicapped as a result of illness or congenital deformity.

A local authority may also make arrangements for the prevention of other illness and for the care and after-care of those who are, or have been, ill. In particular, it may arrange for the provision, equipping and maintenance of training or occupational centres or other facilities, as well as ancillary or supplemental services. It may also arrange for meals to be provided at such centres, as well as meals on wheels for house-bound people. It may also arrange for people who work in training or occupational centres or other facilities to be remunerated; for the provision of social services (including advice and support) to prevent the impairment of the physical or mental health of adults in families where such impairment is likely, and to prevent the break-up of such families, or assist in their rehabilitation; for the provision of night-sitter services; for recuperative holidays; for facilities for social and recreational activities; for services specifically for those who are alcohol- or drug-dependent; and for the provision of laundry facilities for households where a home help is being, or might be, provided (National Health Service Act 1977; LAC(93)10).

Under s.117 of the Mental Health Act 1983, local authorities are jointly responsible with local health authorities for the provision of after-care services for mentally disordered patients who have been discharged from long-term detention in hospital under the Mental Health Act 1983. The duty remains in existence until both authorities are satisfied that the person concerned no longer requires after-care assistance.

A person is disabled for the purposes of receiving community care, if he or she is, 'blind, deaf or dumb, or is suffering from *mental disorder* of any description, or is *substantially and permanently handicapped by illness, injury or congenital deformity* or such other disability as may be prescribed by the Secretary of State' (National Assistance Act, 1948, s.29). Mental disorder means mental illness, *arrested or incomplete development of mind*, psychopathic disorder, and *any other disorder or disability of mind* (National Assistance Act 1948, s.29).

Welfare services

Section 4 of the Disabled Persons (Services, Consultation and Representation) Act 1986 placed a duty on local authorities to assess the needs of disabled people only when requested to do so by a disabled person or his/her carer. However, since the coming into force of s.47(1) of the 1990 Act, if it appears to a local authority, during an assessment of need, that the person who is being assessed is a *disabled person*, the authority is under an additional duty to assess him/her for welfare services under the Chronically Sick and Disabled Persons Act 1970 and NHS and Community Care Act 1990, s.47(2).

The services which a local authority must provide under s.2 of the Chronically Sick and Disabled Persons Act are:

- practical assistance in the home, including home helps, particularly for households where help is required owing to the presence of a person handicapped as a result of illness or by congenital deformity
- a radio, television, library or similar recreational facilities, or assistance in obtaining any of these
- lectures, games, outings or other recreational facilities outside a person's home, or assistance in taking advantage of available educational facilities
- facilities for, or assistance in, travelling to and from home to participate in any of the above facilities
- assistance in arranging or carrying out adaptations to a person's home (such as ramps for wheelchair access or the provision of handrails) or the provision of additional facilities to secure greater safety, comfort or convenience
- holidays, arranged by the authority itself or otherwise
- meals at home or elsewhere
- a telephone and any equipment which is necessary to enable a person to use it, or assistance in obtaining it.

A disabled person must be offered an assessment of his/her need for these services, irrespective of the nature of the need which is initially presented. Most, if not all, individuals with learning disabilities are likely to be entitled to an assessment of this kind.

The nature and extent of the duty to assess

Although s.47 of the 1990 Act placed additional assessment duties upon local authorities, they have, in practice, considerable discretion to determine whether or not they are under a duty to assess a particular person's need for the community care services outlined in the previous section. This is because, in the first place, many of the duties and powers in this field arise in relation only to those who are 'ordinarily resident' in the local authority's area. This could have important implications for those with learning disabilities who live for part of the time in the area of one social services authority, and for part of the time in another area, as a result, for example, of being placed in an out-of-county or out-of-borough residential unit. The meaning of the term 'ordinarily resi-dent' is not defined in the relevant legislation but, according to Circular LAC(93)7 it should be given 'its ordinary and normal meaning'. 'Ordinary residence' has, however, been discussed in a number of judicial cases, and seems to depend upon such factors as continuity and intention. According to Circular LAC(93)7, an adult with learning disabilities should, in any case, be regarded as capable of forming his or her own intentions as to where he or she wishes to live. Where two local authorities are in dispute as to which one of them is responsible for providing a service, the question of a person's 'ordinary residence' must be determined by the Secretary of State.

Second, according to policy guidance,[1] a social services authority should have specific criteria for determining what categories of need should be given priority within the assessment process. There should be procedures in place for screening or filtering referrals for assessment in accordance with these criteria. The Audit Commission has suggested that setting eligibility criteria is the most effective way of shaping a coherent approach to need whilst striking a balance between commitments and budgeted finance. Amongst its suggestions in this field is a framework which authorities can use in making key planning decisions, that is, grouping people with similar needs; identifying numbers in each group; identifying services options for each group; costing services options; calculating total costs against the total budget; prioritising to bring total costs in line with the budget; specifying eligibility criteria that match priorities; and by devolving local budgets that equate to local needs (Audit Commission 1993). Clearly, the language of priorities, and of actions to be taken within available resources, is not the language of rights (Age Concern 1992), and the speed of an authority's response, the type and level of assessment expertise required, and even the extent of involvement by other agencies, may be governed by these criteria.

It is for reasons such as these that social service authorities have considerable discretion in relation to the duty to assess. Nevertheless, discretion must always be exercised properly, and a refusal to assess, or a delay in carrying out an assessment, which appeared to be unreasonable, or irrational or illegal, could be the subject of a challenge by way of a formal complaint to the authority, a complaint to the local authority monitoring officer, a representation to the Secretary of State, or an application for judicial review of the authority's decision. (For a fuller discussion of these processess, see, for example, Public Law Project 1994 and Roberts and Griffiths 1993.)

Participation and assessment

An important aspect of an assessment process is that the person being assessed should be able to participate as fully as possible. According to policy guidance, 'the individual service user, and normally, with his or her agreement, any carers should be involved throughout the process. They should be made to feel that the process is aimed at meeting their wishes' (Department of Health 1990a). Where a person is not able to participate actively, it is even more important that he/she should be helped to understand what is involved and the intended outcome. A social service authority should take positive steps, therefore, to ensure that if a service user has communication problems, whether as a result of mental incapacity, sensory impairment or any other disability, he or she is enabled to participate as fully as possible in the assessment process, as well as in the process of determining service provision (Department of Health 1990a). Where a person has problems in communicating, a facilitator and/or an interpreter, may be needed to ensure that the service user is as fully involved as possible in the assessment.

In the case of *R v North Yorkshire County Council ex parte Hargreaves* CO/878/94 (unreported), it was held that Miss Hargreaves, a severely mentally disabled adult, should have had her preferences taken into account in relation to assessing her need for respite care. Despite all attempts to involve her, Miss Hargreaves had not contributed, on a number of occasions, to discussions at which she had been present. Nevertheless, she had managed to communicate her wishes and preferences in at least two respects. She had indicated that she did not want to receive a particular kind of respite care which the authority was offering her and her carer, and that she did wish to receive respite care at home. Mr Justice Dyson was not satisfied, however, that she had been invited to express her preferences in relation to the two establishments to which she normally went for respite care, as compared with the facilities which were available locally. The social services authority had reached its decision without taking account of Miss Hargreaves' preferences in this respect and, in doing so, it had not taken sufficient account of relevant policy guidance. The authority had, therefore, acted unlawfully in the way it reached its decision on respite care for Miss Hargreaves.

Carrying out an assessment

The Secretary of State has power under the 1990 Act to issue directions to local authorities on how they should carry out an assessment of need. However, as yet no directions have been issued. In the meantime, an assessment may be carried out, 'in such manner and take such form as the local authority consider(s) appropriate' (NHS and Community Care Act 1990, s.47(4)). As a result, it is for local authorities themselves to determine the degree and extent of an assessment, and the scope may be adjusted to take account of any initial finding, with full multi-disciplinary assessments being reserved for the most complex situations.

An assessment should, however, be a process of objectively defining needs and determining eligibility for assistance against stated policy criteria (Department of Health 1989). Need is, 'a complex concept which...[can be used] as a shorthand for the requirement of individuals to enable them to achieve, maintain or restore an acceptable level of social independence or quality of life, *as defined by the particular care agency or authority*' (SSI/SWSG 1991a, p 14) (emphasis added). Need is also

> a dynamic concept, the definition of which will vary over time in accordance with:
>
> • changes in national legislation
>
> • changes in local policy
>
> • the availability of resources
>
> • the patterns of local demand
>
> (SSI/SWSG 1991a, p.14)

An assessment should focus on the difficulties for which an individual is seeking assistance, but it should also take account of all the relevant circumstances, including a person's capacities and incapacities; his/her preferences and aspirations; his/her living situation; the support available from relatives and friends; and any other sources of help (Laming 1992, p.5). It should focus on the needs and strengths of the person being assessed in the context of their everyday life. The aim should be to recognise, 'the individuality of need by challenging practitioners to identify the unique characteristics of each individual's needs and to develop individualised, rather than stereotyped, responses to those needs *within the constraints of local policy and resources*' (SSI/SSWG 1991a, p.13) (emphasis added). Indeed, despite the rhetoric of tailoring services to individual need, a local authority is only obliged to consider an individual's needs in relation to 'community care services'. In effect, a 'needs-led assessment' is not the same as a 'user-led assessment' (McDonald and Taylor 1995).

Nevertheless, in a number of cases, the courts have interpreted the concept of need. In *R v Mid-Glamorgan County Council, ex parte Miles* reported in *Legal Action* in January 1994, a local authority agreed that, in the circumstances of the case, a person's needs could include not only needs which were currently in existence, but needs which might arise at some future date; and in *R v Avon County Council, ex parte M* [1994] 2 FCR 259, which concerned the local authority's assessment of the needs of Mark Hazell, a young man with learning disability, it was held that the concept of 'need' included his psychological, as well as his physical, needs.

Providing services

Since assessment is seen as a service in its own right it must be distinguished from the decision as to whether or not a person has a need for community care and/or welfare services. As a result, after carrying out an assessment, a local authority must take account of the results and decide whether a person's needs call for the provision of services, and if so what packages of care to provide, that is, it must decide on a *care plan* in consultation with the client and other care professionals (Department of Health 1990a):

> The needs-led approach pre-supposes a progressive separation of assessment from service provision. Assessment does not take place in a vacuum; account needs to be taken of the local authority's criteria for determining when services should be provided, the types of service they have decided to make available and the overall range of services provided by other agencies, including health authorities. (p.25)

Indeed, according to the Department of Health, eligibility for services 'may be determined against stated policy criteria' (Department of Health 1990a) helped by a system of banding which assigns individuals to particular categories, although account should also be taken of individual circumstances. 'An authority may take into account the resources available when deciding how to respond to an individual's assessment' (Laming 1992, p.5). In practice, the 'rule of economy is a major influence on definition of need whereby needs-led assessment are required then compromised by what resources can be provided' (Braye and Preston-Shoot 1992, pp.32–33).

Nevertheless, in *R v Gloucestershire County Council exparte Barry: R v Lancashire County Council ex parte RADAR* [1996] 4 ALL ER 42, the Court of Appeal decided that resources are not relevant to the local authority's duty to meet the needs of a disabled person under s.2(1) of the Chronically Sick and Disabled Persons' Act 1970. The duty which arises under s.2 of the 1970 Act is plainly directed towards a particular individual, and to meeting that individual's need. Establishing 'need' is a question of making both an assessment and a judgement; it is not a question of discretion. Once a need has been identified in accordance with s.2, a duty is placed upon a local authority to meet it, and the availability of resources is not an issue. Otherwise, the consequence would be that where a local authority had resources, no disabled person who was resident in that area would be considered to have any need for services under the 1970 Act. In this context, the term 'need' is to be construed according to its ordinary meaning, that is, as a basic or essential requirement.

However, according to this decision, a local authority is entitled to take resources into account when deciding what kinds of service should be provided to meet a person's need. A local authority does not have to provide a more expensive method of meeting need merely because a preference has been expressed by the individual concerned.

A similar interpretation has been placed on the local authority's duty in relation to meeting a person's need for community care services under s.47 (1) of the Act. The local authority may not take resources into account when making the assessment. In this case, however, the extent of the local authority's duty is to *have regard* to the results of the assessment and it may then take account of resources in determining the provision of services (NHS and Community Care Act, s.47 (1)).

Although this decision is to be welcomed, it is likely to be the subject of an appeal by Gloucester County Council to the House of Lords.

The Community Care (Direct Payments) Bill 1995

To what extent will the passing of the Community Care (Direct Payments) Bill 1995 overcome some of the current disadvantages of the community care system? According to Baroness Cumberlege, the aim is to enable local authorities to pay cash to disabled people, within the resources available, rather than provide them with services, where that was appropriate to the person's needs and also what that person would prefer. The individual would not be forced to accept an offer of cash if help in the form of services was preferred. He/she could also opt for a mix of services plus cash. According to Baroness Cumberlege, a local authority will not be allowed to set payments at a level which is insufficient to meet the individual's needs, nor at a level which it knew to be less cost-effective than providing or arranging services itself.

Regulations are to be issued which will set out the categories of disabled people who are to be permitted to exercise choice in this way. Some groups are likely to be excluded in order to prevent an 'inappropriate' use of direct payments, that is, paying for care which is currently provided voluntarily by the person's family and/or friends. The aim of the proposals is not to replace existing support by families and communities, but to provide users with greater choice and control over the services they would otherwise receive from the local authority. Concern has been expressed that people with learning disabilities are to be excluded from this right to choose. If that is so, the Opposition promises to press for the inclusion of all categories of disability, whether physical or mental, within the legislation.

Although any statutory provision which encourages choice must be welcome, there is nothing in the proposed legislation which will overcome the problem that it is the local authority which will decide on an assessment of need, and which will continue to do so in accordance with policy guidance and the decision in the *Gloucester* case. The government has also indicated that the proposed scheme is to be cost-neutral. Ultimately, however, the success of care in the community depends upon proper and adequate funding. It may be too easily assumed that community care is necessarily cheaper than institutional care. In fact, for people with complex or substantial disabilities, providing packages of care which enable them to live independent lives of reasonable quality in the community is far from cheap.

Community care and the enforcement of legal rights

Another issue of importance in the field of community care is the extent to which the new community care provisions enable service users to obtain the services they need. Since local authorities, as the 'lead' authority in the field of community care, are given a range of duties to provide or arrange community care services, it might be expected that where a disabled person was not satisfied with the quality or quantity of the services which he/she was receiving, or had been refused a service which the local authority was under a duty to provide, he/she would have a right to legal redress. Unfortunately, there are relatively few enforceable legal rights in this field.

In general, it would seem that breaches of duty arising in public law are unlikely to create rights of redress by means of an action for damages (see *Wyatt v Hillingdon LBC* (1978) 76 LGR 767), particularly since the courts have been reluctant to intervene in what they perceive as political decisions, such as the allocation of resources. In any case, statutory duties are often set out in the legislation in such general terms that it may be difficult to establish that a duty is owed to a particular person. It has been argued, however, that the courts might recognise a duty to a particular person in relation to some statutory provisions (that is, under s.21 of the National Health Service Act 1977 and under s.117 of the Mental Health Act 1983); or where an authority has assessed a person as needing a specific service but fails to provide it (Gordon 1993).

Judicial review is the process which is most likely to make local authorities liable for the decisions they take in the area of community care. This is a procedure by which the High Court supervises public bodies and ensures that their actions are reasonable, rational and lawful. Where a social service authority fails to act properly in relation to its community care functions, the court may grant an order to quash the original decision, or to make the authority act, or to prohibit the authority from acting.

Judicial review is not concerned, however, with whether a particular decision is good or bad in itself. The court's only concern is to review whether, in reaching its decision, the authority acted reasonably, rationally and legally, for example, that it has not acted beyond its statutory authority, or in a way which is unfair or biased. In *R v London Borough of Ealing, ex parte Leaman, The Times,* 10 February 1984, Mr Leaman applied to Ealing LBC for financial assistance in taking a privately arranged holiday. The request was turned down on the grounds that the council would only grant financial assistance for holidays which it had itself arranged or sponsored. In this case, the court stated that the council's policy had the result of removing the words 'or otherwise' from s.2 (1)(F) of the Chronically Sick and Disabled Persons Act 1970 so that a person could not be given help in relation to privately arranged holidays (see p.162). Since this was contrary to the duty set out in the 1970 Act, the court was prepared to make an order against the council.

Although there is increasing use of judicial review in the area of community care, the procedure also has its disadvantages. In the first place, all the remedies in this field are at the discretion of the court, and may be refused if, for example, an alternative remedy is available. Second, before an action can be brought the leave of the court must be obtained in each case. Third, there is normally a time limit of three months from the time when the matter complained about became known to the applicant, unless there is good reason for the court to extend the period. Fourth, the process can be very long-drawn. Finally, legal decisions, such as in the *Gloucester* case, may help to clarify the nature and extent of a local authority's duty to provide; they also indicate how even in relation to public law procedures, the emphasis is on individual solutions for individual problems, rather than on establishing rights of citizenship for people with disabilities. Nevertheless, given the current state of English law, judicial review is probably the procedure with greatest potential for securing community care provision for people with learning disabilities.

Community care: rhetoric and reality

In his seminal report *Community Care: Agenda for Action* in 1988, Sir Roy Griffiths said that: '...in few areas can the gap between political rhetoric and policy on the one hand or between policy and reality in the field...have been so great' (p.iv). It is doubtful whether, despite the reforms introduced by the NHS and Community Care Act 1990, the situation has improved much since 1988. Indeed, it seems ironic that:

> empowerment as a term has entered the language of community care, since the focus on 'needs' rather than 'human rights' is in direct conflict with the concept of empowerment. The concept of need is an approach that runs through all the legislation and is one which promotes

pathology, inadequacy and inability as the basis for determining who has what services. (Jones 1992, p.38)

The powers of service users remain limited, consisting mainly of a right to information, a right to take part in certain decision-making processes and a right to have their views taken into account, rather than the right to take decisions for themselves. Despite the rhetoric of person-centred planning, and the concept of the 'active consumer' (Centre for Policy on Ageing 1990), decisions concerning the allocation and provision of services lie with social services authorities, based on their assessment of a person's need for services. Indeed, assessment of need, 'as the "keystone" of community care can only result in reinforcing the power imbalance between those using services and those providing them' (Jones 1992, p.38). As with most other forms of social legislation, the new statutory provisions are concerned, primarily, with the delivery of welfare provision to those in need, rather than with establishing a right of entitlement. As Braye and Preston-Shoot have argued: 'In a society which promotes a self-help, enterprise culture, valuing responsibility and the ability to provide for oneself from the fruits of one's labours, to be publicly identified as "needy" has an inevitably stigmatising effect' (Braye and Preston-Shoot 1992, p.25).

Social services authorities have been given powers and duties to provide community care services, but the law, 'only rarely bestows upon an individual the right to receive them. This lack of entitlement leaves people who need services in a peculiarly powerless position, at the mercy of professional judgement and local authority budgets' (Harding 1992, pp.3–4). As the law stands, individuals who need care and support to achieve their full potential, have few clearly established rights to services. It is also the case that services are provided, '…not because people have an active right, but because a passive need has been established. Individual detriment has to be proved rather than membership of a group with rights' (Braye and Preston-Shoot 1992, p.32). Until the legal system provides disabled people with a proper system of enforcement and redress, 'empowerment' will remain the soft currency of rhetoric rather than the hard currency of rights.

References

Age Concern (1992) *Home Help and Care. Rights, Charging and Reality*. London: Age Concern.
Allen, P. (1995) 'From the bottom up: ensuring quality with service users.' In T. Philpot and L. Ward (eds) *Values and Visions: Changing Ideas in Services for People with Learning Difficulties*. Oxford: Butterworth-Heinemann.
Audit Commission (1993) *Taking Care. Progress with Care in the Community*. London: HMSO.
Bewley, C. and Glendinning, C. (1994) *Involving Disabled People in Community Care Planning*. York: Joseph Rowntree Foundation/Community Care.

Braye, S. and Preston-Shoot, M. (1992) *Practising Social Work Law*. Basingstoke and London: BASW/Macmillan.

Centre for Policy on Ageing (1990) *Community Life: A Code of Practice for Community Care*. London: Centre for Policy on Ageing.

Clements, L. (1995) 'Judgement daze.' *Community Care*, 13–19 July, 24–5.

Department of Health (1989) *Caring for People. Community Care in the Next Decade and Beyond*. Cm.849. London: HMSO.

Department of Health (1990a) *Community Care in the Next Decade and Beyond*. London: HMSO.

Department of Health (1990b) *The Care of Children. Principles and Practice in Regulation and Guidance*. London: HMSO.

Gordon, R. (1993) *Community Care Assessments*. London: Longman.

Griffiths, R. (1988) *Community Care: Agenda for Action*. London: HMSO.

Harding, T. (1992) 'Questions on the social services agenda.' In T. Harding (ed) *Who Owns Welfare?* London: NISW.

Jones, A. (1992) 'Civil rights, citizenship and the welfare agenda for the 1990s.' In T. Harding (ed) *Who Owns Welfare?* London: NISW.

Laming, H. (1992) *Implementing Caring for People. Assessment*. CI(92)34. London: Department of Health.

McDonald, A. and Taylor, M.E. (1995) *The Law and Elderly People*. London: Sweet and Maxwell.

Public Law Project (1994) *Challenging Community Care Decisions*. London: Unison/The Public Law Project.

Roberts, G. and Griffiths, A. (1993) *What Can We Do?* Manchester: NDT/Mencap.

SSI/SWSG (1991a) *Care Management and Assessment. Managers' Guide*. London: HMSO.

Empowerment in Formal Settings
The Themes

Paul Ramcharan and John Borland

Inclusive identity and disability-related services

In Section 1 of this book, we saw that establishing a clear sense of self-identity, as well as ensuring inclusion within the ordinary spheres of family life, friendship, education, work and the wider community, is important for people with learning disabilities. But, if self-identity is to be established within the interactional domains in which people generally circulate, then, for people with learning disabilities, inclusion can occur only if such domains are available, accessible and usable. This is equally true in relation to people who are held in secure settings (Chapter 8).

All the informants referred to by Griffiths *et al.* in Chapter 8 are clear that who they are now is a reflection of their personal histories, and of the sometimes damaging relationships which they have had with others in their lives. We may loosely define the aim of the services described in the first two case studies as the 'management of spoiled identity'. What is striking about these accounts is how punitive measures are likely to deepen a person's negative self-image. Such measures often result in a self-fulfilling prophecy because they reinforce the individual's own perception of that 'spoiled identity'.

This is what makes the notion of 'non-negotiables' (Smull and Burke Harrison 1992) so important for the argument set out by Griffiths *et al.* It is a concept which values an individual by providing him/her with a positive self-image as well as directing service personnel to work with the person as he/she actually is, and not the person service workers want him/her to become.

The recommendations made by Griffiths *et al.* on the nature and aims of services within secure settings are based on listening to people who live within them. Nevertheless, many of the lessons they offer could be applied more generally. Their recommendations relate, for example, to: developing systems of professional accountability which prevent physical brutality and abuse; providing skills and life chances that aid rehabilitation and inclusion; working with people's non-negotiables in ways which are understandable to the person concerned; and ensuring that all aspects of service provision are consistent in relation to these. In short, services should work towards promoting positive 'included identities' which a person contributes, as a valued individual, as their gift to their communities.

By using the notion of a 'non-negotiable', Griffiths *et al.* have contributed the notions of both 'autonomy' and 'self-determination' as essential components of an 'included identity'. An important measuring rod for government policy and legislative provisions, therefore, is the extent to which the latter make it possible for people with learning disabilities to exercise autonomy and self-determination within formal service settings.

To what extent does the existing system of service provision meet these requirements? One approach is to ask whether the state assigns such rights to citizens with learning disabilities. A means of measuring this would be to examine the outcomes of those services which are provided specifically for people with learning disabilities. That would require a considerably more comprehensive analysis of service provision than is intended in this more modest contribution to the current debates. A more feasible approach in this context, however, is to examine policy and legislation against the concept of the 'included identity', and to measure the extent to which they are either positive or negative in their effect. This is discussed in the rest of this chapter.

Inclusion and service provision

Dowson (Chapter 6) makes an impassioned plea against perceiving formal service provision as the answer to the supposed problems facing people with learning disabilities. The service sector represents an organisational solution to a perceived social problem, that is, how best to meet the needs of a particular group of people. This assumes that: people with learning disabilities are an identifiable group which should be identified and separated out; and that, in separating them out in this way, the problem will be solved. Indeed, the large welfare and personal social services industry in Britain is founded on such assumptions. It is in relation to this highly bureaucratised and formalised service system that Dowson constructs his critique.

Like Souza (Chapter 1), Dowson does not perceive people with learning disabilities as any different from other people. Why, then, are they placed in specifically designed and costly institutions and organisations which separate them from the rest of society? According to Smull and Burke Harrison (1992):

> Where our goal is to control people within our programs rather than to accommodate them within our communities, we see the past as reflecting the need for increased control. The need for control translates into the need for more direct care and professional staff and the accompanying costs. We then conclude that we cannot afford to serve

these individuals in the community because of the staff needed to control their behaviour. (p.8)

As Dowson implies, such a system produces what McKnight (1986) calls 'an economy of need in need' in which professionals can manufacture a need to sustain themselves and the system of which they are incumbents.

For Dowson, existing services contain three broad problems. First, the structures of services are circumscribed by *formalised* rules which are at odds with the rights of people with learning disabilities to live ordinary lives in the community. In his example of a social services group home scheme, for example, Dowson amply demonstrates the ways in which the right of citizens to buy or to rent homes, or to choose to live with particular people, cannot easily be achieved where the homes are owned by the local authority. This means that it is the local authority which decides who lives there and for how long. This works against the assumptions which most of us have when we choose where and with whom to live, and for how long.

Second, Dowson argues that the service structure allows *informal rules* to emerge and flourish which may run contrary to the exercise of choice and control by those who receive the service. He points to a series of questionable practices, such as service personnel using a person's home as if it was their own; choosing with whom the person should live; and choosing and dictating routines in relation to going to bed, getting up, where the person goes during the day and so forth. Although a structure which allows such informal practices to flourish may also allow some good practices, there is overwhelming evidence that informal rules of this kind act against the existence of ordinary lifestyles.

Third, given that those formal and informal rules are likely to conflict with ordinary choices and aspirations, they are also likely to tie the person into a service culture and environment. Dowson argues that this '*domain of inclusion*' is not justified, that is, it cannot incorporate an 'included identity' nor allow 'autonomy and self-determination'. This means that institutionalised practices live on, and that, '...the campus has broken up, but not the institution itself'. Dowson is arguing that professional '...skills should be used to help people in achieving lifestyles of their own choosing. They should not determine that lifestyle' (Smull and Burke Harrison 1992, p.3). Since service structures largely determine the agenda for people with learning disabilities, they cannot empower, for they will seldom be a reflection of the user's choices and wishes.

In summary, despite some service procedures working in an empowering way (see Chapters 7 and 9), the overwhelming evidence is of an inherent conflict between service aims and practices and individual self-determination, autonomy and integration. Dowson argues that alternative solutions are needed, although these are not stated in his conclusions.

What service users need

Despite the difficulties identified by Dowson, the rationale behind the recent reorganisation of community care in Britain is, '…the empowerment of users and carers' (Department of Health 1989, p.4). This is to be achieved through the development of a mixed economy of welfare, in which one of the functions of local authorities is to enable the development of a flourishing private and voluntary sector alongside statutory provision, hence extending the choice available to service users. With the local authority responsible for fostering the growth of a mixed economy and for the purchasing of services for any individual the, '…extent to which both users and carers have choice is…dictated to a large degree by the extent to which they have a say in the needs assessment and care planning process and in the ways in which the quasi-market is constructed by local authorities' (McGrath and Ramcharan 1996, p.1). To what extent, therefore, does the quasi-market model make for empowerment, and to what extent do procedural rights, in relation to needs assessment and the processes of participation and consultation, lead to empowerment?

Drawing on Hirschman's (1970) discussion of the concepts of 'exit' (i.e. the ability to change services) and of 'voice' (i.e. the ability to make changes in a service already being received), Means and Smith (1994) argue that the mixed economy of welfare may, potentially, provide an opportunity for an 'exit' model of welfare in which users can switch services if they so wish. However, they warn that the often cosy relations between the purchasers and providers of services can lead to monopoly or near-monopoly situations and thus a reduction of choice. They also point to the fact that many services are taken up at times of crisis; that there is often a reluctance amongst the users to change a service which they are using at present; and that purchasers may often make decisions on criteria other than what is in the interests of service users.

This, they report, is in stark contrast to the experience of people using the Independent Living Fund (ILF) in Britain, where consumers themselves bought services by means of vouchers or benefit payments. This 'individualised funding' established an 'exit' model which was unencumbered by third parties, such as local authority care managers. Means and Smith suggest that the ILF model led to many successful packages of personal care, packages which specifically reflected people's wishes. In this model, the consumer him/herself held control over hiring and firing ('exit') and in directing how their service should be delivered ('voice'). In this model, therefore, demands on the service market arise from personal choice. Given that services under the ILF are not dependent on bureaucracies for assessing, contracting and reviewing services and needs, it follows that this method of service delivery is more likely to be quick and efficient.

Whilst the ILF was an exception brought about by changes in the welfare benefit system, Roberts (Chapter 9) suggests that a similar model of 'exit' and 'voice' could be achieved for people with learning disabilities by means of the

Community Care (Direct Payments) Bill 1995. At the time of writing, however, it seems that this mechanism will not be made available to people with learning disabilities. Rather, the responsibility to purchase services will remain with local authority care managers and will be determined by the needs assessment process, a process which, in comparison to the ILF, requires extra tiers of bureaucracy for its operation.

In Britain it is the 'assessment of need' which mediates disability and service provision, and a considerable welfare industry is organised around the concept. A prospective user seeking assessment is a carrier of particular needs which it is considered that the local authority, by means of an assessment, can determine. Dowson (1990) has made the point that 'wanting' something is quite different from 'needing' something. Not only is 'want' more personal, according more autonomy and choice, but it is an outcome. Needs, in contrast provide the means to achieving this outcome. Thus, if I 'want' something (the end goal such as a house), I will have certain 'needs' (for example, the need to set rental or mortgage terms, to find a suitable dwelling and so forth) in achieving this end. By conflating the two, the power for identifying services on the basis of needs assessment is transferred from the service user to the professional.

According to policy guidance the views of both users and carers should be 'taken into account' in the needs assessment process. At the same time, though, need can be understood as, '...a dynamic concept, the definition of which will vary over time in accordance with changes in national legislation, changes in local policy, the availability of resources, and patterns of local demand. Need is thus a relative concept' (SSI 1991, para 13). Given that needs are constrained in these ways it is likely that they will remain a far cry from acting to meet the wishes of the person. The professionals who have control over the process may wield this authority in ways which act against personal choice and autonomy and, as Dowson indicates, against integration and inclusion.

The problem, as Dowson (1991) argues, is that there remains a series of possible conflicts of interest where the local authority controls not only the assessment and purchase of services, but also has control over monitoring, evaluation and review of the services provided. As North (1993) argues, the legislation, '...in essence empowered purchasers rather than service users' (p.136). Ellis (1993) has aptly demonstrated this by showing that assessment is as much about professionals rationing scarce resources as it is about individual needs as assessed. However, front-line workers have sometimes been reported to have had, 'little or no influence on the outcome of completed assessments' and their, 'inability to negotiate for the provision of even very basic services' is thought to require further consideration (Day 1994). As Plant (Plant and Barry 1990) argues: 'There can be no enforceable right to scarce resources and without the idea of enforceability the idea of rights becomes merely rhetorical' (p.22).

At present, the technology of community care needs assessment appears to be soaking up so much of the time of care managers that two important consequences are becoming increasingly evident: first, that there is less time available for counselling or other forms of direct work, and, second, monitoring and review activity is relegated or neglected (Lewis and Glennerster 1996). Hence, there are challenges to be faced not only with the conceptual roots but also the practicalities of needs assessment.

If the process of needs assessment confers greater authority and control on professionals, what legal rights are conferred on users? The considerable social policy literature generated around recent community care legislation in Britain has attracted less attention in terms of its legal underpinning and the extent to which this empowers service users. Roberts (Chapter 9) examines some aspects of this process and the extent to which empowerment may be possible under the new legislation.

Roberts tells us that a request for assessment does not, in itself, give rise to a legal duty to assess. In addition, eligibility criteria, which often determine priorities, are often based upon such extraneous factors as local policies, priorities and resources. She shows, furthermore, how test cases in relation to disputes over needs, '…hardly ever establish additional substantive rights for service users' and that, 'new statutory provisions are concerned, primarily, with the delivery of welfare provision to those in need, rather than in establishing individual rights of entitlement'.

However, Means and Smith (1994) say that, '…the community care re-forms…included a mixture of "exit" and "voice" mechanisms. The whole emphasis of community care planning is that social services…are required to seek the views of others before deciding overall strategic direction…' (p.88). Users and carers were seen to be an essential part of this process. The chapters by both Grant (Chapter 7) and Roberts examine more closely the issues tied up with the right to participation both at the individual and planning levels within services.

In Grant's view, unlike that of Dowson, the service 'domain of inclusion' should be seen as an aspect of everyday life. And, as with other spheres of everyday life, people ought to be actively involved and consulted about any decision which may affect them. If services can facilitate an 'everyday' life in the community, then it seems sensible to think that, not only should this be considered another legitimate domain of inclusion amongst others, but that those people who use such services should have a say in how they are structured and operated. Were these conditions to be met it might counteract the conflicts of interest which Dowson argues may preclude an everyday life in the commu-nity. Grant recognises that participation and consultation within the service sphere is a minor aspect of a person's life but, given that services exist, it is important to make sure that those who make use of them are consulted.

Grant describes the All Wales Strategy for the Development of Services for Mentally Handicapped People (Welsh Office 1983) as a 'beacon of light' which 'has prompted considerable change and innovation in strategies for involving people in services and local policy'. He examines the historical development of policy and some of the problems surrounding the involvement of family carers and service users in individual planning (i.e. working with the user and carer to discuss a service plan) and in the consultation process of developing service plans in each of the Welsh counties. Individual planning, with its focus on working with people to develop service plans and provision, was widely accepted, not only by service personnel but also by families and people with learning disabilities. Once again, however, individual planning was constrained by the mismatch between resources and demand.

Evidence about the wish for involvement in wider consultations was more patchy, although it has been biased towards the participation of carers as opposed to people with learning disabilities themselves. Grant suggests that the most successful forms of participation occur where egalitarian models are adopted. Such models, he argues, concern, '…the sharing of life experience, knowledge, information and insight between all members of the group, users, families, professionals and planners alike'.

Grant's discussion leaves us asking why recent community care legislation has not sought to learn and implement the lessons of consultation from the All Wales Strategy. As Roberts argues, participation in strategic planning under the present community care arrangements has been less than successful. In the preparation of social care plans (a local authority's plan for services which must be produced annually), she points to the difficulties in determining what constituencies individual users or carers represent; the actual power and influence they have in affecting the whole process of planning; and the fact that the plans themselves are seldom produced in a user-friendly format.

As Grant and Roberts suggest, much needs to be done before the procedural rights to consultation and participation are achieved within the present system of service provision and planning. But as Grant points out, such rights should not be the sole preserve of services. Consultation and participation within services, to the exclusion of similar mechanisms in other spheres of a person's life, cannot provide fully for empowerment. Problems therefore arise where consultation and participation within the service sector are exclusively pursued by the service sector as ends in themselves.

By definition, participation in planning is needed only where an organisation is empowered to construct a system of services to meet overall need. If the call on resources was made by users of services themselves, the demand side of the equation would not require a third party to have control over what services should be funded. In this sense the 'quasi-market' (Hoyes and Means 1993) is a construct which gives local authorities the main power in determining the demand for services.

Viewed in this way, participation within services and service planning is seen as contributing to the 'economy of need in need' mentioned earlier. Gomm (1993), for example, sees such participation as a means by which professionals are able to colonise the area of empowerment to protect their own interests, whilst Shemmings and Shemmings (1995) have argued that:

> ...the primary motivation behind the introduction of 'empowerment' and 'participation' into health and welfare organisations is best understood from the marketisation of services...empowerment and participation are a predictable consequence of the creation of the illusion that receiving health or welfare services is no different from purchasing goods at the supermarket. (p.56)

Disentangling the links between formal settings and empowerment

We have dealt, albeit summarily, with three concepts that form the basis upon which services to people with learning disabilities in Britain are constructed, that is, the concept of need, the notion of a mixed economy and the notions of consultation and participation. If empowerment is to be developed out of these, that can happen only within the boundaries set by organisational structures.

Within these structures, it is possible, at an interactional level, to provide people with learning disabilities with greater choice and self-determination. Services may also be ordered in such a way as to value the individual and to work to their agenda, for example through the idea of non-negotiables. Grant shows that empowerment is possible for some service users and carers by means of both individual and service planning. And Roberts' review of recent judicial decisions suggests that legal procedures may provide a limited form of redress in certain circumstances. However, there is a sense in which, despite these possibilities for empowerment, existing legislation and policy is inherently problematic. Procedural and substantive issues remain.

It has been argued that, procedurally, participation in the needs assessment process is a poor relation to individualised decision-making and that needs assessment is a model based on an agenda set by professionals. If, therefore, we accept personal choice of services as a predetermining factor in empowering people with learning disabilities, we are left with a residual problem. The experience of the ILF, and the possibilities of direct payments, mean that in a deregulated market the demand for services will emerge out of the personal choices of users. But how can choice be extended where persons with a learning disability are themselves unable to speak or act on their own behalf? The informality of a system of deregulation may also leave many people unaware of their entitlements and unable to exercise them in a meaningful way. Or they may be placed in a position in which they are open to abuse by others. Possible answers to these questions are discussed in Section 3 of this volume.

At a substantive level, there are questions about the extent to which the market provides for distributive justice. Saunders (1993), comparing levels of absolute poverty in the pre- and post-war period, has argued that standards of income have improved the quality of life of citizens. The market, he suggests, can improve the lot of disabled citizens over time as its effects 'trickle down'. But in a system of 'trickle-down' the effect of the 'gift relation' between government and people with disabilities still requires a mechanism for identifying those for whom entitlements should be made, and we are led to the concept of needs assessment and its labelling and stigmatising effects. The undemocratic sphere of the market is therefore unlikely to benefit those who are most oppressed within society, for theirs is a smaller voice and they have fewer mechanisms for control or for arguing their entitlement to resources. The substantive rights accorded to the consumer within a market-place are likely to be more penalising to those in society who have the least power and influence because, '...social justice will act in an arbitrary and discretionary way...this means the most powerful groups are likely to obtain concessions from government to meet what they see as social justice' (Plant and Barry 1990, p.11).

Perhaps most critical to this discussion of empowerment is that substantively 'need' is a concept which immediately labels and separates the person from the rest of society, conferring upon them the title of 'worthy poor'. To make this situation worse, such worthiness is limited by policy definitions which make the idea of 'need' contingent on national legislation, local policy, availability of resources and patterns of local demand (SSI 1991). Without some recourse to a notion which links entitlement to what constitutes an acceptable outcome for persons with a learning disability, the level of services will be determined by the prioritisation of limited funds. Given that people with learning disabilities have less of a draw on resources than other more powerful groups within society, they are likely to remain disadvantaged and oppressed in economic and social terms. If distributive justice is the key to extending choice, not only in the market-place, but also socially in terms of participation in community life, then it must lie at the very foundation of any notion of empowerment. A system of 'need' is inimical to distributive justice where entitlement is based on prioritising limited resources rather than achieving specified minimum outcomes.

In the Preface, we noted that individual cases of empowerment do not in themselves necessarily produce an empowered lifestyle. Contradictions therefore arise where seemingly empowering actions are taken to be sufficient for an empowered lifestyle for people with learning disabilities. Many of the supposedly empowering aspects which run in tandem with present legislation are themselves a product of the legislation, that is, are an iatrogenic form of service empowerment. For example, it is only where large-scale planning is a bureaucratic requirement that participation in planning becomes necessary; it is only in a professionally based 'needs assessment' process that user participation is warranted; it is only in a mixed economy that choice is arbitrated through a third party; and it is only where entitlements to resources are unspecified that legal solutions are required to establish entitlement where there is dispute.

The existence of a service structure leads to a 'bounded empowerment agenda' which is in itself iatrogenic. Huge effort and resources are placed into trying to achieve empowerment within these service structures as if they were ends in themselves. But on closer inspection, it is clear that there are some inherently disempowering aspects to the so-called rights of users within such structures. As Barnes and Prior (1995) have argued, 'freedom to make choices may sometimes be a positive means of self-expression, but if the context of choosing is divorced from the context in which power in society is exercised, increasing choice cannot in itself be a means of empowerment' (p.54). And as Lupton and Hall (1993) suggest, 'there is a clear contrast between the participation of service users as 'citizens' of a democratic society and their involvement as customers of a social care market place' (p.7).

The seemingly recalcitrant features of present formal service and legal structures which limit the possibilities of empowerment lead us to ask whether there are alternative structural forms which might provide the conditions within which empowerment for people with learning disabilities can be better accomplished. This is the central question to be addressed in Section 3.

References

Barnes, M. and Prior, D. (1995) 'Spoilt for choice? How consumerism can disempower public service users.' *Public Money and Management* July–September, 53–58.

Day, P.R. (1994) 'Ambiguity and user involvement: issues arising in assessments for young people and their carers.' *British Journal of Social Work 24*, 577–596.

Department of Health (1989) *Caring for People: Community Care in the Next Decade and Beyond.* cmnd 849. London: HMSO.

Dowson, S. (1990) *Who Does What? The Process of Enabling People with Learning Difficulties to Achieve what they Need and Want.* London: Values into Action.

Ellis, K. (1993) *Squaring the Circle: User and Carer Participation in Needs Assessment.* London: Joseph Rowntree.

Gomm, R. (1993) 'Issues of power in health and welfare.' In J. Walmsley, J. Reynolds, P. Shakespeare, and R. Woolfe (eds) *Health, Welfare and Practice: Reflecting on Roles and Relationships, 131–138.* London: Sage.

Hirschman, A. (1970) *Exit, Voice and Loyalty: Responses to Decline in Firms, Organisations and States.* Harvard: Harvard University Press.

Hoyes, L. and Means, R. (1993) 'Markets, contracts and social care services: prospects and problems.' In J. Bornat, C. Pereira, D. Pilgrim and F. Williams (eds) *Community Care: A Reader, 287–296.* London: Macmillan in association with The Open University Press.

Lewis, J. and Glennerster, H. (1996) *Implementing the New Community Care.* Buckingham: The Open University Press.

Lupton, C. and Hall, B. (1993) 'Beyond the rhetoric: from policy to practice in user involvement.' *Research, Policy and Planning 10*, 2, 6–11.

McGrath, M. and Ramcharan, P. (1996) Mixing the economy of community care in Wales: purchasing, power and protectionism. University of Wales, Bangor, CSPRD: Working Paper.

McKnight, J. (1986) 'Professionalised service and disabling help.' In A. Brechin, P. Liddiard and J. Swain (eds) *Handicap in a Social World.* Sevenoaks: Hodder and Stoughton; Milton Keynes: The Open University Press.

Means, R. and Smith, R. (1994) *Community Care: Policy and Practice.* London: Macmillan.

North, N. (1993) 'Empowerment in welfare markets.' *Health and Social Care 1,* 129–137.

Plant, R. and Barry, N. (1990) *Citizenship and Rights in Thatcher's Britain: Two Views.* London: The IEA Health and Welfare Unit.

Saunders, P. (1993) 'Citizenship in a liberal society.' In B. Turner (ed) *Citizenship and Social Theory.* London: Sage.

Shemmings, D. and Shemmings, Y. (1995) 'Defining participative practice in health and welfare.' In R. Jack (ed) *Empowerment in Community Care.* London: Chapman and Hall.

Smull, M. and Burke Harrison, S. (1992) *Supporting People with Severe Reputations in the Community.* Alexandria, Virginia: National Association of State Directors of Developmental Disabilities Services Inc.

SSI/Social Work Services Group (1991) *Care Management and Assessment: Manager's Guide.* London: Department of Health/Scottish Office.

Welsh Office (1983) *The All Wales Strategy for the Development of Services for Mentally Handicapped People.* Cardiff: Welsh Office.

PART 3

Empowerment in Different Legal
and Policy Contexts

CHAPTER 10

Capacity and Empowerment

Gwyneth Roberts

Introduction

In relation to empowering people with learning disabilities in their everyday lives, one of the key functions of the law is to achieve a proper balance between, on the one hand, protecting the rights of adults to autonomy and self-determination whilst, at the same time, ensuring proper care and protection for those in society who are either defined as mentally incapacitated, or who are vulnerable to neglect, abuse and exploitation.

The presumption of capacity

A primary assumption upon which, as individual citizens, we base the conduct of our life is that we are able to exercise a considerable degree of personal freedom. That freedom is made up of a number of different elements, one of which is the right to autonomy and self-determination. One of the important legal principles underlying this assumption is the notion of capacity. The common law presumes that *every* adult citizen is endowed with full mental capacity to take decisions for him/herself, and that he/she will be held generally responsible for the consequences.

The assumption of capacity applies equally to people with learning disabilities. As a result, no person with learning disabilities may be deprived of his/her decision-making powers unless it is shown that he/she is mentally incapacitated. In other words, before a person can be treated as mentally incompetent, this fundamental principle must be rebutted by evidence to the contrary. The legal rules, therefore, favour autonomy and self-determination. As the Law Commission[1] has pointed out, it is the right of all people to take their own

---

1   The English Law Commission is a permanent body set up in 1965 with the task of keeping the law under review and making proposals for change where appropriate. The government is not bound by the Law Commission's proposals, which are often in the form of a draft Bill.

decisions if they are capable of doing so, to have someone else to take such decisions for them if they are not, and to protection against abuse, exploitation and neglect of duty by those who have responsibility for them (Law Commission 1991).

Many decisions, especially in relation to personal care, are taken by carers without any formal authority. Where informal arrangements fail or prove inadequate, however, there are few legal mechanisms which can be used to protect the incapacitated person. As a result, although many efficient and ethical decisions are taken informally, so are many of those decisions which lead to the abuse or exploitation of the incapacitated person (Law Commission 1993). To a considerable extent, this is because the legal rules on determining incapacity are currently, 'fragmented, complex and in many respects out of date' (Law Commission 1991, p.5). As a result, some incapacitated individuals find themselves wrongly deprived of their legitimate right to take decisions for themselves, whilst others find themselves exposed to neglect, abuse or exploitation.

It was the number of approaches which it had received over the years in relation to such problems that led the Law Commission in 1991 to begin its investigation of the adequacy of legal and other procedures for decision-making on behalf of mentally incapacitated adults (Law Commission 1991). In this chapter, some of the problems which have arisen as a result of the current legal position are examined in the light of the Law Commission's recent proposals for reform of the law (Law Commission 1995).

The current law on incapacity

At present, the basic common law test of mental incapacity is whether or not a person is able to understand, in broad terms, the nature of a particular decision and its effects. This basic test has become more complex, however, in relation to some areas of decision-making. As a result, there are a number of differences between one area of the law and another. For example, somewhat different tests apply in relation to:

- entering into a contract
- managing property and financial affairs
- making a will
- getting married
- consenting to sexual intercourse
- consenting to medical treatment.

In relation to entering into a *valid contract*, the test is whether a person understands the nature of the transaction which is being agreed. The required level of understanding varies, however, according to the nature and complexity of the contract. As a result, a person may be legally capable of entering into a simple contract, such as purchasing items of food and drink, but legally incapable of entering into a more complex contract, such as a hire purchase agreement. A contract will be binding even where one of the parties lacks mental capacity, unless it can also be shown that the other party was aware, or ought to have been aware, of that fact. And, whatever the circumstances, the incapacitated person must pay a reasonable price for any 'necessaries' which have been supplied to him/her. 'Necessaries', in this context, means any goods or services, such as food, drink or clothing, which are suitable to the person's station in life, and to his/her actual requirements at the time of sale and delivery (Sale of Goods Act 1979, s.3(2)).

Where it appears that a person is *incapable of managing his/her property and financial affairs*, an application may be made to the Court of Protection for a receiver to be appointed who then becomes responsible for dealing with the person's affairs. The application must be based on mental disorder, that is, that the person is suffering from, 'mental illness, *arrested or incomplete development of mind*, psychopathic disorder, or any other disorder or disability of mind' (Mental Health Act 1983, s.1).

The test in relation to *making a will* is whether, at the time when the will is being made, the testator/trix understands the nature of the transaction; the broad extent of his/her property (although not necessarily its value); and any persons he/she ought to have in mind in making the will (*Banks v. Goodfellow* (1870) 39 LR 5 QB 549). Where a person is under the jurisdiction of the Court of Protection, the court may execute a statutory will on his/her behalf. According to the decision in *Re J(D)* [1982] 2 All ER 37, the court's function in such cases is to make a will which the person in question, if acting reasonably, would have made if he/she were notionally restored to full mental capacity, memory and foresight. In *Re C (Spinster and Mental Patient)* [1991] 3 All ER 866, a 75-year-old woman, who had a severe learning disability from birth, had been hospitalised since the age of ten. Her parents left her a substantial estate. It was held that the Court of Protection could draft a will on her behalf according to the way in which she was likely to have disposed of her property if she were not mentally disordered under the Mental Health Act 1983.

In relation to *getting married*, there are two tests of incapacity. The first test is whether, at the time of the ceremony, a person is capable of giving valid consent, that is, whether he or she understands what marriage entails, and the duties and responsibilities which attach to it. The level of understanding which is necessary in this case is relatively low. Indeed, according to the judgement in *Re Park* [1954] P.112, marriage, 'is a simple contract which it does not require a high degree of intelligence to understand'. The second test of incapacity, in relation to marriage, is whether, at the time of the ceremony, a person was suffering from mental disorder within the meaning of the Mental Health Act 1983 of such a kind, or to such an extent, as to be unfit for marriage

(Matrimonial Causes Act 1973, s.12(d)). In either of these cases, the effect of incapacity is to make the marriage voidable at the instigation of either spouse.

In relation to *sexual relations*, the test is whether the person understands the nature of what is being proposed, and its implications. There are a number of statutory offences in this field. For example, it is an offence for a male manager or a male employee at a mental nursing home or hospital, to have sexual intercourse on the premises with a person who is receiving treatment for mental disorder, whether as an in-patient or as an out-patient.

The basic common law rule in relation to *medical treatment* is that the patient must consent to being examined and/or treated, except in cases of urgent necessity, for example, to save a person's life, or to prevent a person from acting in ways which are dangerous to him/herself or others. The test of capacity is whether the patient is capable of understanding the nature and purpose of the proposed medical procedure, and its benefits and risks. The facts of *Re C (Adult: Refusal of Treatment)* [1994] 1 All ER 819, were that C, who suffered from schizophrenia, was compulsorily detained in a special hospital. He suffered from a number of delusions, including a belief that he possessed certain medical skills. One of his legs had become gangrenous to such an extent that his life was said to be in danger. He was transferred to a general hospital where the doctor in charge of his treatment assessed C's chances of survival as 15 per cent unless the leg was amputated. However, C refused to give his consent. A meeting was arranged between C and a solicitor to assess his competence to give a reasoned decision. In the meantime, treatment with antibiotics and conservative surgery averted the immediate threat of imminent death. There remained a possibility, however, that C would develop gangrene again. C applied to the court for an injunction to prevent the amputation being carried out without his express written consent.

The question before the court was whether the presumption of capacity had been rebutted in this case, by evidence that C suffered from mental disorder. It was held that where a person has the necessary capacity to understand the nature, purpose and effect of the treatment which is offered, he/she also has the necessary mental capacity to consent or refuse treatment. The decision-making process consisted of three stages: first, comprehending and retaining treatment information, second, believing it and, third, weighing it in the balance to arrive at choice.[2] This test applied even if the patient's general capacity was affected by chronic mental disorder.

If a patient lacks capacity, there is no legal mechanism for consent to be given on his/her behalf, either by another person, or by the court, although an application may be made to the court for a declaration that proceeding with

---

2   The Law Commission had also proposed a similar approach in para 2.20 of *Mentally Handicapped Adults and Decision-Making* Consultation Paper 129.

the treatment would not be unlawful. This was the situation in *Re F (Mental Patient: Sterilisation)* [1990] 2 A.C. 1 which concerned a woman with learning disability. An application had been made to the court for leave to perform a sterilisation on F. According to the House of Lords' decision in this case, a doctor may treat an incompetent patient without his/her consent on the grounds of necessity where treatment would be in the patient's best interests. 'Best interests' is defined as treatment which is necessary to save a person's life, or prevent deterioration, or to ensure improvement, in his/her physical or mental health. According to Lord Goff, the decision to proceed may involve others besides the doctor.

It must surely be good practice to consult relatives and others who are concerned with the care of the patient. Sometimes, consultation with a specialist will be required and, in others, especially where the decision involves more than a purely medical opinion, an interdisciplinary team will in practice participate in the decision.

Certain categories of non-therapeutic procedures, such as sterilisation, (though not abortion) should, as a matter of good practice, be referred to the court before treatment is given. Where a patient is in a persistent vegetative state, the issue is often whether or not medical treatment which may extend life, but which is unlikely to alleviate the patient's condition, should be continued. The test, according to *Airedale NHS Trust v. Bland* [1993] is whether the continuance of intrusive life support is in the patient's best interests. Doctors who are faced with this situation must seek a declaration from the court in every case.

Specific statutory rules apply to patients detained under the Mental Health Act 1983 (except those detained for short periods). The consent of such patients is not necessary in relation to treatment *for their mental disorder* administered to them by the responsible medical officer (that is, the doctor in charge of their treatment) (Mental Health Act 1983, s.63). The phrase 'treatment for mental disorder' was given a broad meaning by the Court of Appeal in *B v Croydon Health Authority* [1995] 1 All ER 683. Certain treatments are excluded, however, from the ambit of s.63. Where it is intended to administer electroconvulsive therapy (ECT) therapy, or medicine for the patient's mental disorder for a period longer than three months, the patient's independently certified consent, or the agreement of a second, independent, doctor must be obtained. In relation to psychosurgery and the surgical implantation of hormones, the patient's independently certified consent *and* an independent medical opinion must be obtained (whether the patient is detained under the Act or not). The test of capacity, in this context, is whether the, 'patient is capable of understanding the nature, purpose and likely effects of the treatment in question' (s.57(2)(a), s.58(2)(a)).

In addition to the tests discussed above, there are tests of capacity, also, in relation to serving on a jury, voting in an election, and giving evidence in a court of law. As a result, it is now widely recognised that the law on mental incapacity is unsystematic as well as being full of glaring gaps, and that the rules are largely inaccessible and, sometimes, incomprehensible to the lay person (Law Commission 1995). The Law Commission was struck by the description of the existing law, offered to it by the Master of the Court of Protection, as: 'a string bag, which can stretch further and hold more than a basket but which is essentially a group of holes and whose use is therefore more limited' (Law Commission 1995, p.26).

By means of its report and draft Bill, the Law Commission is proposing that this 'group of holes' within which people who lack mental capacity now exist should be replaced 'with a carefully designed and well-constructed legal basket' (Law Commission 1995, p.29).

The need for reform

Given the current position, it is hardly surprising that many carers and service providers, when invited to give evidence before the Law Commission, expressed considerable concern about what they perceived as lack of clear authority in carrying out the everyday tasks of looking after an incapacitated person. They were unsure what they were permitted to do and, conversely, what they had no authority to do (Law Commission 1993). Doctors, social workers and carers all have a claim to have their positions clarified. How are these competing interests to be reconciled? In this context there is, too, the question of appropriate risk-taking as a positive element in a person's life.

The first need is to ensure that the law contains a single, coherent test of incapacity. The second need is to determine the basis upon which proxy decision-making should take place. If these two needs are more appropriately met, it may be possible to achieve a better balance between intrusive and arbitrary intervention in the lives of people with learning disabilities, on the one hand, and the need to protect vulnerable adults from possible harm, abuse or exploitation, on the other. The Law Commission has set out its proposals in a comprehensive draft Bill which is appended to its final report on mental incapacity (Law Commission 1995).

Proposals for reform

In discussing possible ways forward, the Law Commission begins by restating the common law presumption of capacity. The Commission accepts that it would be helpful for any new statutory provisions in this field to include both the existing presumption of capacity, and the relevant standard of proof. As a result, clause 2(6) of the Law Commission's draft Bill expressly sets out a presumption against incapacity, as well as the necessary standard of proof, that is, that 'any question whether a person lacks capacity shall be decided on the balance of probabilities' (Law Commission 1995, p.223). This confirmation of the common law principle and its embodiment in the proposed legislation sets out the terms upon which individuals are to be treated in relation to their decision-making rights.

The test of incapacity

The Law Commission has set out what it regards as the three main approaches to determining whether a person is mentally incapacitated, that is:

- a status test
- an outcome test
- a functional test.

A *status* test, if adopted, would involve treating every individual falling within a particular group or category as mentally incompetent *per se*. For example, it would be possible to treat every person who falls within the definition of mental disorder, as set out in s.1 of the Mental Health Act 1983, in this way. In the Law Commission's view, however, the status approach is quite out of tune with the policy aim of enabling and encouraging people to take for themselves any decision which they have capacity to take, and the 'least restrictive alternative' principle.

The second approach would be to determine capacity on the basis of *outcome*, that is, to measure a person's mental capacity against the possible result of taking a decision in a particular way. If this approach were adopted, it could penalise individuality and might result in conformity at the expense of personal autonomy. It would also place considerable power in the hands of the person who had the task of assessing possible outcome. Whether consciously or not, an assessor might be tempted to impose his/her values and judgements upon the decision in question.

As a result, the Law Commission rejected these possible tests for determining mental incapacity. Instead, it favours a third approach, that is, a *functional* test which, in effect, extends and clarifies the existing common law test. According to this approach, the emphasis is on a person's *capacity to make a decision*, that is to understand its nature and effect, and to choose, where appropriate, from amongst a number of options. Of course, there are disadvantages in a test such as this. Whereas a status test provides certainty, a functional test recognises capacity as a more complex concept which may fluctuate not only over time, but may also be partial and may vary from decision to decision. As Gunn points out: 'Capacity/incapacity are not concepts with clear *a priori* boundaries. They appear on a continuum which ranges from full capacity at one end to full incapacity at the other end. There are therefore degrees of incapacity' (Gunn 1994, p.14). Although application of this test means that those who care for, and have dealings with, people with learning disabilities have to be constantly aware of the nature of the test, it is undoubtedly the one which is most likely to ensure that people with learning disabilities are enabled and empowered to take decisions for themselves.

If these proposals become incorporated into the law, before a decision could be taken out of a person's hands, it would have to be shown that he/she lacked capacity, that is, that he/she was *unable to make a decision* on the matter in question by reason of '*mental disability*'; or was *unable to communicate a decision* because he or she was unconscious, or for any other reason.

A person would be, 'unable...to make a decision by reason of mental disability' if he/she was *unable, at the time, to understand or remember information which was relevant to the decision, and its reasonably foreseeable consequences*. Such information should be provided in broad terms and simple language. *Mental disability* is defined as, 'any disability or disorder of the mind or brain, whether permanent or temporary, which results in an impairment or disturbance of mental function'. Initially, the Law Commission proposed that mental disorder, as defined in the Mental Health Act 1983, should be the threshold test in determining incapacity. It was persuaded, however, that the term had become equated in the minds of many people with the much narrower phenomenon of psychiatric illness, or with the criteria for compulsory detention under the Mental Health Act.

Nevertheless, the Commission felt that including a diagnostic threshold would give significant protection to those who might otherwise be treated as incompetent on the grounds that they had made an unusual or unwise decision, and the use of the term 'mental disability' would stress the need for the condition to have a *disabling* effect on a person's mental capacity (Law Commission 1995). An individual would not be treated as incapacitated because of mental disability simply on the grounds that the decision was not one which a person of ordinary prudence would take. In other words, we should all, as adults, be given a licence to make mistakes, and even be unwise, in some of the decisions we take. Neither should a person be deemed 'unable to communicate a decision' until all practicable steps have been taken – without success – to enable him/her to do so.

Surrogate decision-making

What might be the possible consequences of a person with learning disability being assessed as mentally incapacitated as a result of applying the functional test? In what circumstances, for example, could a surrogate decision be made? The Law Commission lists a variety of decisions which carers have to take from day to day. These range from simple daily decisions such as what an incapacitated person should eat, what he/she should wear, when he/she should go to bed or get up, whether he/she should have a bath or haircut, through to major decisions about where he/she is to live or whether he/she should undergo irreversible medical treatment.

At present, many such decisions are taken in a legal limbo. Freeman has suggested that unless there is a clear locus of authority, decision-making is potentially flawed with deleterious consequences for all affected, not least the incompetent person himself or herself (Freeman 1994). Mechanisms are, therefore, needed to legitimate and regulate the decision-making of carers and service providers.

The incremental approach

The Law Commission proposes an incremental approach to surrogate decision-making through a series of graduated interventions. Such intervention might range from authority to take a single decision on behalf of the incapacitated person to authority being vested by the court in a personal manager (but only if power to make a single decision was considered insufficient). As a general principle, decision-making should take place at 'the *lowest level consistent with protecting the incapacitated person from improper usurpation of his or her autonomy, and from improper decision-making*' (Law Commission 1993, p.5). In exercising the power to appoint a manager, the court would have regard for the principle that a single decision by the court was preferable to appointing a manager, and that the powers conferred on a manager should be as limited in scope and duration as possible, and would not in any case extend beyond a period of five years.

The value of a judicial forum as the ultimate decision-maker has been subject to discussion. The judicial forum proposed by the Law Commission, for this purpose, is a newly formed Court of Protection which would provide a single integrated framework for making personal welfare decisions, health care decisions and financial decisions, with power to make a declaration, to make an order and to appoint a manager, where necessary. Amongst those able to apply to the court on any of these matters would be a person who was incapacitated, or who was alleged to be so.

There are five characteristics which enhance decision-making by a judicial forum which are not present in more informal, more private decision-making processes, that is, that such decisions reside in the public arena; that they are governed by rules and principles, and are required to be reasonable; that decisions reached in this way help to promote independent decision-making; that a judicial forum follows established procedural rules; and that a body of this kind is accountable (Freeman 1994).

General legal authority

The Law Commission advocates the introduction of a general legal authority to act reasonably for the personal welfare or health care of an incapacitated person. This authority could be exercised by any person, if 'in all the circumstances [it is] reasonable for it to be done by the person who does it' (Law Commission 1995, pp.50–51) and the decision is taken in the best interests of the incapacitated person. The general authority would also apply to any situation where there were *reasonable grounds for believing* that a person was incapacitated. The introduction of a general legal authority to act would mean that it would not be necessary to appoint a personal manager for every incapacitated person, since most day-to-day welfare and health decisions would fall within its ambit.

The Law Commission's draft Bill sets out the parameters of a general authority of this kind. It would include the right to pledge the credit of an incapacitated person, and apply his/her money to meet such expenditure. It would also enable a person to be reimbursed or otherwise indemnified for such expenditure. On the other hand, certain decisions would be specifically excluded. The general authority to act would not permit the use or threat of force in order to make an incapacitated person do anything to which he/she objected; nor to permit an incapacitated person to be detained or confined, *whether or not he/she objected.* Nor would the general legal authority permit any action which was contrary to a decision or direction given by a manager appointed by the court, or by a person with continuing powers of attorney.[3]

These exceptions would not, however, preclude taking any steps which were necessary to avert the death of an incapacitated person, or a serious deterioration in his/her condition, whilst seeking a court order.

There are a number of decisions of such a personal nature, however, that they should never be taken on behalf of another person. These are:

- consenting to marriage
- consenting to a sexual relationship
- consenting to divorce following a two year separation
- agreeing to adoption, or consent to the freeing of a child for adoption
- discharging parental responsibilities, except in relation to a child's property
- voting at an election.

In relation to a number of key issues, such as determining whether a person was incapacitated, only the court would have the authority to decide. It would also have the power to resolve a number of other issues, that is:

- where an incapacitated person was to live

---

3   The aim of enabling people to take for themselves the decisions which they are able to take extends also to anticipatory decisions. The Law Commission, therefore, proposes replacing the current provisions for creating enduring powers of attorney by a power to create a *continuing* power of attorney. The appointment could encompass a person's welfare and health care as well as matters relating to property and other affairs, such as conducting legal proceedings.

- what contact, if any, he/she was to have with one or more specified individuals
- in relation to an incapacitated person's statutory right to information (such as access to health records)
- as to statutory benefits and services.

Medical treatment[4]

Certain forms of medical treatments or procedures would require the court's authorisation, or the consent of an attorney or a manager. These include any treatment intended, or reasonably likely, to result in infertility (except where the treatment related to a disease of the reproductive organs, or was intended to relieve the detrimental effects of menstruation); and treatment for facilitating donation by the patient of non-regenerative tissue or bone marrow; and any other treatment or procedure prescribed by the Secretary of State.

Certain kinds of medical treatment would require either the certification of an independent doctor or the consent of an attorney or manager. These would include:

- treatment intended to relieve the detrimental effects of menstruation which was likely to result in infertility
- abortion
- treatment for mental disorder as set out in s.58(1) of the Mental Health Act
- any other treatment or procedure prescribed by the Secretary of State.

In relation to patients who are in a persistent vegetative state, the Law Commission proposes that the discontinuation of artificial nutrients and hydration would be lawful only where certain statutory requirements had been met.

The 'best interests' test

On what basis should a surrogate decision be taken on behalf of an incapacitated person? The Law Commission proposes that the primary test should be the 'best interests' of the incapacitated person.[5] Such intervention should, however, be as limited as possible, and concerned to achieve what the person him/herself

---

4 The Law Commission recommends that a competent person aged 18 or over should be able to make an advance statement refusing medical care and treatment other than 'basic care' should he/she become incapacitated. 'Basic care' is defined as care to maintain bodily cleanliness and to alleviate severe pain, as well as direct oral nutrition and hydration.

5 Decisions made in order to protect other people which *are not* in the best interests of the incapacitated person would be dealt with under the Mental Health Act 1983.

would have wanted. Although it rejected 'substituted judgement' as the basis for surrogate decision-making, that is, attempting to reach a decision on the basis of what an incapacitated person him/herself would have decided, the proposed checklist contains elements of a substituted judgement test. The test also emphasises the importance of encouraging personal autonomy, and the 'least restrictive alternative'. The term 'best interests' is not defined in the draft Bill, but Clause 3(2) lists four factors which a decision-maker should have in mind in reaching a decision or taking any action. These are:

1. The ascertainable past and present wishes and feelings of the person concerned, and the factors that he/she would take into consideration if able to do so.

2. The need to permit and encourage the incapacitated person to participate, or to improve his or her ability to participate, as fully as possible in anything done for, and any decision affecting, him or her.

3. Where it is practicable and appropriate to consult them, the views as to the person's wishes and feelings, and what would be in the person's best interests of:

    a) those named by the incapacitated person for this purpose

    b) anyone (such as a spouse, relative, friend or other person) who cares for the incapacitated person, or who is interested in his/her welfare

    c) the donee of a continuing power of attorney (cf footnote 3, p.194)

    d) any manager appointed for the incapacitated person by the court.

4. Whether the purpose for which any action or decision is required can be as effectively achieved in a manner less restrictive of the person's freedom of action, that is, the least restrictive alternative should be used.

Carson (1993) has suggested that, while the 'best interests test' as formulated by the Law Commission implies that mentally incapacitated people must be positively valued, there are doubts about how it would work in practice. For Carson, the basic question is how would it be possible to know whether a person was or was not taking the criteria into account? The appeal, he suggests, is to finer feelings: 'It is like charity; allowing people to feel good without recognising any responsibility' (p.307). According to Carson:

> The Law Commission's proposals will tackle practical problems in so far as they will shower empowerment upon formal and informal carers. But just because complaints and litigation do not arise, it would not be appropriate to assume that problems were not occurring. The disputes are unlikely to see the light of day. (p.318)

In his view any new legislation should be concerned with the quality of the decision taken, with whether those exercising care and authority act properly, and should attempt to ensure that those exercising care and authority were made accountable in justifying their action. However, as Carson himself concedes, such a provision would not be without definitional problems (Carson 1993).

Carson would go further than the Law Commission in placing positive duties on those who exercise care and authority in relation to incapacitated people. He argues that it is not, 'just the practical or instrumental role of such proposed legislation that is important but its capacity to provide symbols, the associations, the legally authorised and supported ways of regarding people with disabilities and the duties of carers' (Carson 1993, p.305).

The legal framework should be more than simply a regulating instrument. It ought to have a more positive promotional role in empowering mentally incapacitated people.

The problem, however, is whether such procedures would be workable in practice, raising as they do issues of enforcement and intrusion. As Ungerson (1993) has argued:

> citizenship is essentially placed in the public domain...carers are physically located in the private domain...particularly where we adopt a notion of citizenship that emphasises rights, we run into difficult water as soon as we try to operate a notion of rights within the domestic and private domain. (p.144)

In the Law Commission's view, such intervention should be limited to public law procedures to protect vulnerable adults from abuse and neglect.

Public law procedures

The second major question to be considered by the Law Commission is how, at the same time as promoting and encouraging independence, autonomy and self-determination, vulnerable adults can be protected from possible neglect, abuse or exploitation. The Law Commission's initial discussions took place against public concern over the case of Beverley Lewis, a young woman with a severe learning disability whose mentally ill mother had obstructed the efforts of the authorities to provide Beverley with the services she needed. Many of those who responded to the Law Commission's consultation documents considered that the existing law was ineffective in protecting people with disabilities, and other vulnerable people, from abuse and neglect. It was also inadequate in its approach to issues of autonomy and individual rights. Indeed, the legal provisions were seen as counter-productive, being so draconian that they were seldom used (Law Commission 1995). The Law Commission has responded with a number of proposals for the protection of vulnerable people who are at risk.

In the first place, the Law Commission proposes the creation of a new offence of ill-treating or wilfully neglecting a person in relation to whom the offender has been given powers by virtue of the proposed legislation. Second, it proposes a number of new public law procedures in this field. The Law Commission acknowledges that community living has exposed many vulnerable people to new, or at least different, dangers. In spite of the increasing awareness of abuse, there are a number of problems in this field, such as the lack of a standard definition of the term, under-reporting of the incidence of abuse, and the attitudes of professionals, such as lawyers and social workers (Griffiths, Roberts and Williams 1993). In particular, a number of those giving evidence to the Law Commission expressed concern about what they termed the 'abusive normalisation' of some disabled people, as the result of an ideology of non-intervention on the part of service providers and advisers which placed the autonomy principle above everything else (Law Commission 1995).

KAREN AND MICHAEL

Some of the possible effects of 'abusive normalisation' may be seen in the case of Karen and Michael who, having met at a hostel for disabled people, got married in July 1989. Karen was a lively woman with Down's Syndrome, whilst Michael was more seriously disabled. They were given a two year training programme and were then allocated a council flat, although the social services department was aware that they had problems in planning balanced meals and in paying bills.

Within weeks, it had become apparent that they were incapable of looking after themselves. The flat was burgled and became infested with rats. They stopped washing, and lost other skills they had acquired over many years. A specialist social worker was assigned to help the couple, but failed to persuade them that they needed assistance. Karen's father tried to help but became frustrated at the apparent reluctance of social workers to take action to stop their condition from deteriorating further. After six months, the couple's standards of dress and hygiene had declined to an alarming level. The social worker said that she would continue to try to assist them, but that it was up to the couple how they lived their life. It was an argument repeated often over the next three years as they descended into deeper squalor. According to Karen's father, it was the social worker's complacency which shocked him: 'She kept talking about their rights as citizens, to do what they liked. But I kept pointing out that they were abusing themselves...'. He gave up trying to keep them clean, believing that the problem would only be resolved if it reached crisis point.

The couple began buying goods on credit and bills went unpaid. They ran up debts of more than £2500. They were fined for not possessing a television licence and summonsed for non-payment of water rates. There was another burglary. Things went missing, including their social security benefit book; the gas meter was broken into. By this time, Karen had lice and black crusts in her matted hair. She had only one set of clothes, no shoes or underwear. There was mould all over the ceilings of the flat where they were living and the lavatory was coated in a yellow crust.

What Karen and Michael so desperately needed, and what they were not persuaded to accept, were sufficient support and community care services to enable them to live a reasonable life in the community. In the face of their obvious vulnerability, what action would have been available to a local authority in these circumstances? At first sight, guardianship under the Mental Health Act 1983 would seem the obvious mechanism for providing them with protection as well as positive social support. An application for guardianship under s.7 of the Mental Health Act 1983 may be made in relation to a patient who is, 'suffering from mental disorder, being mental illness, severe mental impairment, psychopathic disorder or mental impairment...of a nature or degree which warrants...reception into guardianship'. 'Severe mental impairment' means state of arrested or incomplete development of mind which includes severe impairment of intelligence and social functioning and is associated with abnormally aggressive or seriously irresponsible conduct. Mental impairment is defined in the same way except that, in this case, impairment must be 'significant' rather than 'severe' in its extent.

When, in the 1970s, the government was considering how the existing mental health legislation should be reformed, arguments were put forward for substantially extending the existing concept by introducing additional short-term and long-term powers. These were not accepted. As a result, the powers of guardians are currently restricted to three specific areas: requiring the patient to reside at a place specified by the authority or person named as guardian; requiring the patient to attend at places and times as specified for the purpose of medical treatment, occupation, education or training; and requiring access to the patient to be given to a doctor, approved social worker or any other specified person, at the place where the patient is currently residing. It could be argued that the powers which exist at present make no allowance for flexibility in the relationship between the patient and his/her guardian, nor for varying degrees of intervention geared to the varying needs of particular individuals. Even more fundamental is the lack of any positive duty on the part of the guardian to support, assist and encourage the patient towards greater independence. As a result, guardianship under the Mental Health Act would hardly be helpful in this case. The Law Commission does not propose a radical revision of the powers of a guardian, but that the 1983 Act should be amended to give a guardian additional powers to convey the patient to a residence which he/she specifies.[6]

---

6   The Law Commission recommends that the Mental Health Act 1983 should be amended so that only a social services authority could act as guardian.

Under s.135 of the Mental Health Act 1983, any person can apply to a magistrate for a warrant to authorise a police officer to enter premises, if necessary by force, and without the consent of the occupant, to remove a person thought to be mentally disordered, with a view to making an application for his/her admission to a place of safety. A person can be detained in a place of safety under this section for a maximum period of 72 hours. Before a warrant is issued, the magistrate must be given information on oath by an approved social worker that there is reasonable cause to suspect that a person believed to be mentally disordered has been or is being ill-treated, neglected or kept otherwise than under proper control; or, being unable to care for him/herself, is living alone. An approved social worker and a doctor must accompany the constable when executing the warrant. The use of s.135 would hardly have been useful in the case of Karen and Michael since access to the premises where they were living was not in question.

Another procedure which is available to a district local authority, on the certificate of a community physician, is to make use of s.47 of the National Assistance Act 1948, as amended by the National Assistance Act (Amendment) Act 1951. Section 47 provides for the removal to suitable premises of a person in need of care and attention who is suffering from grave chronic disease, or being aged, infirm or physically incapacitated, is living in insanitary conditions, and is not able to provide him/herself with proper care and attention and is not receiving such care from another person. As the Law Commission points out, these powers are rarely used, since they are regarded as inflexible and stigmatising. It proposes that they should be repealed and replaced by a new scheme giving clearer and more appropriate powers to social services authorities to protect incapacitated, mentally disordered and vulnerable people.

The Law Commission's proposals are linked to the recently introduced provisions in the field of community care. Their purpose is to provide better protection for people over the age of 16 who are deemed 'vulnerable', that is, those who are, or may be, in need of community care services by reason of mental or other disability, age or illness; and who are, or may be, unable to take care of themselves, or who are, or may be, unable to protect themselves against significant harm or serious exploitation. In this context 'harm' is defined as ill-treatment (including sexual abuse and forms of ill-treatment that are not physical); the impairment of, or an avoidable deterioration in, physical or mental health; and the impairment of physical, intellectual, emotional, social or behavioural development.

Where a local authority had reason to believe that a vulnerable person, in its area, was suffering, or was likely to be suffering *significant harm* or *serious exploitation*, it would have a duty to *make such enquiries as were necessary* to determine whether this was the case, and if so, whether to provide or arrange community care services, or take some other action to protect the person from harm or exploitation.

If an authorised officer[7] of the local authority had reasonable cause to believe that a vulnerable person, who was living in premises in the area, was *at risk*, he/she would be able *to enter and inspect the premises* at any reasonable time, and interview the person concerned in private. An authorised officer would also be able to apply to the court for an entry warrant authorising a police constable, accompanied by the officer, to enter specified premises if:

- he/she had reasonable cause to believe that a person, who was living there, was vulnerable and 'at risk'

- granting the warrant was necessary to enable the officer to gain access to the vulnerable person.

An application could also be made to the court for *an assessment order* if:

- the applicant had reasonable cause to believe that a vulnerable person was 'at risk'

- the order was required in order that the local authority could assess whether the person was 'at risk' and, if so, whether community care services should be provided or arranged or other protective action taken.

An authorised officer would be able to apply to the court for a temporary protection order if a vulnerable person was likely to be 'at risk' unless removed to, or kept in, protective accommodation for a short period. A temporary protection order would authorise a person's removal to protected accommodation for a period of up to eight days, that is, for the shortest period needed to protect the individual. The court would also be able to direct that he/she should be assessed. Where a person had been removed in this way, it would be the local authority's duty to return him/her to the place from which he/she had been removed, as soon as practicable and consistent with the person's interests.

None of the above orders would be granted, however, if the authorised officer knew, or believed, that the person concerned objected or would object to their use, *unless there was reasonable cause to believe that he/she suffered, or might be suffering, from mental disability*. In effect, vulnerable individuals who were suffering from learning disability but not lacking in capacity would have the right to refuse such intervention if they so wished. The aim of the proposals is to make available a battery of procedures to protect vulnerable individuals from abuse and neglect, whilst at the same time protecting the autonomy and rights of competent individuals.

---

7   Only certain social services officers with relevant training and experience would be authorised to act in this way.

The Law Commission's Report: A Charter for the Future?

The current legal position on mental incapacity sits uneasily within a social context where there is increased emphasis on a 'rights' agenda and citizen advocacy, and growing concern about the possible abuse of vulnerable adults (Law Commission 1995). In the field of mental incapacity, the dilemma is to achieve a balance between two images. The first is the image of the independent autonomous adult at risk of being either patronised or underestimated, or, worse, having to accept a regime designed on the basis of someone else's idea of what he/she can or cannot, should or should not do. The second is the image of helplessness which leads to the need for powers of intervention and protection (Parkin 1995). People with learning disabilities are amongst the groups most likely to be disempowered and disenfranchised by the uncertainties of the current law. Measured against the following principles, how effectively do the Law Commission's recommendations provide a method of reconciling these two images?

The recommendations:

1. Favour a presumption of competence confirming the basic right of individuals to take decisions for themselves.

2. Recognise the principle of normalisation, that is, that people who are incapacitated should be treated as much as possible like other adult citizens and be encouraged to make decisions for themselves if they have the capacity to do so.

3. Recognise the need for the least restrictive intervention in the lives of those who lack mental capacity.

4. Encourage maximum self-determination coupled, however, to protection from exploitation.

To a considerable extent, therefore, the Law Commission's final recommendations present a substantial step forward which, if implemented, would strike a far better balance between, 'self determination and paternalism, rights and welfare, autonomy and protection' (Law Commission 1995, p.113). As the Commission has argued, reform of the law is now a matter of urgent necessity. It is hoped that the government will recognise this need by accepting the Law Commission's recommendations, and so remove many people with learning disabilities from the social and legal limbo in which they are currently placed.

References

Carson, D. (1993) 'Disabling progress: the Law Commission's proposals on mentally incapacitated adults' decision-making.' *The Journal of Welfare and Family Law 5*, 304–320.

Freeman, M. (1994) 'Deciding for the intellectually impaired.' *Medical Law Review 2*, Spring, 77–91.

CAPACITY AND EMPOWERMENT 203

Griffiths, A., Roberts, G. and Williams, J. (1993) 'Elder abuse and the law.' In P. Delcamer and F. Glendenning (eds) *The Mistreatment of Elderly People*. London: Sage.

Gunn, M. (1994) 'The meaning of capacity.' *Medical Law Review 2*, Spring, 8–29.

Law Commission (1991) *Mentally Incapacitated Adults and Decision-Making: An Overview*. Consultation Paper 119. London: HMSO.

Law Commission (1993) *Mentally Incapacitated Adults and Decision-Making: A New Jurisdiction*. Consultation Paper 128. London: HMSO.

Law Commission (1995) *Mental Incapacity*. Law. Com. No 231. London: HMSO.

Parkin, A. (1995) 'The care and control of elderly or incapacitated adults.' *Journal of Social Welfare and Family Law 17*, 4, 431–444.

Ungerson, C. (1993) 'Caring and citizenship: a complex relationship.' In J. Bornat, C. Pereira, D. Pilgrim and F. Williams (eds) *Community Care: A Reader*. London: Macmillan.

CHAPTER 11

Citizenship and People with Disabilities in Canada
Towards the Elusive Ideal

Marcia Rioux, Michael Bach and Cameron Crawford

Introduction

Struggles over who will secure citizenship and the entitlements that status will bring have defined the political landscape of many nations in the 20th century. Conventionally understood to be a status that brings basic civil and political rights, the women's movement and the civil rights movement have successfully challenged laws and policies that excluded people from exercising these rights on the basis of their sex or race. The dilemma for women and for people of colour is that enjoyment of these rights has not on its own been sufficient to address the systemic inequalities they face. Nor have the social and economic rights necessary to challenge the inequalities faced by marginalised groups been fully institutionalised.

The critique of the exclusionary framework of civil and political rights, and of a limited view of what counts for citizenship, has focused on women and people of colour (Pascall 1986; Williams 1989; Young 1990). Much less has been written about how people with disabilities have been excluded from the status of citizen, and the nature of citizenship rights that would secure their equality and inclusion in society. The welfare state looks very different from the vantage point of women and people of colour who do not have disabilities, and it constructs the inequalities of these groups in a distinct manner. This chapter looks at how citizenship and equality have eluded people with disabilities in the welfare state era in Canada. It also looks at how a new framework to secure citizenship and equality has emerged in the past 20 years through developments in legislation, policy and jurisprudence. It is on the basis of this framework that policy proposals for income and social services are made in the latter sections of this chapter. These proposals seek to secure the citizenship for people with disabilities that public policy has done so much to undermine.

The roots of the welfare state in Canada can be found in the English Poor Laws, which established a distinction between the worthy and the unworthy poor. Through the evolution of this distinction in the succeeding 400 years or so, the state established some obligation to care for those considered to be worthy poor and unable to work – elderly people, the ill and people who were disabled. The implications of this distinction have most often been analysed from the perspective of those considered 'unworthy' – able-bodied and 'able-minded' men and women, those who were deemed able but unwilling to work. For those who fall into this category the welfare state has been minimalist and residual and has reflected the 'less-eligibility' principle.[1] Without recognition of the structural factors which have led to unemployment, poverty, ill-health and illiteracy, welfare state provision has entangled people and families in a web of meagre provision, disentitlement, discretionary benefits, contradictory eligibility rules, surveillance and targeted programmes (National Council of Welfare 1987; The Roeher Institute 1988, 1990). These have had the effect of entrenching rather than ameliorating inequality.

From the perspective of the 'worthy' poor – a category which has tended to include a large proportion of people with disabilities – the welfare state has provided minimalist provision in some respects, but 'residual' it has not been. Often the problem has been one of 'overfunding' and 'over-serving' rather than underfunding. A different set of obligations was established for the worthy poor than for those considered unworthy. These obligations could only be exercised by constructing legal and social differences between the worthy and unworthy poor that have served to legitimate different treatment and different obligations (Rioux 1994). Thus, the obligation the state took on in establishing the category of worthy poor has become a double- and triple-edged sword for people with disabilities. Under the legal and social regime of the worthy poor, people with disabilities became the object of charity, but at the cost of basic citizenship rights (Rioux 1993). Considered incompetent to function in society – this being the ticket to becoming 'worthy' – the welfare state established systems of segregation for people with disabilities – segregation from their families, from educational institutions, from the labour market, from political participation, from the exercise of rights of self-determination and from communities. The monuments to the 'disabled but worthy' poor are the institutions, special schools, vocational workshops and segregated classrooms. The costs of being worthy poor have been high for people with disabilities (extremely high rates of unemployment, violence and abuse, illiteracy, poverty, illness, social isolation and discrimination).

---

1   This principle was explicitly stated in the 1834 revisions of the Elizabethan Poor Laws. This principle required that public support for an individual guarantee a lower standard of living than that of the poorest paid labourer. BPP 127.

In the immediate post-war period the framework of obligations for the welfare state in Canada entrenched the worthy/unworthy distinction with the emphasis on security, citizenship (understood as civil and political rights) and democracy. These became the pillars of the Canadian state, and provided the basis for massive investment in building the institutional infrastructure for welfare provision (The Roeher Institute 1993). Whilst Marshall's (1949/1963) broader notion of citizenship (to include social and economic rights) was being formulated in this period, the figure of the 'citizen' that remained entrenched was that of the self-made, rational and independent individual exercising basic democratic and legal rights. A democratic state and society was to be constituted by such individuals securing for themselves, and largely on their own, 'the good life'. Because many people with disabilities did not meet the tests imposed by such a concept of citizen, they were to be taken care of through the 'security' pillar of the welfare state – investment in institutional facilities, special education, segregated vocational training and employment, and community services exclusively for persons with disabilities grew substantially in the post-war period. In this way the post-war framework for securing the welfare and well-being of Canadians institutionalised exclusion for people with disabilities.

The cracks in the post-war framework for well-being began to emerge in the 1960s, and claims for its restructuring gained momentum from the 1960s through the 1980s, first from the civil rights and women's movements, and later from the growing disability rights movement.

A new foundation of rights was established in Canada and internationally in response to such claims. The entrenchment of the rights of people with disabilities within human rights legislation, and the entrenchment of Constitutional equality rights for people with disabilities within the Charter of Rights and Freedoms (Canada 1982)[2] have had important consequences in Canada. These rights are now legally entrenched on an equal basis with others: women, people of minority races, cultures and religions, and older Canadians. The prohibition against discrimination under provincial human rights statutes has in the past 15 years been extended from issues of employment for those with physical handicaps to include services, facilities and accommodation for people with both mental and physical handicaps – making these statutes a much more expansive instrument of rights protections. Canada is also signatory to a number of international agreements which affirm political, social and economic rights for people with disabilities, including the United Nations Universal Declaration of Human Rights (1948); the United Nations Convention on the Rights of the Child (1989); the United Nations World Programme of Action Concerning Disabled Persons (1983); the UN Declaration on the Rights of Disabled Persons

---

2   Section 15 'Equality Rights' in the Charter of Rights and Freedoms provides that all persons are equal before and under the law without discrimination on grounds including physical and mental disability.

(1975); and the United Nations Standard Rules on the Equalisation of Opportunities for Persons with Disabilities (1993). Established in the post-war period, these agreements provide a set of international commitments to guide nation states in the pursuit of social well-being.

A new framework for citizenship and social well-being

The emergence of a new framework for social well-being in Canada is rooted, then, in a number of developments in the post-war period: the obligations found in human rights protections established in the past 50 years; the universal entitlements of the post-war welfare state; and the established critique of the worthy/unworthy poor distinction as a basis of state provision. The key elements of the new framework are self-determination, democratisation, and equality. In the Canadian context, these principles are reflected in statutory instruments such as the Canadian Charter of Rights and Freedoms, the recently repealed Canada Assistance Plan, statutory human rights provisions, the Canada Health Act (which aims to ensure universal access to needed health care), and employment equity legislation that seeks to secure greater equality in employment for women, aboriginal persons, persons with disabilities and visible minorities.

Together these statutory instruments and provisions articulate the social, economic and political foundations that are considered in Canada to be necessary for the well-being of individuals, communities and society as a whole. They establish basic protections which respect the integrity of individuals, communities and Canadian society. They define the decision-making processes to enable participation and to respect the integrity of diverse groups. As well, these provisions recognise the importance of fairness and distributive justice in society. The guiding principle which these provisions articulate to ensure respect and integrity is that of self-determination. To guide the formation of decision-making processes, appeal is made to the principle of democratisation. To guide a fair distribution of benefits and advantages in Canadian society, these instruments declare the principle of equality.

People, communities and societies hold the principle of self-determination as one of their most cherished values. Claiming and exercising the right to self-determination can enable them to make choices that realise their vision for a good life and a good society. In a society increasingly defined by cultural, linguistic, ethnic and other differences, the promotion of self-determination is essential if there is a commitment to respecting these differences. Without mutual respect for self-determination these differences become the basis for conflict rather than dialogue and cooperation. The exercise of self-determination is not simply a good idea from a sociological perspective; its importance to the very definition of what it means to be a person has been recognised for centuries in ethics and in law (Kymlicka 1989). However, it cannot be the only element of a framework for social well-being, because people and groups cannot be self-determining all on their own. People with disabilities and many groups experience frustration because they continually encounter institutional barriers to exercising self-determination. The traditional categorical and targeted pro- grammes established for people with disabilities under the welfare state in Canada have for the most part removed their rights to self-determination, and vested decision-making authority in government bureaucrats who administer social assistance, or government social workers, community service providers, and public and private guardians.

The basis for the social commitment to self-determination is articulated in the international human rights instruments to which Canada is a signatory, and in the rights entrenched in the Charter of Rights and Freedoms to life, liberty and security of the person. Commitments to collective rights of self-determi- nation are also embedded in the Constitution and the Charter.

Democratisation is a second element of the framework which began to emerge for social well-being. The struggles through which diverse people and groups in Canada have sought to obtain recognition for themselves and for their aims have been defined as, 'the politics of recognition' (Taylor 1992). Democratisation makes a constructive politics of recognition possible. It goes beyond the conventional meaning of the term 'democracy' and refers to the process of enabling the democratic participation of individuals and diverse groups in a wide scope of decision-making processes that directly affect their lives and their well-being. Seeking and granting recognition to diverse groups and regions in public policy decisions are very much a part of our history and continue to be at the heart of the dilemmas of public policy and politics in Canada (Drover and Kerans 1993). The underlying principle of a democratised government, society and economy is participation in decision-making. The economy would not rest on 'global forces' or 'market pressures'. It would rest on the idea that economies should serve people and communities. It would assume that social and economic equality is the norm by which economic arrangements are to be judged in order to challenge the inequalities fostered by current arrangements (Heilbroner 1992).

Social well-being is achieved in a society where democratisation is an integrating force. There are existing obligations and commitments in Canadian society that provide the foundation for democratisation. The right to vote, collective bargaining arrangements, and individual and collective rights en- trenched in the Charter, are all important aspects of this foundation. Canada's first Constitution in 1867 provided a foundation for democratisation and mutual recognition by granting status in institutions and decision-making processes to both French and English communities. The process of democratis- ing institutions to give greater representation to the communities that make up Canada has continued. Québécois and aboriginal nationalist movements have sought recognition for their cultural and linguistic differences and have sought forms of collective representation in order to improve their status. Their claims have challenged conventional interpretations of equality rights, the federal state and the collective rights the state should recognise (Jenson 1993).

Equality is the third element of social well-being, when it is defined as the absence of barriers to mutual respect and recognition between people, 'who are equally free from political control, social pressure and economic deprivation and insecurity to engage in valued pursuits, and who have equal access to the means of self-development' (Lukes 1980, p.218). To a large extent, our institutions are not designed to enable this kind of equality to be practised in our society. This is largely because the 'formal' interpretation of equality that has predominated in public policy and court rulings requires treating similar cases in similar ways. However, this formal interpretation no longer responds to the demands for equality made by diverse groups in Canadian society. It is difficult, if not impossible, to claim that people with disabilities are 'situated' in society in the same way as people without disabilities.

Challenges to this formal understanding of equality have been advanced in recent years (Smith 1986). Since the introduction of the equality provisions of the Canadian Charter of Right and Freedoms (Canada 1982), courts in Canada have begun to rewrite the standards of equality. In particular, significant judgements have been handed down by the Supreme Court of Canada,[3] such as that of *Andrews v. Law Society of British Columbia*.[4] In that judgement, the Supreme Court determined that the principle of equality does not necessarily imply similar treatment; it may require treating people differently. In this view, the differences arising from nationality, gender, race and ethnicity, religious belief, disability and so on, are not a reason to deny people the support they need to exercise their self-determination. If people are to exercise self-determination, institutions in society should be structured to recognise, respect and support the presence of diverse languages, identities and cultures (Kymlicka 1989; Young 1990).

This evolving framework for citizenship and social well-being has provided the basis for overturning 400 years of law and policy which has resulted in exclusion for people with disabilities. The impact of the legal entrenchment of this framework has been both direct and indirect. Successful legal challenges have been important; so too have been the indirect ways in which the legal entrenchment of rights has influenced policy and attitudes. There has been a shift away from the traditional way of viewing people with disabilities and the introduction of much more systemic analysis of the discrimination they face. The notion that disability is a result of individual pathology has given way to,

---

3   The Supreme Court of Canada is Canada's highest court. Cases heard in lower courts, including the provincial Supreme Courts, can be appealed to higher courts, ultimately to the Supreme Court of Canada for a final judgement.

4   *Andrews v. Law Society of British Columbia* (1989) 1 SCR 143; 56 DLR (4th).

at the least, a nominal recognition of the roots of inequality in the state organisation of environmental and social relationships.

There are many examples of this shift in Canada. For instance, in the early 1990s a federal government House of Commons committee was mandated with the investigation of human rights and disability, a contrast to earlier such committees mandated with responsibility for health and disability. Legal and policy questions have been raised about the fairness of keeping people in segregated workshops. Provincial and federal governments have developed policies that plan for the closure of large institutions. Governments are beginning to establish legislative and policy provisions for 'assisted' and 'supported' decision-making as an alternative to the removal of rights through guardianship.[5] Hospitals are being challenged, legally and ethically, on their policies of refusing treatment to new-borns and other persons with severe disabilities (Endicott 1988, 1990). Protocols have been introduced by some provincial attorneys-general to ensure that people with intellectual and other disabilities can give evidence in court and therefore receive the same access to justice as others (see, for example, Deparment of the Attorney General and Department of the Solicitor General 1991).

Successful legal challenges to the denial of rights have also been forthcoming in the past 15 years. In 1986, the Supreme Court of Canada ruled in the *Eve* case that people who have an intellectual disability cannot be required to undergo sterilisation, for non-medical reasons, where such a procedure is authorised by any third party, including parents or next of kin, the Public Trustee or the administrator of a facility. This judgement was made on the basis that such an intrusion on the rights of a person could never be in their best interests.[6]

In 1983, the Supreme Court of British Columbia ruled that Stephen Dawson, a six-year-old boy, had the right to life-sustaining medical treatment to which his parents had refused their consent.[7] In 1982, an Ontario District Court judge denied an application by Justin Clark's parents to have him declared mentally incompetent so his father could be designated as his guardian and prevent Justin from exercising his choice to leave the institution where he had been for all his 18 years and live with friends in Ottawa.[8]

---

5   The governments of Manitoba and the Northwest Territories have recently passed legislation enabling persons to use assistance in decision-making as an alternative to meeting the strict and exclusionary standards of competence. How far such provisions go in enabling people with intellectual disabilities to maintain their rights to self-determination remains to be seen.

6   *Re Eve* (1986) 2 SCR 388.

7   *Re Stephen Dawson* (1983) 3 WWR 618 (BC Supreme Court).

8   *Clark v Clark* (1982) 40 OR (2d) 383 (Co.Ct.).

In 1987 a basic democratic right of citizenship was restored to those with an intellectual disability when the Federal Court of Canada struck down the clause in the Canada Elections Act that disqualified from exercising the right to vote every person, 'who [was] restrained of his liberty of movement or deprived of the management of his property by reason of mental disease'.

In January 1991, the Quebec Human Rights Commission found the administration of Pavillon Saint-Théophile of Laval, an institution for people with an intellectual disability, guilty of exploiting its residents. The 88 people who lived in the centre were awarded $1 million to be split between them: $700,000 in compensation for moral damages for enduring humiliation and attacks on their dignity; and $300,000 in compensation for the intentional exploitation to which they had been submitted. The administration of the centre was found to have misused government funds and to have treated residents in a manner described as, 'punishment, deprivation and infantilisation'. The case established that justice for people with disabilities includes treating them with respect and protecting their fundamental rights.[9]

The recent Ontario Court of Appeal decision in the *Eaton* case found that denying a choice for a child with an intellectual disability to go to the neighbourhood school was not an issue of pedagogical theory, or even the right to education, but was in substance a denial of the equality right found in the Charter of Rights and Freedoms.[10]

All of these legal cases reflect a shift towards ensuring the social well-being of people with disabilities: their self-determination; participation in decisions that affect their person and their life; and equality with others regardless of their differences.

Policy directions for income and social services

With a new conceptual and legal framework in place to challenge the exclusionary legacy of the welfare state, people with disabilities and their advocacy organisations are challenging how income support and social services are funded and delivered – the mainstays of the welfare state in Canada. It is well recognised that the 'system' of providing for disability-related income and other supports to the over four million Canadians with disabilities is sorely in need of reform. The reforms to date have been characterised more by 'hit and miss' than by a coordinated and just approach to the allocation of benefits. For example, some programmes can compensate for lost wages in the event of disability, such as Workers' Compensation, Unemployment Insurance Sickness Benefits, Canada Pension Plan Disability Benefits, private long-term disability

---

9   Commission des droits del personne du Quebec c Centre d'accueil Pavillon
    St-Théophile (1991), 16 CHRR D/124.
10 *Eaton v Brant (County) Board of Education* (1995) 22 OR 93D)1.

insurance and auto insurance. Disability-related social services and other benefits may be available under Canada Assistance Plan-funded programmes (for example, supports funded by welfare dollars) and extended health care arrangements. Still other programmes focus on promoting the labour market integration of individuals with disabilities who qualify, by providing vocational counselling services, funding for vocational training and job-finding assistance, resources for accommodating the work place, and financing on-the-job personal supports.

Each of the many programmes that contain provisions for persons with disabilities has its own means of determining whether individuals have disabilities, the extent and form of disability and the levels of benefit for which they qualify. Individuals are denied access to necessary supports on grounds as diverse as their age, the cause, nature and severity of their condition, their attachment to the labour market and their involvement in training or education. Where individuals do not have access to necessary supports, they often find themselves denied a myriad of other opportunities for personal development, social participation, economic security and well-being.

How, then, should the currently confused, administratively costly, cumbersome and inconsistent policy and programme arrangements be re-conceptualised and re-designed in order to be more consistent with the framework for citizenship and social well-being that has emerged in the past 20 years and been outlined in this chapter? Building upon a number of policy studies and policy positions outlined by disability organisations in Canada (The Roeher Institute 1988, 1990, 1992, 1993), the model outlined in this chapter proposes an integrated policy framework and delivery system to cover direct costs that are specifically related to disability and to ensure the delivery of disability-related supports that are appropriate to individual requirements (Rioux and Crawford 1994).

Because the programme would be designed to promote equality of social and economic participation of Canadians with disabilities, it would be a national programme but could be provincially administered. Programme criteria would ensure responsiveness to individual requirements, accessibility, equity and portability of support, geographically and from situation to situation; and be publicly supported. These criteria would provide a basis for clear, enforceable national programme standards.

The proposed system would provide support for the additional costs of disability. It would target persons who are not eligible for Workers' Compensation, who are not privately insured in the event of disability, who are not eligible for disability compensation under war veterans' programmes, or whose disability pension or insurance coverage is inadequate to address their disability-related requirements.

The system would not be a basic income support programme. Instead, disability-related policy and programmes would be removed entirely from a welfare framework. This would give an alternative to the many people with disabilities who have no option but to apply for welfare in order to qualify for essential disability supports. Through the new programme arrangements proposed here, such individuals would be able to qualify for the attendant services, personal support workers, wheelchairs and other supports they require without programme criteria that deny them access to the labour force, adult training, educational upgrading and other social and economic opportunities that are available to the non-disabled public. Structuring programmes in this manner goes at least some way to breaking the welfare state legacy of the worthy poor and the concomitant segregationist and institutionalised practice and provision.

Individuals with disabilities whose income for basic necessities falls below the established social minimum[11] would, like other persons and on equal terms, have access to welfare programmes. However, because disability-related supports would be provided through an entirely different system designed to maximise individuals' social and economic inclusion and participation, we anticipate that, over time, significant numbers of people with disabilities who are now attached to the welfare system would find a much greater proportion of their income through participation in the paid labour market. In other words, we are suggesting a cost-effective policy and programme approach to disability that, in time, has the potential to reduce welfare expenditures. There is evidence of increased labour force participation of people with even severe disabilities when their needs for support are adequately met (The Roeher Institute 1992).

It is in separating the funding of disability-related supports from the restrictive and exclusionary welfare system, that a basis can be established for a system that promotes social well-being. The model that we propose involves two basic elements, each with a distinct funding allocation stream:

- demand-side funding: dollars would flow to consumers who would use these dollars to acquire the support and services they need. In economic terms these dollars would be the means of generating effective 'demand' in an evolving 'market' of human services

- supply-side funding: dollars would flow to providers of disability-related social services and other supports, thereby generating and sustaining the capacity to respond to consumer demand.

---

11 Currently, the 12 Canadian provinces and territories have established 12 different formulations of an acceptable social minimum. However, the underlying commonality is the assumption that if a person's income is less than what they require for basic necessities such as food, shelter and utilities, the individual has a legitimate claim on state largesse if they have no other access to income. These key provisions are entrenched in federal law under the Canada Assistance Plan. Provinces are at liberty to interpret these provisions as they see fit. Accordingly, the size of provincial/territorial largesse, and the formulae for calculating the income threshold below which 'need' is presumed valid, vary considerably from region to region.

Demand-side funding

Funding the demand side is an adaptation of 'individualised funding', a notion that has been widely discussed in the disability community and has received considerable attention in policy circles. A significant proportion of funding would be 'attached' directly to individuals who face disability-related costs. This has proven to be an effective means of making social services more responsive and accountable to consumer demand (The Roeher Institute 1993). It introduces market forces and related efficiencies, lacking at present, into the social services sector. It is a means of containing costs in the sense that funds are allocated to actual requirements of individuals and over-serving can thereby be avoided.[12] Demand-side funding has the additional advantage of providing enormous social and economic flexibility to the individuals being funded.

Three kinds of arrangement could be used for the purpose of recommending to government the suitability of individual claims for funding:

1. Self-articulation: people with disabilities or their advocates fill out a 'Support Schedule'[13] themselves and provide this directly to the government claims settlement.

2. Community review: people with disabilities consult with counsellors or staff in community organisations that are accredited by government to review claims and to make recommendations to government claims settlement concerning eligibility for funding.[14]

---

12 The inflexibility of funding mechanisms and programme requirements has meant that people with disabilities are often required by service agencies to use support options (for example, 24 hour care in a residential facility) where more independent living arrangements and reduced levels of paid support would meet their individual needs.

13 The Support Schedule would itemise commonly utilised human and other supports (for example, attendant services; wheelchairs). For each class of support (for example, human support), the Schedule would detail typical rates and unit costs at fair market values in local/regional economies. The Schedule would introduce elements of fairness and transparency, currently lacking, in terms of the total value of supports available to qualifying individuals with disabilities. The Schedule would also help individuals and community agencies prepare cost estimates that are reasonable.

14 The proposed funding model assumes that the final decision concerning the approval of funding will be made by government. Claims settlement officers would perform this role. However, they would base their decisions on recommendations by claims reviewers who operate at arm's length from government. In this way, the decision-making about the reasonableness of a given claim and about funding would not be driven principally by the funding system's internal pressures (for example, cost containment). System pressures currently drive much of the decision-making about supports because system counsellors, who often have little background in disability, are mandated with the decision-making role and typically do not consult others in the process.

3. Approved diagnostic assessments: on a fee-for-service basis, an accredited professional administers and interprets standardised tests and confirms that a particular good or service is required.

People with disabilities would have the discretion to choose the approach or approaches most appropriate to their circumstances. Applications under any of these arrangements would be at the individual's discretion. Each would be accorded equal status and authority, and none would be accorded preference.[15] Since funding decisions are ultimately a governmental responsibility, a government agency would be vested with the responsibility for settling claims. It would assess the overall 'fit' of stated requirements in relation to previous claims and 'typical' cases. People with disabilities would have the option of appealing any unfavourable decisions. Individuals would have access to a fair and efficient appeal process in the event that they have been denied access to a support they perceive as necessary. Individuals would also have access to an appeal when the supports for which they have been deemed eligible do not meet their perceived requirements. The appeal process would be conducted at arm's length from the department responsible for claims settlement and funding.

In order to ensure that consumers are spending disability-related support dollars in a manner consistent with their requirements, there would be a formal agreement (for example, a letter of understanding) between consumers and the government funder. The contract would set out how the funds are to be spent, reporting requirements and other standard features of contracting provisions. In the interests of efficiency, however, the contracts would be prepared in plain language to avoid unnecessary confusion and litigation costs. In the same way, contracts or letters of understanding should detail what consumers expect of providers, the terms and conditions of delivery, and so on.

People with disabilities would have the option of preparing their own contracts and letters of understanding or of engaging the services of community

---

15 However, it is likely that first-time claimants would require support for their claim, either by community reviewers (for example, representing persons with mobility impairments) or by some other assessor (for example, an optician). Without some form of external validation for a claim, government officials would be unlikely to authorise funding unless they were to conduct their own detailed review of the claim. The proposal aims to move government officials out of the detailed claim review process except where a particular claim seems anomalous or where a community review process/assessor is forwarding unusually high numbers of anomalous claims.

Once it has been established that an individual's requirements are stable (for example, they have a permanent disability resulting from a spinal cord injury that requires a given level of attendant services weekly and a particular mobility device), there should be no problem in the individual by-passing the detailed review/assessment process and simply filing their claim for settlement. In fact, this would be the most efficient and cost-effective route, administratively speaking. A limited number of random, detailed audits could be conducted to ensure effective resource management, in much the same way that the Canadian tax system accountability measures operate.

agencies for assistance. They would also have the option of making their own
logistical arrangements with service providers or of enlisting the services of
community agencies for this purpose. That is, individuals who prefer to
self-manage their supports without assistance from others would have the
option of doing so.

Individuals whose requirements are funded would have the latitude to
negotiate favourable terms from service providers and vendors of devices within
the parameters of their costed support package. Individuals would also have the
latitude to hire individuals who are not on staff with a providing agency,
including family members, to provide support services.

The demand-side funding arrangements proposed here would contribute to
the achievement of social well-being in a number of ways. It would provide
individuals with the means by which to make decisions about the nature of the
disability-related supports they require and how these would be delivered. It
would increase the opportunities for people with disabilities and their organisations to participate in decisions about the allocation of funding disability-related supports through the community review process. Finally, demand-side
funding would contribute to equality of outcomes for individuals by providing
a basic entitlement to disability-related supports in a manner responsive to
individual need and choice.

Supply-side funding

Exclusive reliance on demand-side funding (i.e. funds directly allocated to
consumers) to finance the supply of disability-related community services
would be unwise and unworkable for several reasons. First, consumers would
be left with much, if not all, of the responsibility of identifying and arranging
for needed supports if services to assist with such logistics were not already
funded and available in the community. Many consumers are not in a position
or are disinclined to spend what may amount to considerable time, skill and
effort to make such arrangements.

In addition, the supply of disability-related services would hinge largely on
how effectively people with disabilities were able to network with one another,
to organise amongst themselves a coherent aggregate demand for specific
services, and to 'market' their collective spending power to potential service
providers. The mere presence of a service delivery system ought not to depend
chiefly on the ability or willingness of people with disabilities to engage in such
efforts.

In the absence of organised public commitment to a basic infrastructure of
services, the entire field of disability-related social services would also be
extremely unstable and vulnerable to cash flow crises. Some services would
simply go out of business due to mismanagement or periodic, unavoidable
fluctuations in consumer demand, regardless of how well those services might
be addressing the needs of particular individuals at any given moment. Critical

gaps in service would also likely persist, especially in thinly populated areas of the country.

Given the limitation of demand-side funding, some ongoing public provision must be made to ensure that a range of disability-related services are available for consumers to purchase. This can be facilitated without mitigating the principle that the capacity of services to thrive will depend primarily on the extent of consumer demand. The proposed means of ensuring a range of services is for government to provide direct transfers to cover *administrative* (including clerical, managerial, secretarial, training and retraining) expenses of service providers. Individuals with disabilities, using funds allocated to them under the programme, would provide the user fees that would be the critical determinant of service providers' ongoing economic viability. To the extent that consumers actually use services, the services can flourish. To the degree that consumer demand is lacking, the core funding commitment for the providers can be reviewed and reallocated to other organisations as warranted.[16]

Service providers could be funded on an annual cycle and be subject to in-depth review every five years. Clear service standards would be developed and used as a means of guiding the service review. Consumer evaluation and feedback mechanisms would be implemented to assist in the programme review process. Eligible agencies and organisations would include those that specialise and provide services in the field of disability, including self-help and representative (for example, advocacy) organisations. However, agencies and organisations that do not currently have the capacity to focus on disability, but which seek to develop such a capacity, would also be eligible. That is, a generic service agency such as a provider of homemaker or counselling services that can adapt its operations and demonstrate a capacity to meet the needs of persons with disabilities effectively would qualify for core funding. This would provide a means of building general community capacity to include and facilitate the participation of people with disabilities effectively, to further the goals of integration. The size of the core grant would be linked to the anticipated level of consumer usage.

The community services for which a publicly funded supply-side commitment is required to cover *administrative* (including secretarial, managerial,

---

16 In all likelihood, consumers would opt to purchase services from the most competent and responsive providers available to them. Service-providing organisations would have some incentives, therefore, to ensure the professional development of their respective labour pools. They would also have some incentives to ensure good relations between agency management and labour so that negative spill-over effects of sour relations do not result in a weakening of consumer demand. In the event that the providing organisation is unionised, the union would have some incentives to examine its demands to ensure these are compatible with the requirements of the people it is serving.

clerical, training and retraining) expenses, but which would depend largely on consumer demand for their economic viability, include:

- services to assist individuals with disabilities with the planning, contracting and logistical requirements they face whilst attempting to secure necessary supports

- attendant, communication and other personal services

- rehabilitation services

- counselling services to assist individuals and families to come to terms with the impact of disability

- labour market integration and work activity services for individuals who face unusual difficulties integrating into the paid labour market

- consultation services that are required to assist employers, public and private programmes to devise accommodations that will enable people with disabilities to participate on equal terms with others.

To ensure that communities systematically anticipate, plan for and make adequate provision for the disability-related services that will be required in the future, research data and analysis are also essential. Communities must have regular access to data concerning the disability-related requirements that are already present and funded in a given locale. The tracking and analysis of long-range trends in the demand for, and utilisation of, formally organised disability-related social services is also needed.

Aggregate data from agencies mandated to review and recommend eligibility, as well as data from claims settlement, would be systematically organised and made available to communities for the purposes of forecasting and planning. On the basis of their analysis, they would make recommendations to government concerning the kinds and volume of organised services that are likely to be required at a given point in the future, with the associated budgetary implications. Relevant community organisations in the disability and social services sector would have to be mandated for this purpose.

We consider the data gathering, analysis, community forecasting and planning functions to be essential services. Accordingly, we propose that they be funded entirely as such by government. The agencies mandated to conduct these research services would be accountable to government and to local communities, including persons with disabilities and their respective organisations. In particular, the input of people with disabilities would be sought on how effectively the organisations mandated with the research and forecasting roles are performing those functions.

A sustained public review and funding commitment is also required to ensure that generic services and opportunities in the community (for example, recreation programmes, employment centres and post-secondary educational institutions) are adapted to facilitate the participation of people with disabilities; and so that new services and opportunities are designed on the premise that people with disabilities will have equitable access in the first instance. A broad review of the community's capacity to include persons with disabilities would be conducted in conjunction with the review and forecasting of demand for specialised services that focus on disability. However, we propose that the financing of this broader review not be derived from dollars that are earmarked for the individual cost offset programme, or for the development of community services that have a particular focus on disability.

The proposal, then, looks for a new approach to supply-side funding. We maintain that it is no longer acceptable for the state to invest the major share of public resources in services, then require individuals with disabilities to queue up for those services, with the providers acting as the gatekeepers to public support. Instead, the proposal calls for supply-side funding that will ensure the availability of services but on terms and conditions that ensure the system is responsive to the consumer's legitimate aspirations for self-determination, democratisation and equality. The supply-side arrangements would also ensure that the state has an ongoing capacity to anticipate future demand for services and to make appropriate provision for that eventuality. Provinces are at liberty to interpret these provisions as they see fit. Accordingly, the size of provincial/territorial largesse, and the formulae for calculating the income threshold below which 'need' is presumed valid, vary considerably from region to region.

Conclusion

A social security system that is designed to meet the needs of those who have been excluded from social and economic participation will support the greater needs of society generally and allow all citizens to participate together in the social well-being of Canadians. We believe that the proposed model for reforming the provision of disability-related supports is a timely and realistic means of achieving those objectives. An integrated policy framework and delivery system to cover direct costs that are specifically related to disability would ensure the delivery of disability-related supports in a way that secures self-determination and is appropriate to individual requirements. In this, our model moves beyond the rigidities imposed by the present system and focuses on what works rather than on what does not work. The rigidities imposed by the extant system with its paternalistic, welfarist, institutionalising, and segregating impacts may, through the above model, be transformed so that the principles of self-determination, democratisation and equality come to characterise the lives of people with disabilities.

Canadians with and without disabilities can achieve citizenship and social well-being through a policy framework that permits social, environmental and occupational inclusion for all members. A coordinated policy approach to ensuring the well-being of people with disabilities both depends on, and

mandates, cooperative partnerships amongst individuals, governments, voluntary organisations and professionals. It is through such an approach that
citizenship can become a reality rather than an elusive ideal for people with
disabilities.

References

Canada (1982) Charter of rights and freedoms. Part I of the Constitution Act, 1982,
being Schedule B to the Canada Act 1982 (UK), Ch11.

Department of the Attorney General and Department of the Solicitor General (1991)
*Protocol for Investigation and Prosecution of Cases Involving Persons with Special
Communication Needs.* Nova Scotia: 12 April 1991.

Drover, G. and Kerans, P. (eds) (1993) *New Approaches to Welfare Theory.* Aldershot:
Edward Elgar Publishing Company.

Endicott, O. (1988) 'It is still a capital offence to have Downs Syndrome.' *Entourage 3,*
3, Summer, 17–22.

Endicott, O. (1990) *The Right of Persons with Intellectual Handicaps to Receive Medical
Treatment.* Toronto: Canadian Association for Community Living, January.

Heilbroner, R. (1992) *Twenty-First Century Capitalism.* Concord (Ont): Anansi Press.

Jenson, J. (1993) *Deconstructing Dualities: Making Rights Claims in Political Institutions.*
Prepared for a Seminar in Social Welfare Theory, Aylmer, Quebec.

Kymlicka, W. (1989) *Liberalism, Community, and Culture.* Oxford: Clarendon Press.

Lukes, S. (1980) 'Socialism and equality.' In J. Sterba (ed) *Justice: Alternative Political
Perspectives.* Belmont (Calif): Wadsworth Publishing Company.

Marshall, T.H. (1963) 'Citizenship and social class.' In T.H. Marshall (ed) *Sociology at
the Crossroads and Other Essays.* London: Heinemann.

National Council of Welfare (1987) *Welfare in Canada, The Tangled Safety Net: A Report
by the National Council of Welfare.* Ottawa: The National Council of Welfare.

Pascall, G. (1986) *Social Policy: A Feminist Analysis.* London: Tavistock Publications.

Rioux, M. (1993) 'Exchanging charity for rights: the challenge for the next decade.'
British Institute of Learning Disabilities No. 89, June.

Rioux, M. (1994) 'Towards a concept of equality of well-being: overcoming the
social and legal construction of inequality.' In M. Rioux and M. Bach (eds)
Disability is not Measles. Ontario: The Roeher Institute.

Rioux, M. and Crawford, C. (1994) *The Canadian Disability Resource Program: Offsetting
Costs of Disability and Assuring Access to Disability-Related Supports.* An Occasional
Paper, North York: The Roeher Institute.

Smith, L. (1986) 'A new paradigm for equality rights.' In L. Smith, G. Côté-Harper,
R. Elliot and M. Seydegart (eds) *Righting the Balance: Canada's New Equality Rights.*
Saskatoon: Canadian Human Rights Reporter.

Taylor, C. (1992) *Multiculturalism and 'The Politics of Recognition': An Essay.* Princeton
(NJ): Princeton University Press.

The Roeher Institute (1988) *Income Insecurity: The Disability Income System in Canada.*
North York (Ont): The Roeher Institute.

The Roeher Institute (1990) *Poor Places: Disability-Related Residential and Support Services.* North York (Ont): The Roeher Institute.

The Roeher Institute (1992) *On Target? Canada's Employment-Related Programmes for Persons with Disabilities.* North York (Ont): The Roeher Institute.

The Roeher Institute (1993) *Direct Dollars: A Study of Individualized Funding in Canada.* North York (Ont): The Roeher Institute.

Williams, F. (1989) *Social Policy: A Critical Introduction: Issues of Race, Gender, and Class.* Cambridge: Polity Press.

Young, I.M. (1990) *Justice and the Politics of Difference.* Princeton: Princeton University Press.

CHAPTER 12

Empowerment and the Limitations of Formal Human Services and Legislation

Errol Cocks and Judith Cockram

Introduction

In the late 20th century, people with disabilities, along with many other groups of citizens of Western society, are so deeply connected to, and embedded within, modern formal human service systems, that it is incomplete to contemplate their past, present or future without taking account of that context. It is certainly not possible to consider the issue of empowerment without analysing its context. An analysis taking account of the formal human service context may chronicle the reasons why people with disabilities need to be freed from the oppression of the 'imperial' service system. It may describe the struggles of the system to improve itself. Or it may assert the need for people with disabilities to try to remain outside the system.

Modern formal human services represent powerful social institutions. There are at least two views of this power. In one the overt purposes are to address the problem of certain groups of people who are perceived not to be easily assimilated into the values and life of modern Western cultures. Despite their long history, such services have grown in their power and influence since the Enlightenment and the adoption of materialistic science as a fundamental steering principle. Moreover, since World War II and the emergence of the 'serviced society' (McKnight 1976, 1986), the growth of service systems has accelerated so that for the first time in human history, there is major economic reliance upon them. It can therefore be considered that their primary concern has become the production of goods and services and the allocation of resources (Hoggett 1990).

Another view of human services lies in their conceptualisation as a major strategy for wealth recycling within our post-primary production patterns of labour through provision of services to both valued and impaired people (Wolfensberger 1989). At the same time, the power of these institutions has

been enhanced through the adoption of bureaucratic, professional and technological means, and a union with judicial sources of legitimacy. These purposes
are a far cry from a conception of human services as looking after the well-being
of vulnerable people and facilitating their empowerment and self-determination. Rather, there may be discerned in this view an implicit purpose around
the creation and maintenance of dependence and the control of social deviance.

Human service systems, however defined, remain shaped and governed by
many sources of legitimacy, possibly the most important of which is the law.
This is illustrated clearly in the concept of protective services that focus on both
formal service and legal frameworks to address limited capacity and vulnerability. Ferguson (1978) has provided a definition of such protective services:

> Adult protective services is one level of a comprehensive adult service
> system. It is a full access service that is distinguished by the 'protective'
> characteristics of the person served and uniquely, but not in every
> instance, involves a modulated substitution of the client's
> decision-making power by that of another person who is willing to
> use professional authority as well as legal and judicial authority to
> secure or to provide necessary medical, social, or legal services based
> on the least restrictive alternative and gradualism. (pp.37–38)

Two aspects of this definition are important here. The first is the high
correspondence between protective services and formal human services. The
second is the invocation of both professional and judicial authority. But there
remains a contradiction between the two. Habermas (1989a) wrote in considering the purposes of the role of the state in the welfare of its citizens:

> In short, a contradiction between its goals and its method is inherent
> in the welfare state project as such. Its goal is the establishment of forms
> of life that are structured in an egalitarian way and that at the same
> time open up arenas for individual self-realisation and spontaneity. But
> evidently this goal cannot be reached via the direct route of putting
> political programs into legal and administrative form. *Generating forms
> of life exceeds the capabilities of the medium of power* (emphasis added). (p.59)

This draws attention to the problem of the incoherency between means and
ends of modern formal human services which is the primary focus of this
chapter.

In this chapter we discuss a conceptualisation of empowerment that we
consider appropriate for the purpose of analysing the relationship between
people with learning disabilities and service systems. We then provide a brief
analysis of some of the key assumptions that underpin the high order bureaucratic, professional and technological models that make up the dominant
paradigm of modern formal human services as outlined previously. This is
discussed from the perspective of empowering people with learning disabilities.
Consideration is then given to three lower order models that strongly influence

contemporary human service practices: the 'economic/commercial', the 'rights' and the 'advocacy' models. Finally, the role of the law and legislation as a major strategy for human service reform is critically examined.

Empowerment

Since this chapter is about the relationship between empowerment and human services, we begin with a brief consideration of empowerment. This is a term that has become very trendy in contemporary disability literature, although its meaning is unclear and usually cloaked either in scepticism or romanticism. In the specific context of people with learning disabilities (and possibly universally), we suggest that empowerment consists of two basic freedoms: freedom from avoidable and unnecessary constraint, and freedom to develop towards one's human potential.

In a strategic sense, empowerment needs to be considered within three contexts: personal, systemic and societal. Thus, empowerment at a personal level means freedom from the avoidable constraints that come from one's impairments and from the limiting attitudes of other people; at the systemic level it means freedom from the misguided actions of formal human services and other social institutions; and at the societal level societal values and ideologies that promote vulnerability and disempowerment. This notion of empowerment is therefore based upon the idea that there are many people who experience heightened vulnerability and have special needs because of their impairments.

Following on from Wolfensberger and Thomas (1994), we suggest that there are four types of 'universally relevant liberating actions'. Since one source of disempowerment is dependency, an appropriate response is the enhancement of competency in order to promote a sufficient level of independent functioning. A related issue is that not all dependency is necessarily burdensome or disempowering – for example, the dependency of the young child on its parents or of ageing parents on their adult children. Whether or not dependence is perceived to be an acceptable or unacceptable human state will be influenced significantly by personal and societal ideologies on the matter. Arguably, dominant modernistic societal values around materialism and individualism mean that dependency is perceived to be an undesirable state even to the extent of denial of personal vulnerability or need. Independence could lead, for example, to children becoming more, rather than less, vulnerable. A second liberating strategy addresses the enhancement of people's social image in that a positive social image is likely to enable other liberating strategies to occur, such as more valued lifestyles. A third strategy is to remove unwarranted constraints and restrictions on people, particularly where these occur because of hostility, overprotection or the lack of recognition of personal capacities. The fourth strategy suggested by Wolfensberger and Thomas is addressing vulnerability through the voluntary commitments and collective actions of ordinary people.

In summary, empowerment needs to be addressed within personal, systemic and societal contexts in ways which avoid unnecessary constraints on the individual and which maximise their human potential. This freedom can be achieved by the enhancement of competence and social image, the removal of constraints and by mobilising voluntary commitment and collective action. Questions therefore arise as to whether human services can fulfil these roles, and whether the contradictions that we will argue exist between such services and legislation provide necessary conditions, means and ends to bring these to fruition. This requires a consideration of modern formal services, the law and the relationship between them.

The paradigm of modern formal human services

Human services are influenced by the particular set of circumstances which characterise modern Western society, particularly those that increase personal risk and vulnerability. There is a considerable body of literature that describes and interprets the current high level of social conflict experienced in Western cultures (see, for example, Bell 1973; Cocks 1987; Dicken 1986; Habermas 1989b; Korten 1984; Michael 1983; Williams 1982; Wolfensberger 1989). Much of the debate about the nature of modern society is incorporated in the literature on modernity and post-modernity (Sztompka 1993). Modern Western society is described as 'transitional' and 'turbulent'. Both characteristics contribute to heightened personal and social vulnerability for some groups of people.

In an analysis of the relationship between formal human services and society, Cocks (1994) defined societal turbulence as:

> ...social conditions which are characterised by a very high rate of social change that occurs in many fundamental areas of human experience simultaneously. Change occurs not only in the areas that are linked directly to technological transformations, for example, in transport and communications, but in patterns of living and in fundamental social institutions such as the family. In addition, critical challenges occur within the ethical and moral fabric...exemplified by the dilemmas in the area of socio-biology...where technological advances which assume an imperative to implementation, outstrip the capacity of people and social institutions such as the law to cope. Turbulence also incorporates increasing complexity and the uncertainty that confronts society, for example, in the depletion of natural resources, lessened public confidence in traditionally-respected public institutions and the apparent rise in social problems such as poverty, unemployment and crime. (pp.18–19)

Within this context, a dominant paradigm of modern formal human services has emerged that consists of the assumptions and resulting practices and outcomes associated with three powerful societal models – bureaucracy, professionalism and technology. A model is conceptualised here to mean a framework, useful to describe and analyse human services, consisting of a set of beliefs and assumptions about important and relevant issues. These issues include high order beliefs about the nature of 'humanness' and society and about the nature of and the solutions to the problems being addressed, as well as those people to whom such solutions are directed. A model also includes processes or methods by which service content is provided; and outcomes for people and society. We are indebted to Wolfensberger and Thomas (1994), who developed this framework. The bureaucratic, professional and technological models are relatively high order models in the sense of influencing society broadly and not only human services. An examination of some of the assumptions of these models places the notion of empowerment of vulnerable people in context. It also places in view the contradictions between formal human services and the nature of empowerment as outlined in our introduction. Cocks (1994) described ten such assumptions:

- Modern formal human services are based on an assumption of personal and community inadequacy. Amongst other consequences, this has contributed to a focus on seeking out that inadequacy, giving high legitimacy and power to formal processes that measure and document that inadequacy, and, through processes of role expectancy and circularity, fostering learned helplessness. This assumption has also contributed to social policies that have removed vulnerable people from their perceived inadequate communities and families, given power to formal systems and subjugated personal freedoms.

- Formal human services are perceived to be essential in addressing human and social problems. This has encouraged the handover of responsibilities that traditionally have been the province of the individual, family or some other informal institution, to formal human services in their various guises. Formal approaches are likely to be accorded more authority than informal systems which are then likely to be disempowered and disenfranchised.

- Objectivity is perceived to be a necessary characteristic of good services. This assumption is inherent in each of the three contributory models: bureaucracy, through its historical effort to overcome particularism and nepotism and move towards universalism and equal treatment; professionalism, through the requirement of detachment; and technology, through its derivation in positivistic science. The implications include a suspicion that personal involvement and rewards for human service practitioners are inversely proportional to their distance from the client, that is, the further removed the better the reward.

- Human and social problems require professional help, in part because such problems are very complex and beyond the capacity of ordinary people to comprehend or master. This assumption, in concert with others, contributes to the ever-increasing degrees of specialisation and complexity in the human resource functions of formal human services, the establishment of complex and specialised industrial systems to meet the needs of those specialists, and the tendency for goal displacement from addressing of client to addressing of system needs.

- Modern formal human services are based on the assumption of the necessity for large-scale and centralised planning and intervention. The tendency of formal systems is to get larger, even when overt policies may speak of dispersal of services and decentralisation of decision making. At the same time, a view is established of small, localised and informal efforts as being wasteful and redundant. There is more likely to be concern for economies of scale rather than diseconomies of large scale.

- A major purpose of human services is assumed to be the efficient management of human and social problems, especially through the application of technological, managerial interventions. The management rather than the solution to problems may contain an implicit assumption that the problems cannot be solved, or at least are beyond the capabilities of formal systems to do so. A particularly dysfunctional characteristic associated with this assumption is the incessant organisational restructuring occurring in modern formal human services that incurs considerable policy and personnel discontinuity and cost.

- Modern formal human services are assumed to be more efficient and effective if they are content- or value-free. This assumption, actually built into the policies and practices of most large government human service bureaucracies in Australia (for example, the senior executive services of many Australian public services), adopts the approach of naive positivism in which informality and explicit, positive human values are likely to be disparaged. Associated closely with this assumption is the belief in the importance of management 'science' and the adoption of pragmatic social policies.

- There is a clear assumption that modern formal human services are necessarily very expensive and that the major imperative for funders is to seek financial efficiencies (perhaps through policies of

privatisation and market-based social policies). For providers, the
imperative is to acquire more funding.

- Although services pursue explicit policies of equity, in fact the
  paradigm assumes correctly, given the characteristics of the total
  system, that there will never be sufficient resources to provide for
  need and therefore some people must wait for services and others
  will never receive them. Solutions are less likely to be seen in a
  diagnosis of iatrogenic problems such as the underpinning service
  models, than they are to be put down to resource shortages.

- Finally, modern formal human services operate in an intensely
  political environment in which there are multiple stakeholders, as
  many as possible of whom must be appeased. In this situation,
  particularly without strong advocacy, people who are weak,
  powerless and vulnerable are unlikely to be given high priority
  within this market.

In summary it can be contended that there is a drift towards increased
professionalisation, bureaucratisation and technological solutions. This drift
acts, not to remove constraints and restrictions, but rather to intensify them; it
acts as a vacuum drawing in the attachments and relations which are antecedent
to voluntary commitment and collective action; and, in accomplishing this 'drift
to disempowerment' it also accomplishes the negative social image associated
with the ownership of people with learning disabilities by the segregated
human service systems.

Human service models

The 'drift to disempowerment' is characterised by the increase in bureaucratisation, professionalisation and increased technology. But within this drift,
human service workers have over the past two decades begun to move away
from their association with the medical model and developmental models of
disability towards other models. We will discuss three that are strongly influencing human service policies and practices and which impact on empowerment
issues: the economic/commercial model; the rights model; and the advocacy
model.

The economic/commercial model

Since the 1980s, the economic/commercial model has been growing in
influence in policy, legislation and practice in human services. This is not the
first time. Wolfensberger (1975) described the 'economisation' period in North
American institutions in the late 19th century during which institutions became
larger and, utilising the labour of inmates, more self-sufficient in the quest for
financial efficiency. This movement overlapped with the period of the 'indict-

ment' in which people with learning disabilities and others became the targets of the eugenics movement. Although history may not repeat itself in any precise manner, we would be foolish to discount the past in denying the possibility of a modern equivalent of the 'indictment' or a new eugenics effort, allied with the growth of socio-biological technological imperatives.

The model is well illustrated by the following extract from the annual report of a large human service bureaucracy in Australia:

> [The agency] now employs just over 7,500 full-time equivalent staff, more than 6,500 of them engaged in direct service to many tens of thousands of individual clients in the course of a year. Many of these clients receive intensive, individually planned and often costly customised services. No two clients make identical demands on the system. [The agency's] 'production lines' share a common logic with a manufacturing 'custom shop', building one-off products to order, but employing mass production methods to a significant extent. Whether the product is physical objects or human services, the logic of organisation and control is identical (Community Services Victoria 1991, p.5)

The economic/commercial model conceives of people with disabilities as 'customers' who know what they need and whose needs should be satisfied. The major problem addressed by this model is insufficient resources to meet their demand. In the context of human services, an interesting conundrum is created by the notion that service provision is actually 'supply-driven', that is, reflecting the dominance of the service providers. Nevertheless, the solution to the problem, no matter whether caused by demand or supply, is perceived to be better managed resources. This leads directly to managerial solutions largely focused on organisational and system restructuring. There is a long list of these measures, most of which originated in business schools (for example, management by objectives, zero-based budgeting, strategic management, total quality management, quality assurance).

The nature of reform promoted by this model draws heavily on economic concepts and measures. The disability field becomes a market, or more accurately, a 'quasi-market' (Hoggett 1990; Le Grand 1993), because in fact it cannot operate as a true market in the conventional sense largely because the customers actually exert little influence, are represented by the very agents who constitute the market, and are presented with little real choice. Other contemporary trends include the user paying, purchaser–provider splits (which essentially redistribute power and influence between those who already have it), and case-mix whereby quality is defined in terms of average unit service costs and equated with quantity of output. This model has spawned many service technologies around planning processes (for example, individual programme, education or habilitation plans; general and individual service plans; lifestyle plans, personal futures plans); and the 'management' of customers (for example, case management and service brokerage). At the organisational level, the economic/commercial model is hard at work ensuring that human services are constantly restructured, outsourced, downscaled and decentralised, whilst human resource and financial and strategic management components of formal human services burgeon as demand for their services increases to manage and control the confusion.

There are many issues associated with this model, with three being of particular importance. First, the perception of vulnerable, powerless people as 'customers' is very problematic. Our perception is that this model has encouraged a move away from acknowledging the role of actual knowledge and experience of disability towards a technical, objectified, 'human values-free' notion of human service. People are perceived to be 'units' and commodities, a view of human beings that denies their 'humanness' and is hardly concerned with issues of empowerment. As the individual is commodified so the person at the centre of empowerment is subjugated to the quasi-market system.

Second, the central strategy is fine-tuning a system that may in fact be intrinsically dysfunctional in order to make it more efficient, and third a major concern with the implementation of this model within a broader context of economic rationalism and cost-cutting is in fully meeting the needs and wishes of people who are very vulnerable or who have high support needs. It is simply uneconomical to serve this group properly. Le Grand (1993) refers to this as the incentive for the service system to engage in 'cream skimming' and 'problem dumping' (pp.20–22).

The rights model

The rights model is arguably the most significant contemporary influence on modern policy and legislation, although we believe that the economic/commercial model is on the verge of taking its place. The rights model is based on certain implicit assumptions, some of which are allied to those underpinning empowerment. People with disabilities are perceived to be 'consumers' (the term illustrating how closely this and the economic/commercial model are related), whose human and consumer rights must be respected. This model conceptualises the central problem as being the denial of those rights by society and its institutions. Amongst the most important of rights is that of 'choice'. This may even take precedence over protection from harm. The solution proposed by this model is to implement measures that guarantee that rights are respected and more choice is provided. The major strategies of the rights model incorporate social policy, rights covenants and legislative development, focusing on social justice, equity and access, equal opportunity and anti-discrimination. Desired outcomes are that consumers' rights are respected, that they are 'empowered', and that they achieve a good 'quality of life'.

Some key issues with this model include the following:

- To what extent are assumptions about 'consumers' applicable to people who are vulnerable and limited in power and influence?

- This model may contain a somewhat naive, over-reliance on the efficacy of formal measures, such as policy and legislation. The analysis of legislation as a reform strategy considered later in this chapter is relevant here.

- The solutions sought by this model contribute significantly to the overall complexity and opaqueness of modern formal human services. The volume of highly technical legislation and regulation alone limits accessibility for ordinary people and fosters the growth of highly trained technicians and professionals who hold knowledge and power.

- The rights model does not easily incorporate acknowledgement of vulnerability. In some contexts there may even be a denial of disability or a claim that disability is only socially constructed

- The rights model may not acknowledge that with rights come responsibilities. This is crucial for people who may really lack the capacity to exercise the responsibilities that accompany certain rights. Thus the de-institutionalisation and inclusion movements may create situations in which some rights of vulnerable people are respected but to their overall detriment – that is, they are 'abandoned with their rights'. We know of a person who was de-institutionalised from a large government institution containing about 500 people in the early 1980s in Victoria, Australia. He was relocated to a special accommodation house, privately run for profit, with about 200 people. Although a successful de-institutionalisation project for the bureaucracy, he has experienced regular bashings on pension day as he is preyed upon by others, many of whom may have been de-institutionalised themselves.

- The notion of choice requires considerable analysis. The provision of more choice options for one group – people with learning disabilities, for example – may reduce the choice options for others, such as carers. In a real sense, liberating processes often result in benefits for one group at the expense of others. The guarantee of a minimum level of support to a highly devalued and vulnerable group may be of higher priority than provision of choice. This raises the question of choice as a means or as an end (Le Grand 1993).

The advocacy model

The advocacy model has emerged in the disability field particularly since the late 1960s, although its influence is much more recent, possibly dating from the early 1980s. This model is based on an acknowledgement that some people and groups experience heightened vulnerability. This may lead to social devaluation which is associated with certain negative consequences for people, including experiences of rejection, de-individualisation and loss. The nature of the problem is the risk, or actual experience, of social devaluation. This model supports actions at the individual, system and societal levels that safeguard the valued place of people in society.

Many of the key methods of the advocacy model are incorporated within protective services and legislation. There is also a range of advocacy types including individual advocacy, systemic advocacy, legal advocacy and citizen advocacy (Wolfensberger 1977; Wolfensberger and Zauha 1973). The advocacy model may include key principles particularly focused on the priority of the needs of the vulnerable person and the minimisation of conflicts of interest.

Some of the key issues with this model include the following:

- Concern that the model may overprotect and thus contribute to limiting the opportunities for growth and development for the vulnerable person.

- Confusion about what constitutes advocacy as opposed to other legitimate and useful activity.

- The loss of independence of advocacy efforts as they come under the influence and control of formal human services. This is certainly a significant risk when advocacy efforts receive funding from government sources.

The 'drift to disempowerment' described earlier is tempered by the new professional ethos associated with economic-, rights- and advocacy-based models which, nominally at least, contribute to empowerment. Yet, on a closer examination, we have demonstrated that major contradictions still occur within these models. The internal coherence of the human service systems claiming to be instigating empowerment practice, is therefore highly suspect. This is made even more stark when consideration is given to legislative strategies for reform and, further, the relation of these strategies to human service provision.

Legislative strategies for reform
Inherent contradictions in the law
The law, to the extent that it is concerned with individual freedoms on the one hand and societal regulation on the other, clearly has a central influence on the issue of empowerment. In addition, modern Western social legislation has become concerned with issues of social justice, as well as the actual provision of services and other supports. This is certainly the case in Australia, for example. Of the constraints on what can be achieved by the law, and by formal

human services, are the inherent contradictions and conflicts which result from its multiple purposes.

In modern society, the law, expressed through legislation, will impact on the lives of vulnerable people in many apparently contradictory ways. The law exerts control, provides entitlements, protects from exploitation and harm, punishes and potentates. Historically, the role of law has been ambivalent in its intent to serve citizens, especially those with limited power, and serve society, especially those who possess power. Technically, legislation has always been complex and abstruse, requiring people of considerable training, and high status and reward to administer it. The law has varied greatly in accessibility, both because of its technical nature and because of its cost. The law and its machinery mean to conserve, not to radicalise or empower.

Yet paradoxically, the very conservatism and order of the law may create circumstances in which people who traditionally have been disempowered and disenfranchised may become more free. It is clear, however, that the law, like formal human services, reflects values and ideologies and is but a means to an end, rarely reaching beyond the intentions of the dominant interests in society. The ideological context determines whether laws support apartheid, in one setting, and universal enfranchisement in another, or educational segregation rather than integration. In one jurisdiction, the law may support access and equity for people with disabilities, and in another, perhaps by default, contribute to exclusion and lack of opportunity. We perceive a modern trend towards reification of the law through legislation in human services that appears uninformed by the historical context, which denies the limitations of the law, and which reflects an implicit intent to control within the broad environment of turbulence and uncertainty.

Both the law and human services are important social institutions, the roles of which reflect a fundamental tension between sustaining and protecting society and doing the same thing for its citizens. It is interesting to note that the principle of the least restrictive alternative (Turnbull 1981) that has been so influential in attempted service reform for people with disabilities in a number of jurisdictions, had its origins in the judicial rulings of the US Supreme Court in the early 19th century which attempted to limit the extent of control of the state over its citizens (Burgdorf 1980). In the context of human services, the least restrictive alternative has been used through legal systems to attempt to free people from institutions and to get children with disabilities into education.

In human services, generally, and services for people with learning disabilities in particular, there has been phenomenal legislative development in Australia in the past two decades or so. Both the volume of new legislation and the ever-increasing areas of influence strongly suggest that various interests, particularly governments and their bureaucracies, are using legislation as a major strategy to underpin their efforts to reform and reconstruct the disability field.

In addition, Western legislation is being used as a model in countries with non-Western cultures.

Some assumptions that underpin legislation as a reform strategy

There are some unifying assumptions that underpin these developments. However, there appears to be limited theoretical and conceptual development accompanying the growth of legislation as a reform strategy, and few attempts systematically to determine their effectiveness. The correctness of the assumptions built into such reforms are likely to affect their success in terms of the criteria of empowerment outlined earlier:

- If legislation reflects a society's intentions, those intentions will enhance the position of vulnerable people. This assumes that the dominant societal values and ideologies are positively inclined towards people with disabilities.

- Social reform is facilitated by strategies that are highly formalistic, complex, hierarchical and centrally managed. The 'top-down' and controlling nature of legislative reform may affect the participation, understanding and commitment of ordinary citizens to the reform purposes.

- It may be argued that social reform is largely facilitated by processes that aim for uniformity and standardisation in the project in terms of both methods and outcomes. For example, a characteristic of modern enabling legislation is to impose universal standards, often at the cost of flexibility and sensitivity to individual situations and needs.

- The development of specialised legislation may assume that generic legislation is inadequate in addressing the needs of special groups.

- There is sufficient consensus amongst key stakeholders, particularly in terms of understanding of the needs of people, the nature of the problem and ways to address the problem. An associated assumption is that the legislation has the support of the immediate, and the broader societal, constituency. Legislative reform may be undermined or even perverted if this is not the case.

- There are sufficient financial and human resources to implement the legislative purposes. At present, in Australia, possibly the most significant constraint on the implementation of anti-discrimination acts and adult guardianship measures is insufficient financial and political commitments from governments.

- There is sufficient will to implement the legislative purpose.

Given these assumptions, questions arise as to how legislation is and, indeed, has been ordered, and whether it can produce empowerment.

Below we draw on five types of legislation (protective, enabling, rights-based, generic and universal) and examine their relevance to people with learning disabilities. The actual legislation may fall into more than one type. It is useful to consider that legislation has an historical development that incorporates three broad emphases. Early legislation reflected a protective purpose with the ongoing tension between protecting people and protecting society. During the 19th century, with the development of formal human service systems, a second emphasis was with control and regulation, both of vulnerable people and services. A third emphasis has become apparent, particularly since the 1960s, that is, concern for rights. All three foci continue to influence and shape contemporary legislation.

Protective legislation may be specific to people with learning disabilities or may incorporate this group along with other groups. The purpose of such legislation is to protect or safeguard personal vulnerability and/or a person's estate. Examples of this legislation include the creation of guardianship for adults and children, property trusteeship, ombudsmen, and the provision of public advocacy.

Protective legislation has a long history. The eleventh century doctrine of *parens,* for example, set forth the monarch's responsibility towards his or her subjects: 'If an attempt is made to deprive any wise man in orders of a stranger of either his goods or his life, the king shall act as his kinsman and protector...unless he has some other' (Kittrie 1971, p.9).

In England, *Perogatavia Regis,* written in the 13th century, set forth various royal rights and duties towards people who lacked capacity, distinguishing between 'natural fools' and persons who were *non compos mentis.* Matters were dealt with by the Court of Chancery before being transferred to the Court of Wards in 1540 (Neugebauer 1978).

In medieval England, responsibility for people who lacked capacity was held by families, the church and lords of the manor. As this welfare system disintegrated, the various Poor Laws from the 16th through to the 19th centuries brought about a shift of social welfare responsibilities to the state and contributed to the development of a welfare infrastructure and the first modern human service systems. The Poor Law of 1834 was described as:

> ...the most important piece of social legislation passed in the 19th century. It established a new model of administrative machinery – nationally centralised decision-making on substantive issues of policy, professionalised civil servants, bureaucratic rationality. In essence it was the first recognisable modern welfare system. (Marcus 1981, p.53)

Protective legislation became an integral part of protective services and the development of modern formal human service systems. The extent and nature of direct state involvement in protective services have been subject to considerable examination and critique under the rubrics of the 'welfare state' and the 'therapeutic state' (see, for example, Beilhartz, Considine and Watts 1992; Gaylin *et al*. 1981; Habermas 1989a; Kittrie 1971; McKnight 1986; OECD 1981; Szasz 1974). This critique essentially explores the nature of tensions existing between the state and its citizens in order to address the fundamental conflict of interest between protecting the vulnerable person from society and protecting society from the vulnerable person.

The conflict will inevitably express itself in all social legislation. For example, in adult guardianship legislation, in spite of the development of the notion of limited guardianship based on the least restrictive alternative principle in the 1970s, there remains a major concern with interfering with a person's self-determination (Appelbaum 1982; Carney 1985; Ferguson 1978).

In the 19th and 20th centuries, in association with the eugenics movement, the emphasis of the law clearly was to protect society from various groups of people who were perceived to be a threat – social, economic and genetic. Sterilisation laws were common throughout the Western world. For example, a sterilisation law was on the statute book in Western Australia as late as 1929 (1939 in Victoria), although it was not implemented because of economic preoccupations (Fitzgerald 1988). The problem here lies in balancing the interests of different elements of society. Legislation which requires the identification of special interests and laws separates the vulnerable from the rest of society, thus creating and sustaining those interests as different.

In contrast to protective legislation, enabling legislation is specific to one or more groups of people with disabilities and aims to reflect and implement aspects of government policy, regulation or funding. In Australia, there are disability services Acts at commonwealth, state and territory levels that spell out governing principles and funding policies for disability services. Other examples of such legislation exist in countries which have variously legislated to regulate the employment of people with disabilities, for example, restricting the employment of masseurs to people with visual impairments (see, for example, the Korean Welfare Law for People with Mental and Physical Disabilities 1981–1989), or stipulating a minimum proportion of disabled people in private enterprise (see, for example, the Japanese Disabled Persons Employment Promotion Law 1960–1987). There are therefore a number of possible ways which allow courts legally to pursue disabling and exclusionary policies which militate against maximising the potential choices of people with learning disabilities.

Moreover, rights legislation which may promote inclusion and self-determination is seldom taken up fully by national governments, even where adopted rights are conferred without any form of apparent redress. Often based on universal or specific statements of rights (see, for example, the 1968 Declaration of the General and Specific Rights of the Mentally Retarded of the International

League of Societies for the Mentally Handicapped; the 1971 UN Declaration of the Rights of Persons with Mental Retardation; and the 1975 UN Declaration of the Rights of Disabled Persons), this legislation aims to assert and/or protect the rights of people with learning disabilities, amongst other people and groups. Some examples include anti-discrimination, human rights and equal opportunity Acts. An interesting example of a relevant universal statement of rights that refers to specific minority groups, including people with disabilities, is the 1981 Constitution of India.

Generic legislation affects most or all people in a society and includes specific mention of people with learning disabilities. Examples include education, mental health, criminal and social security Acts. This legislation may contain statements of entitlement. However, in the Australian context, legislation rather protects the political and bureaucratic interests and rarely expresses their obligations. For example, there is no piece of educational legislation in Australia that supports the right or entitlement of children with learning disabilities to education in regular settings with their age peers. Throughout Australia at the present time, many parents of children with disabilities are trying to do battle with the huge educational bureaucracies to gain access to services.

There are some pieces of legislation, which may be referred to as 'universal legislation', which apply across a society that potentially impact positively and negatively on people with learning disabilities to a greater extent than other people. For example, in some Australian jurisdictions, occupational health and safety Acts may turn homes for people with learning disabilities into work places and prevent paid carers from involving the people for whom they care in their own family and friendship networks. Industrial relations Acts may lead to the reinstatement of abusive carers in institutions for highly vulnerable people. On the other hand, administrative appeals mechanisms may provide additional avenues for people with learning disabilities to challenge bureaucratic decisions. Freedom of information legislation (however difficult to access successfully) may enable a person with learning disabilities to gain access to useful information. Financial audit and administration Acts may provide some safeguards against the bureaucratic wastage of scarce funds for services. Consumer protection legislation may provide necessary support. One might also expect the exponential and expensive growth of technical experts in these areas – administrators to administer and lawyers to develop and interpret – as illustrating one sort of empowerment at least.

As noted in relation to some of the examples just outlined, legislation as reform has provided a contemporary agenda and debate which rekindles arguments about the relative, and often contradictory, needs and interests of various stakeholder groups and citizens within Australian society. More worrying are recent attempts by countries without a history of such social legislation to import it from Western democracies without consideration of the contradictions pointed out in the proceeding debate. This 'human service super system'

(Wolfensberger 1992) creates a powerful tendency for major trends in human services to be exported across localities. This growth is occurring in many countries, even including cultures in the Asia Pacific region that have no history or experience of social legislation. There are a number of important issues likely to influence the success of Western-style legislation in differing cultures:

- As most modern Western social legislation is significantly rights-based, the socio-political environment of the culture is crucial. For example, some cultures have limited experience of social democracy, the principles of which may underpin legislation.

- Legislative strategies may be influenced by the historical place of people with disabilities in the culture and what disability is believed to be.

- In cultures with rapidly developing economies, we have observed the adoption of Western legislative initiatives (for example, in the area of employment for people with disabilities or anti-discrimination) largely as the adoption of technology with insufficient understanding of the underpinning values and principles.

- The Western context for social legislation is that of a highly developed formal human service system, well established within the culture. This context may be a necessary framework for certain legislation. It may also be the case that the adoption of a legislative strategy is accompanied by the development of such a structure. Another reflection of the human service 'super system' is the use of common service expressions (for example, 'group homes' or 'sheltered workshops') in Boston, Manchester, Paris, Auckland, Melbourne, Seoul, Tokyo, Hong Kong or Singapore.

Contemporary disability legislation in Australia, whilst bringing issues of rights, protection and enablement on to the agenda, continues to legitimise the professionally based, technologically driven and bureaucratised formal human service delivery patterns. In summary, social legislation reform continues to provide the legislative conditions which support and continue to foster the 'drift to disempowerment' within formal human services. To the extent that the conditions within which this drift flourish, so too will contradictions which make the enhancement of competency and social image, the removal of constraints and restrictions, and the growth of the voluntary commitment and collective action of the public, remain illusory. In the light of this, one is certainly led to a critical stance in relation to empowerment as a leading concept for the coming millennium.

Conclusion

The empowerment of a group of people whose common life experiences include heightened vulnerability and social devaluation cannot be considered in isolation from the formal systems within which they are deeply embedded and which influence their lives so much. Many of the characteristics of formal systems are intrinsically oppressive and controlling, serving purposes, possibly legitimate, that do not necessarily give priority to the interests of vulnerable people. The dependency of modern Western societies on formal human services and various forms of social legislation is of great magnitude, and it is virtually impossible to conceive of a paradigm responding to the needs of vulnerable people that does not include the modern welfare project with its intrinsic contradictory means and ends. The utility and veracity of a concept of empowerment in this context, therefore, requires close critical examination. At the same time, we must not lose sight of the imperative to address the immediate and pressing needs of people with learning disabilities in a broad environment of turbulence and ılık.

References

Appelbaum, P. (1982) 'Limitations on guardianship of the mentally disabled.' *Hospital and Community Psychiatry 33*, 3, 183–184.

Beilhartz, P., Considine, M. and Watts, R. (1992) *Arguing about the Welfare State.* North Sydney: Allen and Unwin.

Bell, D. (1973) *The Coming of Post-Industrial Society. A venture in social forecasting.* New York: Basic Books, Inc., Publishers.

Burgdorf, R. L. (1980) *The Legal Rights of Handicapped Persons. Cases, Materials, and Text.* Baltimore: Paul H. Brookes.

Carney, T. (1985) 'New civil guardianship laws – another view.' *Law Institute Journal* September, 956–959.

Cocks, E. (1987) 'Human services for people with intellectual disabilities in an era of turbulence and "altered consciousness".' *Australian and New Zealand Journal of Developmental Disabilities 13*, 3, 133–140.

Cocks, E. (1994) *Encouraging a Paradigm Shift in Services for People with Disabilities.* Perth: Centre for the Development of Human Resources, Edith Cowan University.

Community Services Victoria (1991) *Annual Report 1990/91.* Melbourne: CSV.

Dicken, P. (1986) *Global Shift: Industrial Change in a Turbulent World.* London: Harper and Row.

Ferguson, E. (1978) *Protecting the Vulnerable Adult: A Perspective on Policy and Program Issues in Adult Protective Services.* Ann Arbor: Institute of Gerontology.

Fitzgerald, M. (1988) 'Preventing the unfit from breeding: The Mental Deficiency Bill in Western Australia.' In P. Hetherington (ed) *Childhood and Society in Western Australia, 144–160.* Nedlands, WA: University of Western Australia Press.

Gaylin, W., Glasser, I., Marcus, S. and Rothman, D. (1981) *Doing Good: The Limits of Benevolence.* New York: Pantheon Books.

Habermas, J. (1989a) *The New Conservatism. Cultural Criticism and the Historians' Debate.* Cambridge: Polity Press.

Habermas, J. (1989b) *The Structural Transformation of the Public Sphere. An Inquiry into a Category of Bourgeois Society.* Cambridge: Polity Press.

Hoggett, P. (1990) *Modernisation, Political Strategy and the Welfare State: An Organisational Perspective. Studies in Decentralisation and Quasi-Markets No 2.* Bristol: School for Advanced Urban Studies.

Kittrie, N. (1971) *The Right to be Different: Deviancy and Enforced Therapy.* Baltimore: Johns Hopkins Press.

Korten, D.C. (1984) 'People-centred development: toward a framework.' In D.C. Korten and R. Klaus (eds) *People-Centred Development.* USA: Kumanan Press.

Le Grand, J. (1993) *Studies in Decentralisation and Quasi-Markets. Quasi-Markets and Community Care.* Bristol: School for Advanced Urban Studies, University of Bristol.

Marcus, S. (1981) 'Their brothers' keepers: an episode from English history.' In W. Gaylin, I. Glasser, S. Marcus and D. Rothman (eds) *Doing Good: The Limits of Benevolence 29–66.* New York: Pantheon Books.

McKnight, J. (1976) 'The professional service business.' *Social Policy 8,* 3, 110–116.

McKnight, J. (1986) 'Social services and the poor: who needs who?' *Utne Reader,* Feb–Mar, 118–121.

Michael, D.N. (1983) 'Competence and compassion in an age of uncertainty.' *World Future Society Bulletin,* Jan/Feb, 1–6.

Neugebauer, R. (1978) 'Treatment of the mentally ill in medieval and early modern England: a reappraisal.' *Journal of the History of the Behavioural Sciences 14,* 158–169.

OECD (1981) *The Welfare State in Crisis.* Geneva: Organisation for Economic Co-operation and Development.

Szasz, T. (1974) *Law, Liberty, and Psychiatry: An Inquiry into the Social Uses of Mental Health Practices.* New York: MacMillan.

Sztompka, P. (1993) *The Sociology of Social Change.* Oxford: Blackwell Publishers.

Turnbull, H.R. (1981) *The Least Restrictive Alternative: Principles and Practices.* Washington, DC: American Association on Mental Deficiency.

Williams, T.A. (1982) *Learning to Manage our Future. The Participative Redesign of Societies in Turbulent Transition.* New York: John Wiley and Sons.

Wolfensberger, W. (1975) *The Origin and Nature of our Institutional Models.* Syracuse: Human Policy Press.

Wolfensberger, W. (1977) *A Balanced Multi-Component Advocacy/Protection Schema.* Ontario: Canadian Association for the Mentally Retarded.

Wolfensberger, W. (1989) 'Human service policies: the rhetoric versus the reality.' In L. Barton (ed) *Disability and Dependency, 23–41.* London: Falmer Press.

Wolfensberger, W. (1992) 'Deinstitutionalisation policy: how it is made, by whom, and why.' *Clinical Psychology Forum 39,* 7–11.

Wolfensberger, W. and Thomas, S. (1994) *Liberation of Handicapped or Societally Devalued People.* Workshop presented in Ottawa, Canada.

Wolfensberger, W. and Zauha, H. (1973) *Citizen Advocacy and Protective Services for the Impaired and Handicapped.* Toronto: National Institute on Mental Retardation.

CHAPTER 13

Citizenship, Empowerment and Everyday Life
Ideal and Illusion in the New Millennium

Paul Ramcharan, Gwyneth Roberts,
Gordon Grant and John Borland

Introduction

In the Preface to this book it was suggested that one of the aims was to design a possible scenario for empowerment which, rather than attempting to fit people to grand theories about the state and its responsibilities, would stimulate the state to provide forms of empowerment which reflect the everyday lives and lifestyles of people with learning disabilities. It has been suggested that developing an 'included identity' for people with learning disabilities in their everyday lives is of vital importance, as is the right to participation within different life spheres and self-determination. In this chapter *one* scenario from amongst a considerable number of possibilities is discussed in relation to the concept of empowerment for citizens with learning disabilities. In this scenario 'citizenship' is argued to be a precondition of an included identity. Citizenship, it is argued, is founded upon an entitlement to resources which guarantees a minimum level of well-being.

There are two ways in which people with learning disabilities might be 'disappeared'. The first would be to follow a theory of eugenics which denies the value of biodiversity or, as Peters (1996) points out, to intern, hide or exclude people from mainstream society:

> Aggressive interventions take the form of ritual performance in eradication of disability/disease, and are not limited to the medical community. From its origins, special education has segregated, sheltered and denied opportunities to children and youth with disabilities... Over the last century scholars within academic disciplines have refined these cultural symbols and ritual performances

in theories of the 'Other' – perpetuating and reinforcing the idea that certain classes of people, by definition, are not quite human. (pp.217–218)

It is only within a system in which some people are seen as 'not quite human' that certain individuals can be denied rights which are accorded to other people.

Since at least the passing of the Poor Laws in the last century, the Great Internment (Foucault 1971) meant that, for a considerable period of time, people with learning disabilities, as well as those with mental health problems, were hidden from the sight of society in workhouses and large asylums. However, more recently the public conscience has reacted against such institutionalised and disacculturated forms of existence (Barton 1959; Goffman 1961). By rendering the alternative simply unthinkable, community care has, as Bean and Mouncer argue (1993), become legitimised as an alternative form of care. The more recent 'conscientisation' of people with mental health problems, people with physical disabilities and, latterly, people with learning disabilities, (i.e. raised awareness about their place in society), has made the Great Internment no longer tenable as a legal and social policy. Moreover, the discourse of rights has made their lack of rights more visible. Within this discourse Nagler (1993) has characterised the continued internment of people with disabilities within the community in terms of, 'the social disadvantages arising from isolation, segregation and discrimination of minority groups [which] have perpetuated the sense of inequality and powerlessness of these groups' (p.33). It is in this sense that people with learning disabilities may be 'in' our communities, but not 'of' them, and without the necessary supports, or economic or social power to contribute to community life. As Nagler goes on to say the, '…ethic and goal for all minorities is equality, integration and social justice' (p.33).

The second strategy through which learning disability might be 'disappeared' contrasts starkly with the eugenics, aggressive interventions and internment described above. In this second strategy lie the ideas of equality, integration and social justice. In this respect it is the stigmatising label which will 'disappear', leaving the individual simply as a 'citizen'. But in this 'brave new world' there must be a clear understanding of what duties and responsibilities accrue both to the citizen and to the state, and what civic structures will produce an 'included identity', 'choice' and 'autonomy'. As these concepts have informed much of the writing in this book, some of the problems and prospects for inclusion, choice and autonomy are considered below.

The citizenship and rights agenda

Dalrymple and Burke (1995), reviewing Norton's (1978) notion of the 'dual perspective', argue that oppression occurs when the structures of civil society, based as they are on the values of dominant groups, are at odds with the day-to-day aspects of a person's ability to function within their family, leisure and other spheres of life. This dialectical interplay has been a key theme of this book. According to Dalrymple and Burke:

> If we are to combat oppression we need first to understand the mechanisms that result in people being denied access to resources... Secondly we must try to provide the means by which individuals can regain control of their lives. The law can be seen as a vehicle for change.
> (1995, p.18)

So, in what ways can the law provide a basis for citizenship rights? Means and Smith (1994) suggest that, 'many in the disability movement believe that the way forward...is to argue for a rights-based approach...' (p.97). So what legal form should these rights take?

Models of equality

Nagler has argued that the UN Declaration of Human Rights has, '...served as an impetus for the disabled to seek legislation which will enshrine their position as equals within mainstream society' (1993, p.34). Yet, in reviewing the effect of the Americans with Disabilities Act which draws on the UN Declaration, he shows that its call for, 'equality of opportunity, full participation, independent living and economic self-sufficiency' have not been translated into reality. The result has been the continued exclusion of disabled people from the mainstream of American society and continuing inequality. We are thus led to ask what this elusive ideal of 'equality' consists of, and what legal forms it might take. Both Rioux (1994), from the point of view of people with learning disabilities, and Gooding (1994), from the point of view of disabled people in general, have carried out a useful analysis of models of equality and human rights. Certain aspects of their analyses are discussed below.

One way by which equality can be achieved is through equality of treatment by, for example, implementing legislation against racial and sexual discrimination which calls for equal treatment in relation to both race and gender. But as Gooding points out, a 'formal equality' model does not take into account the structural inequalities which exist in society. The model focuses, rather, on individual acts of discrimination and suggests that people of equal merit should be treated in the same way. Ironically, therefore, the formal equality model may be of greatest benefit to those individuals from amongst disabled people who are themselves most able. For people with learning disabilities, who remain socio-economically disadvantaged and excluded from the systems through which such merit is achieved, the 'formal equality' model does nothing to liberate them from such oppression. As Rioux points out, the exclusion of children with learning disabilities from mainstream education is justified by arguing that, unlike non-disabled children, they cannot gain from such an education. The 'formal rights' model does not, therefore, provide sufficient empowerment of people with learning disabilities.

The immediate common-sense response to the fact that equal treatment for individuals does not deal with structural inequalities is to suggest forms of special treatment or compensation for certain groups. The many possible approaches to such a model of equality might be subsumed under an 'equality of opportunity' rubric. This 'liberal theory' posits that, '...preferential treatment...is justified because of past injustice. Affirmative action is justifiable...to provide equal opportunity to those groups who have been historically hindered and precluded from participation' (Rioux 1994, p.79). Reviewing the Canadian Charter of Rights and Freedoms, Rioux shows that some gains have been made under this model since it confers substantive, as well as procedural rights, such as the right to treatment as well as to refuse treatment, and a right to vote.

Affirmative action, which is largely relevant in relation to the work place, may involve employing and training of group members who are under-represented in the work force. For affirmative action to work, a continuous audit of participation and the setting of targets for recruitment become necessary. In doing so the effects of discrimination which is not immediately apparent, that is, 'indirect discrimination', can be taken into account. In this context, preferential treatment should be understood as one means of broadening the range of applicants for employment and as a means of removing those barriers which have led to white, able-bodied men being disproportionately represented in the labour market.

Gooding, a member of the Rights Now campaign which lobbies for increased rights for disabled people, puts forward a number of reasons for adopting a rights discourse based on affirmative action. She points out that, although reducing welfare benefits may be legitimate, violating the rights of an individual is not. Moreover she argues:

> As long as the exclusion, segregation and second-class treatment of disabled people is seen as their individual problem, caused by their physical or mental impairment, the solution will continue to be posed in terms of medical cure or charitable dependency. To recast it in terms of structural discrimination is to present the solution in terms of changes to society. (1994, p.44)

She suggests that the rights discourse, like the women's movement and black civil rights, constitutes a 'first phase' which moves away from individualised and pathological models with their segregationist, charitable and paternalistic approach. Whilst this procedure may be a necessary first step, there are difficulties in seeking to transfer the argument made by Gooding to people with learning disabilities.

Work and the materialist mentality

Gooding's argument implies that the term 'disabled people' includes those with 'physical and mental impairments'. She therefore includes people with learning disabilities within the disability lobby. In the disability lobby's view it is by overcoming the disabling effects of society that inclusion can be achieved for 'disabled people' in the work place and the community. Yet, as Rioux points out, affirmative action assumes the ability to recognise shared group characteristics, and it is not clear what such characteristics might be for people labelled as having a learning disability.

In addition, one of the negative aspects of affirmative action is that members of the targeted group must declare themselves to be members, thus reinforcing the stigmatising effects of the label. In a system in which there is competition for employment, people with learning disabilities may suffer a double discrimination in relation both to non-disabled people and in relation to those who are physically, but not mentally-impaired. Gooding does not accept this argument. Bynoe, Oliver and Barnes (1991) argue that whilst all disadvantaged groups are affected by the 'social bias' and the 'differential impact of neutral standards', there are two further barriers to work, that is, 'surmountable impairments' which are barriers which can be overcome with appropriate modifications to the environment, and 'other barriers' where the impairment itself precludes participation. Of these two latter categories Gooding argues:

> I would dispute the validity of creating a legal category of 'insurmountable barriers'. It is based on the social myth of the existence of a hard and fast distinction between able-bodied and disabled people, rather than recognising that people possess a spectrum of abilities. (p.48)

Gooding therefore implies that the whole spectrum of abilities is demanded within a competitive market. But, in a competitive market, it is the individual's productive potential which enables him/her to access the work force, and this may exclude some abilities within the wider spectrum. The difficulties with Gooding's approach are well demonstrated within normalisation and social role valorisation theory. Emerging in northern European countries in the early 1960s, normalisation was seen as a means through which services might, 'create an existence for the mentally retarded as close to normal living conditions as possible...' (Bank-Mikkelson 1980, p.56). The term was adopted by Wolfensberger in the North American context and initially came to be seen as using culturally normative means to culturally normative ends (Wolfensberger 1972). It was later argued to be about, '...the creation, support and defence of valued social roles for people at risk of devaluation' (Wolfensberger 1983, p.234), and with this came its new name – social role valorisation. But, as with all normative theory, difficult questions arise when trying to identify what exactly such norms or valued social roles are, or should be.

This is highlighted in Wolfensberger and Glenn's (1975) manual for assessing services which proposes that everyone with a learning disability should attain the 'culturally valued analogue' (CVA) in their lives as adults. Such a CVA, they suggest, is to be found in fully paid employment. It is hardly necessary to visit many service settings to know that they will score nothing or near zero against such a criterion. In addition, the social role valorisation model is inherently stigmatising to people with learning disabilities if they are neither in, nor able to access, such paid work. A white, middle-class, materialist and normative theory underpins this limited conception of what is valued. Yet, the importance of work and entitlement to resources is vital. As Twine argues:

> Any discussion of citizenship is by implication a discussion of power, and at the centre of power relations in industrial societies is the system of production and its associated system of distribution... Democratising power and control must involve reducing inequalities of resource distribution as resources are a crucial form of power in a market society. (Twine 1994, p.105)

So how might such work and entitlement be accorded? Over and above maximising the likelihood of success in the employment market via education, through affirmative action or through supported employment initiatives (cf Beyer 1995 for a useful review), it is necessary, therefore, to develop a broader value base which is more likely to foster inclusion in the work place. Extending the notion of what constitutes 'work' therefore becomes a vital ingredient in the fight for inclusion. Abberley (1996) comments:

> If we must look elsewhere to a paradise of labour for the concrete utopia...it is not on the basis of classical analysis of social labour...that aspirations and demands of the disability movement run profoundly counter to the dominant cultural problematic of both left and right. This is not a matter of choice, but of the future survival of alternative, impaired modes of being. (p.77)

But what happens where inclusion is possible within a work place, but the person's productivity does not warrant full pay? If employers are expected to make up the difference to eliminate the effects of socio-economic deprivation and oppression, there is likely to be little incentive to include people with learning disabilities. Governments are unlikely to legislate to, '...remedy structural discrimination...to impose the costs of "social engineering" on "innocent" employers' (Gooding 1994, p.51).

In this situation questions arise as to how entitlement to resources can be conferred in order to overcome such effects. The question arises at a key juncture, given the prominence of the market within Western democracies today. For example, the emphasis on the work ethic within the European Community has meant that, '...citizens are citizens-as-workers, not citizens-as-human-beings'. As such, 'social policies...cannot deal coherently with needs arising from conditions that may be unconnected with work' (Meehan 1993, p.147). According to Gooding, the failure to link social policy to employment rights has meant that not one binding European law or directive relating to employment and disabled people has yet been passed.

Another aspect of the pure model of marketisation is the emergence of the concept of the 'active' citizen looking after his/her own interests and those which are held in common with others, for example by means of Neighbourhood Watch Schemes for the protection of property. In Britain, the 'active citizen' is also embodied in the Citizen's Charter, which reflects, 'the unbundling of the state and [the] turn to private sector thinking... This narrow definition of citizenship...is more accurately called a consumer's charter' (Marr 1995, p.264). The concept is also linked to the call for more self-help and social responsibility. Thus Green (1996), for example, argues that, 'We should aim...to base a policy of assisting the less fortunate not on 'rights', which are demands that other people [through taxation] be compelled to render assistance but on duties, which reach within us all for our better nature' (pp.123–4), whilst Herrnstein and Murray (1994) in their highly controversial text argue that the:

> largest reason for wanting to scrap job discrimination law is our belief that the system of affirmative action in education and the workplace alike, is leaking a poison into the American soul. The increasing proportion of ethnic minorities...make it more imperative...that we return to the melting pot and colour blindness as an ideal. Individualism is not only America's heritage. It must be its future. (p.508)

The opportunities which would be denied ethnic minority groups by the above model would be even greater for people with learning disabilities. In a system where the 'active citizen' is encouraged, those who are less able to act without help will be penalised. As rights are increasingly defined in terms of consumerism, they are increasingly geared towards those who are wealthy enough to consume; and, where individual responsibility is unduly extended, there is further alienation, oppression and exclusion as the existing responsibility of the state for its most vulnerable citizens becomes reduced.

Enablement and entitlement

In a society which is based on notions of distributive justice, it is our contention that *where equality of opportunity ends the right to entitlement to resources must begin.* In this context, Rioux's (1994) proposal for an 'equality of well-being' model is particularly potent. A significant characteristic of this model is that it is based on achieving specifiable outcomes which constitute a minimum acceptable level of citizenship. In a model of this kind, there is no need to identify and separate out people with learning disabilities. Rather, they are citizens who are entitled, as such, to a level of well-being to which all citizens have a right. As Rioux argues, 'well-being has a number of components including equal achievement of self-determination, participation and inclusion in social life, and the exercise of fundamental citizenship rights' (p.86). The 'equality of well-being' model would free people to contribute to society in ways which are not necessarily productive in economic terms, whilst at the same time maintaining a level of entitlement to resources which would not disenfranchise them in comparison with other members of the population. An 'equality of well-being' approach, however, raises a host of difficulties, some of which are discussed below.

For example, if self-determination is at the heart of citizenship, should people with learning disabilities be allowed to choose institutional and other segregated settings rather than integration in the community? In arguing for an 'equality of well-being' model, Bach suggests that, 'the parameters within which we exercise our self-determination are not entirely open-ended' (1994, p.142). For Bach, 'choice' of segregation releases the person from both the duties and opportunities that accompany citizenship. However, without such duties and opportunities there can be no citizenship. The arguments put forward in the interlinking chapters also show how choices are circumscribed by laws and policies, and that informed choices must be made within such set agendas. The development of self-identity is as much circumscribed and determined by the legal and policy contexts within which choices are made, as it is a reflection of a person's unencumbered choice of lifestyle.

In an 'equality of well-being' model, self-determination is therefore promoted within a legal and policy framework which limits choice and self-determination to those concomitant with inclusion in mainstream schooling, the work place and the community. For Bach this is the price that citizens must pay with respect to their entitlement to resources. It also reflects one of the defining features of citizenship for the rest of society where inclusion in schooling, the employment ethic and participation in the community are seen as valued goals. As a result, legislation and policy which is inclusive may be seen as a 'just distribution of conditions' under which self-determination can be exercised, a social contract between the state and its citizens which does not discriminate on the basis of disability. And as Cocks and Cockram (Chapter 12) have argued, it is in this way that laws can be empowering as well as constraining.

But perhaps the most difficult and enduring problem with an 'equality of well-being' model of citizenship is to know how and when well-being and citizenship are achieved, and hence the level of entitlement which is needed in order to bring these about. Traditionally, for people with learning disabilities, the service sector has been seen as particularly important in achieving these ends.

Enablement and the service sector
Commenting on some of the historical origins of existing welfare structures, Cocks and Cockram (Chapter 12) offer a pessimistic view of the ability of the

service sector to empower people with learning disabilities. They argue that existing service systems reflect a 'drift to disempowerment' characterised by bureaucratisation, professionalisation and increased technology. Legislation is likely to reflect this, rather than enhance the interests of people with learning disabilities. In short, it is not sufficient to provide the conditions for empowerment by conferring rights through legislation if, at the same time, the service sector prevents this from happening. This leads us to consider whether there are other service models which might lead to empowerment and which mirror the 'equality of well-being' model outlined above. In Chapter 11, Rioux, Bach and Crawford addressed themselves to one such model.

First and foremost, the model proposed by Rioux *et al.* would remove disability-related policy and programmes from within the welfare framework. In this way the necessity for people to declare themselves dependent and to carry the stigmatising labels which such dependency creates would be abolished. The model would operate alongside welfare benefit payments, a further entitlement made to those whose basic income is below a socially acceptable minimum. As with independent living arrangements, for which Morris (1993) has advocated, disability-related supports would be designed to maximise people's inclusion in education, work and other community facilities. The success of such services could then be measured in relation to their ability to ensure that individuals achieve an independent lifestyle. Though the research process might differ, the techniques for measuring such outcomes would be no more complex than those currently used to measure service outcomes. What is at issue, however, is what constitutes a minimum acceptable level of independence. That remains a matter of ethics as well as a question of political expediency.

Rioux *et al.* argue that, over time, naturally evolving community support and success in employment would be the result of their model, serving the public good and promoting efficiency within the system. The burden on welfare payments would be reduced as people become economically empowered through the work place and socially empowered within their communities. It would also release resources from the bureaucratised and professionalised service sector. In the words of Morris (1993):

> It would appear that a shortage of resources is the major straightjacket on the extent to which community care reforms will promote independent living. However, it could be questioned as to whether the actual level of resources is the major problem or whether it is the nature of the current service provision which ties up resources in particular ways which are incompatible with independent living. (p.178)

Rioux *et al.* perceive their model as operating within a market system with the advantages of the market's economic efficiencies, and as acting in a way which does not 'over-serve' the people in receipt of such services. On the demand side of the equation, people would apply for individual funding for services, either through self-articulation, community review (i.e. through accredited local community organisations) or by buying-in approved diagnostic assessments from professionals, choosing the approach most appropriate to their circumstances. In this model needs assessment by professionals is only one of a number of choices available to the service user, and a choice which remains under their control. Services could also be bought from the service sector, from personal assistants or from other community supports, within a costed service package. In this manner the most appropriate supports for the task would be provided in any given circumstance, freeing the person to choose for themselves from the possible options on offer.

But if 'choice' and 'self-determination' are to be achieved, how, under such a system, would people with learning disabilities be able to exercise choice and know which disability-related services to buy? In asking this question, we are led back to some of the basic dilemmas facing *some* people with learning disabilities who are unable to make choices for themselves. Rioux *et al.* refer to 'people with disabilities or their advocates' in making applications for services. It is also likely that within the model some people with learning disabilities may provide community review, acting as expert members of community organisations which decide on applications for funding. But how other forms of advocacy should be organised and implemented for the majority of citizens with a learning disability is highly problematic. Whilst there may be no one 'correct' answer to this problem, some solutions may be better than others.

One approach might be through formal representation. Had sections 1 and 2 of the Disabled Persons (Services Consultation and Representation) Act 1986 been implemented, they would have provided for the appointment of an advocate or representative to speak on behalf of a person in relation to service needs. Had section 3 been implemented, it would have placed a duty on local authorities to respond to such representations. Although there is no formal provision for advocacy and representation under the Act, it is still possible for people with learning disabilities to have independent advocates, although the nature and extent of their formal authority to act may be unclear (Ramcharan 1995). An additional problem relates to the success of advocacy schemes in recruiting a sufficient number of unpaid independent advocates.

The Law Commission has proposed a number of statutory mechanisms in relation to people who suffer from mental incapacity. As Roberts (Chapter 10) implied, the Law Commission's proposals would simplify, clarify and codify the law in this area. The Law Commission proposed a functional test of incapacity, that is, of a person's ability to understand the nature and effect of decisions, including the ability to choose between options, as a means of deciding whether a decision should be made on their behalf. Substitute decisions of this kind must be taken in the person's 'best interests', whether by families, by a manager appointed for the purpose or by a newly established Court of Protection. For proponents of the Commission's work, the proposals offer a useful mechanism for decision-making in relation to those persons who are deemed to be mentally incapacitated as well as mechanisms for the resolution of actual or potential conflict. Using a case study, Roberts also points to the possible simplicity, the procedural fairness, and the merits of a system which balances risk-taking against overprotection for some of the most vulnerable people in society.

The proposals of the Law Commission are unlikely to satisfy some critics who might suggest that the minority of people declared 'incapacitated' would be unduly stigmatised. There are concerns too that where decision-making is handed to professionals this may perpetuate the 'medical model' in which 'best interests' are taken on the basis of professional values and not individual rights. As Inclusion International (1995) argues, 'people with disabilities...should not be made subject to paternalistic decisions in their "best interest"' (p.9).

The proposals of the Law Commission, whilst dealing with substitute decision-making, raise questions about how it might be possible to extend the opportunities through which people with learning disabilities might come to their own preferred decisions. Some forms through which such empowering practice might be achieved are outlined below.

One approach would be to tap in to those closest to the individual, those who care 'about' the person, rather than simply 'for' them. The idea of 'circles of friends' (Perske and Perske 1988) or 'Joshua Committees' (Brandon 1991) made up of the people closest to the person, whether family, friends or advocates, provide useful models in this respect. Such groups are more likely to know and to be wholly dedicated to the person's interests and to maximising their quality of life and well-being. They are likely to know the person and their wishes better than professionals who may not meet on a regular basis to discuss a person's needs, and, as a group, may be able to balance out the interests which are represented in the person's everyday interactions. Groups such as these may be aware not only of the person's choices, but also any changes in his/her circumstances, providing a system which is finely tuned to fluctuations in a person's service needs and wishes. It may also be possible for such groups to draw on concepts such as a 'living will', a statement of life wishes, 'advanced directives' or 'non-negotiables' (see Chapter 8) as a means of providing a value base from which the person and his/her circle of friends can make service and other life choices. An additional possibility would be to introduce a service brokerage model (Brandon 1991; Dowson 1990) in which informal groups work with a broker (who is independent of service-providing organisations), to determine service options and organise delivery of any services which are deemed relevant.

However, there is always the possibility of conflicts of interest arising between the person with learning disabilities and his/her family and other members of such informal groups. This is more likely, as Morris (1993) suggests, where existing service provision is geared towards balancing formal service care with the informal care provided by families. This means that the state implicitly relies upon families, mainly women, to undertake caring roles. Services for an *adult* with a learning disability which are provided to him/her as a fully-fledged independent citizen in his/her own right are less likely to result in conflicts of interest if services are not delivered with a view to balancing informal and formal care. In Morris' view, a person's right to services should be dictated by the personal supports needed to foster independence and inclusion and not in ways that create dependence on other family members. This would leave family members free to pursue their own interests whilst still providing the loving family context which Barnes discusses in Chapter 5.

Within an 'equality of well-being' model, key problems still remain where people with learning disabilities are unable to speak and act for themselves. Inclusionary legislation and policies, and the provision of responsive disability-related services which guarantee opportunities for 'exit' and 'voice', seem more likely to maximise the conditions under which self-determination and autonomy can be exercised. But, ultimately, it must be remembered that for some individuals, advocacy and substitute decision-making are required. How these are organised is likely to be a key challenge for the future.

As well as making proposals relating to the demand for services Rioux *et al.* also suggest that the supply side of service provision should be dictated by consumer demand for disability-related services and/or generic services which are likely to promote independence or further the goals of integration. The question is not therefore how a local authority or other third party should set about developing the supply of services but, rather, how to make the system responsive to the overall service demand of citizens.

Rather than leaving citizens to organise services for themselves, or organising services on the basis of aggregated need, Rioux *et al.* propose that public funding should be used to cover, 'administrative (including secretarial, managerial, clerical, training and retraining) costs'. A community service organisation would allocate funds to services to reflect demand, and any services which did not attract funds would need to change their operation or go out of business. This would reflect the power of the consumers to take decisions for themselves. Control of service demand would thus lead to empowerment for individuals in a way not possible under present community care arrangements in Britain.

There are anxieties, however, over the ability of widely dispersed individual citizens to organise in such a way as to attract government resources. The authors suggest that service standards, consumer feedback and reviews would be needed in order to measure what is needed to improve individual services. In addition, aggregate data-gathering, community forecasting and evaluation of the success of initiatives in creating opportunities in the community, would be part of government-funded research. They suggest that research of this kind could be used to make recommendations to government about the volume and type of services likely to be required, and any associated costs.

Empowerment in everyday life: a summary

Oppression, inequality and exclusion are not inborn characteristics of individuals, nor predetermined experiences, nor a function of individual impairment. They are socially produced phenomena to which socially contrived solutions can be applied. People with learning disabilities, the service sector, families and the community, all have a contribution to make in alleviating some of the effects of oppression, inequality and exclusion. At present, however, the potential for action of this kind is unduly constrained by the conditions within which these parties act. This explains why it is entirely possible for a multitude of empowering practices to be implemented without empowerment being achieved. Empowerment in everyday life cannot happen unless the structures and institutions of civil society are themselves empowering, rather than constraining. It is in this sense that we agree with Twine (1994) who argues for a model of empowerment based on social interdependence:

> ...social interdependence implies, first, that human beings can only be properly understood by appreciating that, although they have freedom potentially to make themselves, they do not do so in circumstances of their own choosing... Choices are always made within a framework of constraint... Yet human beings can, in principle, mould the framework of constraint within which they make their choices. (pp. 1–2)

The task remains one of finding a social contract which is least constraining and which is premised on a notion of equity and distributive justice. Within this approach, Twine (1994) highlights the importance of moulding the conditions within which people make choices. What, in that case, constitutes these necessary conditions?

Drawing on the experiences of citizens with learning disabilities described in Section 1, it is suggested that an 'included identity' is an essential prerequisite for setting the conditions upon which legislation and policy should be framed. An 'included identity' cannot be fostered by laws or services which are themselves exclusionary, segregationist or labelling.

The chapters in Section 2 examined the degree to which contemporary service models meet the criteria for an 'included identity'. In the interlinking chapter at the end of Section 2, it is suggested that there exist many conflicts of interest between the wishes of users and the values of the service system. Thus, bureaucratic and professionalised service structures often work against user choice; the notion of 'need' is a stigmatising concept, requiring the user to declare themselves a member of the 'worthy poor' in order to access resources; placing responsibility for developing a mixture of service options on third parties such as local authorities militates against a pure model of 'exit' and 'voice' in which the demand for services is made purely by users themselves; and it was also suggested that existing forms of empowerment practice within contemporary service systems are 'iatrogenic', that is, being a product of the system itself. Barnes and Prior (1995) have argued the need to:

> ...distinguish the potential for empowerment of service users from the possibilities of more general empowerment of citizens. Prioritising the extension of choice in public welfare services is a policy objective of, at best, narrow application with severely limited benefits in the form of user empowerment, and at worst a recipe for disempowering people already experiencing disadvantage, stress and uncertainty. (p.58)

It is therefore argued that whilst the empowerment of some individuals through participation and consultation mechanisms is possible, these are no substitute for the complete transfer of control to people who use services.

In other words, choice is a commodity within the service market, the parameters of which are set by professionals and their organisations. Whilst there is some success with the application of this model, there is also considerable constraint which prevents people with learning disabilities developing an 'included self-identity'. Since the concept of 'choice' is very much at the heart of this argument, it is suggested that the concept of 'self-determination' should be seen as a necessary aspect of both the empowerment process and of achieving an 'included identity'. A number of political, legal and policy scenarios through which 'self-determination' and an 'included identity' might be achieved are discussed in Section 3 and in the first sections of this chapter.

As a consequence, it is concluded that where attempts to provide opportunities are exhausted, entitlement should begin. Implicit in this model of empowerment is therefore a further concept, that of 'distributive justice' linked to a minimum outcome of well-being for all citizens. At the point at which a minimum level of citizenship becomes a right, the person with learning disabilities disappears and the citizen enters the frame. This is the defining feature which characterises the disability-related service system proposed by Rioux *et al.* in Chapter 11. This is a substantial step away from the systems, policies and practice of community care which exist in Britain today, since it proposes a transfer of control over services to the people who use them. Whilst it may seem radical it is nevertheless still being argued that we, '...require state-provided or state guaranteed services...but we should not try to reinvent yesterday and go back to forms of welfare institutions which, with the best intentions, actually put very little power in the hands of those they were designed to help' (Plant and Barry 1990, p.32).

But how is empowerment to be realised? As argued in the interlinking chapters of this volume, in the first instance it will be accomplished through 'border-crossing' as described by Souza (Chapter 1), whereby a person fights for his/her right to inclusion within mainstream society and where success becomes difficult for those who hold power to ignore. But whilst 'border-crossing' may be possible for the few, it is not a solution for the many. At the end of Section 1 it is argued that 'border-crossing' is possible only where a person recognises the importance of inclusion and accommodates this within his/her self-concept and identity. Given that exclusion is dominant, the likelihood of an identity of this kind developing for every individual with learning disabilities is greatly reduced, since self-concept and identity are likely to be shaped by the experiences of such exclusion.

Another strategy, therefore, is to find a means of linking personal identity with political identity. In this respect, Peters (1996) argues for:

> ...a new disability identity – one that needs to integrate the personal and the political...one identity depends on the other...these identities must rest on the foundations of self-love and spiritual models, as opposed to sociological models that rest on foundations of the 'victim' mentality, deviance and the Other as passive object. (p.231)

To achieve this, alliances must be formed so as to place pressure for change on the institutions of civil society. As Abberley (1996) says:

> the aim of a social movement is not simply to react against existing inequalities, but rather to work towards changing the norms and values of cultural and social life...for action to produce new elements of social structure it must work through and against pre-existing institutions and cultural forms. (p.75)

However, with whom such alliances are formed is open to debate, and needs to be considered carefully by organisations run by and for the interests of people with learning disabilities. Ward (1995), for example, has suggested that:

> As organisations of people with learning difficulties become stronger, alliances between them and organisations of other disabled people will continue to grow as they jointly campaign against discrimination that all disabled people encounter in our society and push for anti-discrimination legislation which is needed to ensure their rights. Increasingly attention will, hopefully, be given to equal opportunities for all people with learning difficulties. (pp.16–17)

But, as has been argued above, equality of opportunity and policies of anti-discrimination may be insufficient since, in relation to these, personal merit remains the arbiter of the right to entitlement. As a result, citizens with learning disabilities are likely to be the losers. When links are being formed with other organisations and groups, important questions concerning the terms upon which such alliances are made, and the nature of the shared agenda, become crucial.

In this final chapter we argue a particular concept of citizenship as the key to empowerment. According to this concept, there should be no discrimination between one individual and another, nor between one class of individuals and another. It is based upon an entitlement to resources which are distributed in such ways as to ensure for all members of society a minimum level of well-being. It is suggested that this notion of well-being is related to inclusion within the family, community and the civil structures of our society. We would argue that when it is tied to the notion of a minimum well-being, citizenship allows a sufficient degree of leeway for people to be able to choose and determine their identity without unnecessary encumbrance from the state or its functionaries.

But a final note of caution must be struck. Abberley warns against the, 'appeal to unity and theoretical consistency' in considering the opportunities for work for disabled people. Similarly, it is suggested that the vast majority of citizens with learning disabilities will only be able to achieve full inclusion in society when educational, community and work places are restructured to enable that to happen. For a small minority, however, such inclusion may be counter-productive. Whether inclusion should be an end in itself, whatever its effects on the individual, poses another vital question which, if ignored, could lead to the further oppression of society's most vulnerable citizens.

In the Preface to this book the question: 'What will the structure/institution/service/citizen relationship look like in an empowering society?' (Baistow 1995, p.44), was posed. We hope, and indeed believe, that this text provides a clearer picture of the complex set of relationships upon which an empowering society must be based. The idea of citizenship based on an equality of well-being has been proposed. Such well-being is dependent upon sufficient entitlement to resources to prevent oppression and inequality, and maximise self-determination and participation. Within this model participation and inclusion in the life of our society are seen as both a right and a responsibility of the citizen. Such participation and inclusion, therefore, provide the conditions under which citizens with learning disabilities make choices about their everyday lives. A considerable number of questions remain in relation to the processes, mechanisms and actual experiences which result in an empowered lifestyle.

Finding the answers to questions such as these provides us with an important challenge as we move into the next millennium.

References

Abberley, P. (1996) 'Work, utopia and impairment.' In L. Barton (ed) *Disability and Society: Emerging Issues and Insights, 61–82.* Harlow: Addison Wesley Longman.

Bach, M. (1994) 'Quality of life: questioning the vantage points for research.' In M. Rioux and M. Bach (eds) *Disability is not Measles: New Research Paradigms in Disability, 127–152.* Ontario: The Roeher Institute.

Baistow, K. (1995) 'Liberation or regulation? Some paradoxes of empowerment.' *Critical Social Policy 42,* 34–46.

Bank-Mikkelson, N. (1980) 'Denmark.' In R.J. Flynn and K.E. Nitsh (eds) *Normalisation, Social Integration and Community Services.* Austin, TX: Pro-Ed.

Barnes, M. and Prior, D. (1995) 'Spoilt for choice? How consumerism can disempower public service users.' *Public Money and Management,* July–September, 53–58.

Barton, R. (1959) *Institutional Neurosis.* Bristol: Wright.

Bean, P. and Mouncer, P. (1993) *Discharged from Mental Hospitals.* London: Macmillan Press in association with MIND.

Beyer, S. (1995) 'Real jobs and supported employment.' In T. Philpot and L. Ward (eds) *Values and Visions: Changing Ideas in Services for People with Learning Difficulties.* Oxford: Butterworth-Heinemann.

Brandon, D. (1991) *Direct Power: A Handbook on Service Brokerage.* Preston: Tao Publications.

Bynoe, I., Oliver, M. and Barnes, C. (1991) *Equal Rights for Disabled People – The Case for a New Law.* London: Institute for Public Policy Research.

Dalrymple, J. and Burke, B. (1995) *Anti-Oppressive Practice: Social Care and the Law.* Buckingham: The Open University Press.

Dowson, S. (1990) *Who Does What? The Process of Enabling People with Learning Difficulties to Achieve what they Need and Want.* London: Values into Action.

Foucault, M. (1971) *Madness and Civilization: A History of Insanity in an Age of Reason.* New York: Plume Books.

Goffman, E. (1961) *Asylums: Essays on the Social Situation of Mental Patients and Others.* Harmondsworth: Penguin.

Gooding, C. (1994) *Disabling Laws, Enabling Acts: Disability Rights in Britain and America.* London: Pluto Press.

Green, D.G. (1996) *Community Without Politics: A Market Approach to Welfare Reform.* London: IEA Health and Welfare Unit.

Herrnstein, R.J. and Murray, C. (1994) *The Bell Curve: Intelligence and Class Structure in American Life.* New York: The Free Press (1996 edn).

Inclusion International (1995) *Safeguarding the Rights of Persons with Disabilities. Response to the Documents Issued until September 1994 by the International Bioethics Committee of UNESCO.* Brussels: Inclusion International.

Marr, A. (1995) *Ruling Britannia: The Failure and Future of British Democracy.* London: Michael Joseph Ltd.

Means, R. and Smith, R. (1994) *Community Care: Policy and Practice.* London: Macmillan.

Meehan, E. (1993) *Citizenship and the European Community.* London: Sage.

Morris, J. (1993) *Independent Lives: Community Care and Disabled People.* London: Macmillan.

Nagler, M. (1993) 'The disabled: the acquisition of power.' In M. Nagler (ed) *Perspective on Disability: Texts and Readings on Disability, 33–36.* Palo Alto: Health Markets Research, (second edition).

Norton, D.C. (1978) *The Dual Perspective.* New York: Council on Social Work Education.

Perske, R. and Perske, M. (1988) *Circles of Friends: People with Learning Disabilities and Their Friends Enrich the Lives of One Another.* Nashville: Abingdon Press.

Peters, S. (1996) 'The politics of disability identity.' In L. Barton (ed) *Disability and Society: Emerging Issues and Insights, 215–234.* Harlow: Addison Wesley Longman.

Plant, R. and Barry, N. (1990) *Citizenship and Rights in Thatcher's Britain: Two Views.* London: The IEA Health and Welfare Unit.

Ramcharan, P. (1995) 'Citizen advocacy and people with learning disabilities in Wales.' In R. Jack (ed) *Empowerment in Community Care, 222–242.* London: Chapman and Hall.

Rioux, M. (1994) 'Towards a concept of equality of well-being: overcoming the social and legal construction of inequality.' In M. Rioux and M. Bach (eds) *Disability is not Measles.* Ontario: The Roeher Institute.

Twine, F. (1994) *Citizenship and Social Rights: The Interdependence of Self and Society.* London: Sage.

Ward, L. (1995) 'Equal citizens: current issues for people with learning difficulties and their allies.' In T. Philpot and L. Ward (eds) *Values and Visions: Changing Ideas in Services for People with Learning Difficulties, 3–19.* Oxford: Butterworth Heinemann.

Wolfensberger, W. (1972) *The Principle of Normalization in Human Services.* Toronto: National Institute on Mental Retardation.

Wolfensberger, W. (1983) 'Social role valorisation: a proposed new term for the principle of normalization.' *Mental Retardation 21*, 234–349.

Wolfensberger, W. and Glenn, S. (1975) *PASS 3: Program Analysis of Service Systems. Handbook and Manual.* Toronto: National Institute on Mental Retardation.

The Contributors

Michael Bach is Senior Researcher on public policy and disability at the Roeher Institute, Canada's national institute for the study of public policy affecting people with disabilities. He is also Assistant Professor (part-time) in the Faculty of Environmental Studies at York University, Ontario.

Marian Barnes is presently Senior Lecturer in the Health Services Management Centre at the University of Birmingham. At the time of writing her article Marian was Senior Lecturer in the Department of Sociological Studies at the University of Sheffield in England.

Michael Bayley is Associate Vicar St Mary's Dramall Lane with Highfield Trinity, Adviser to the Bishop of Sheffield on care in the community and Honorary Lecturer in social administration, University of Sheffield.

John Borland is Senior Lecturer in sociology in the School of Sociology and Social Policy, University of Wales, Bangor.

Liz Byrne is a clinical psychologist with the learning disability service of Guild Community Health Care Trust, Preston, Great Britain.

Judith Cockram is a research officer at the Centre for Disability Research and Development, Faculty of Health and Human Sciences, Edith Cowan University, Western Australia.

Errol Cocks is Director at the Centre for Disability Research and Development, Faculty of Health and Human Sciences, Edith Cowan University, Western Australia.

Cameron Crawford is Assistant Director of the Roeher Institute. His main areas of work are statistical and policy analysis of labour market, income programmes, and social services and criminal justice issues relating to people with disabilities.

Jackie Downer is a self-advocacy development worker with Lambeth Accord.

Steve Dowson is a freelance trainer and consultant in social care.

Margaret Flynn is Assistant Director of the National Development Team and a Prince of Wales Fellow of the Royal College of General Practitioners.

Gordon Grant is Co-director at the Centre for Social Policy Research and Development at the University of Wales, Bangor.

Sian Griffiths is a former project worker for the National Development Team. She is currently undertaking clinical psychology training at Sheffield University.

Kevin Hynes is a social worker with the learning disability service of Guild Community Health Care Trust, Preston.

Morag McGrath is Senior Research Fellow at the Centre for Social Policy Research and Development at the University of Wales, Bangor.

Paul Ramcharan is Research Fellow at the Centre for Social Policy Research and Development, at the University of Wales, Bangor.

Marcia Rioux is Executive Director of The Roeher Institute. She lectures in Canada and internationally on human rights and disability. She is also an adjunct professor of social policy in the Faculty of Environmental Studies at York University, Toronto, Ontario.

Gwyneth Roberts is Senior Lecturer in social policy in the School of Sociology and Social Policy at the University of Wales, Bangor. Her particular interests are in the areas of legal and social policy and how these affect the lives of people with learning disabilities.

Anya Souza has previously been involved with work in self-advocacy with Young People First and with other organisations run by and for people with learning disabilities. Anya has made a number of appearances in the media discussing issues which directly affect the lives of people with learning disabilities.

Jan Walmsley is a lecturer in learning disability at the School of Health and Social Welfare at the Open University.

Index

Learning to Listen

Positive Approaches and People with Difficult Behaviour
Herbert Lovett, Ph.D.
ISBN 1 85302 374 4 pb

'[the author] reflects on the history of the management of difficult behaviour
and provides many fascinating examples of the extraordinary ways in which
previous generations have tackled similar issues…historical analysis is inter-
woven with vivid accounts of people who have been referred to him for advice.
But this book is more than a set of case studies. Lovett hopes that we will be
stimulated to reassess how we relate to our clients and to reflect on our own
experience and practice…this book is to be strongly recommended.'

– Community Care

'The analysis of how labelling, politics and control have dominated the
provision of care is full of insight. The book is relevant to day-to-day
interventions, while providing points for consideration when local services are
being planned.' *– Nursing Times*

'…offers alternatives to professionals dealing with people with intellectual
disabilities… He [the author] shows that, by building an atmosphere of mutual
trust and respect, many of the more unpleasant answers to behavioural problems
can be avoided.' *– In Touch Newsletter*

Hearing the Voice of People with Dementia

Opportunities and Obstacles
Malcolm Goldsmith
Preface by Mary Marshall
ISBN 1 85302 406 6 pb

'…informative and revealing…a challenging - and at times very moving –
book.' *– The Health Service Journal*

'The reader is given a wide range of perspectives on how to communicate with
people with dementia… this is an easy read and raises the reader's awareness
about what it must be like to experience dementia. I feel this book would be
very useful for people who want to know more about dementia and communication.' *– Nursing Times*

'One of the strengths of this book is that it is written for staff and volunteers
rather than for an academic audience. It is a thoroughly good read.'

– from the preface

Jessica Kingsley *Publishers*
116 Pentonville Road, London N1 9JB

Children with Autism

Diagnosis and Interventions to Meet their Needs
*Colwyn Trevarthen, Kenneth Aitken, Despina Papoudi
and Jacqueline Robarts*
ISBN 1 85302 314 0 pb

'...the authors make a comprehensive study of autism, balancing theory with practice and presenting a clear picture of what it means to be autistic, and what can be done to improve the capabilities of the autistic child.'
— In Touch Newletter

Autism: An Inside–Out Approach

An Innovative Look at the 'Mechanics' of 'Autism'
and its Developmental 'Cousins'
Donna Williams
ISBN 1 85302 387 6 pb

'This must be the book most long awaited by therapists working with people with autism... The sensory and perceptual difficulties that challenge autistic people, together with strategies for tackling them, are described in depth. The case histories are illuminating and the review of professional approaches to autism as seen and experienced from the inside is of great interest to the working therapist. I liked the author's very personal form of assessment and her description of an ideal environment in which to work with autistic people. The appendix contains a list of hints for dealing with a variety of problems. The range is vast and touches on subjects as diverse as hairwashing and problems with textures.' *— Therapy Weekly*

'A clear and effective writer, Williams is able to describe her experiences with rare clarity, depth and understanding. Her new book titled Autism: An Inside-Out Approach takes us further into the disability and offers new opportunities to further our understanding. She adds new dimensions to our insights of the problems people with autism have with connections, control, and communication. After reading her exciting new book I know I have many new ways of thinking about my clients and their needs. I want to thank Donna Williams for another splendid triumph and suggest that any student of autism should run to their nearest bookstore and add this to their list of readings.'
*— Professor Gary B Mesibov, University of North Carolina,
and Director, North Carolina Autism Program*

Jessica Kingsley *Publishers*
116 Pentonville Road, London N1 9JB

Invisible Victims

Crime and Abuse Against People with Learning Disabilities
Christopher Williams
ISBN 1 85302 309 4 pb

'Clear advice is offered in relation to crime prevention and how best to make use of press reporting and the courts should a crime occur. This is an excellent reference book. Key points are presented in useful summaries and the addresses of many relevant organisations are provided... This publication should be read by everyone interested in the rights of people with learning disabilities.'
— *Nursing Times*

'Williams ably describes the situation and the wide range of crime, abuse and victimisation which can take place... This publication will be an excellent source book.' — *Community Care*

'the book is a valuable contribution to the body of specialist information available about people with learning difficulties.' — *Connect Bulletin*

Dyslexia

How Would I Cope? 3rd edition
Michael Ryden
ISBN 1 85302 385 X pb

Reviews of the previous editions:

'A book to be commended to everyone. There are very few books written for ordinary members of the public on Dyslexia, but this one gives a very clear insight into the difficulties and frustrations experienced by those suffering from this disability.' — *Disability News*

'Written from personal experience, this book clearly describes and illustrates how written communication can appear to a dyslexic person. The reader gains an increased awareness of the problems and understanding of how difficulties can be minimised. This book reinforces positive attitudes, and will be of interest to parents, teachers and employers.' — *Disabled Living Foundation*

'...well written and beautifully printed. The style is direct and informative and could help not only parents and teachers but young people struggling to understand why they are encountering problems with reading, writing and spelling... This is a useful text for anyone who wishes to learn more about this pervasive and important problem.' — *Rehab Network*

'As this clear and concise book demonstrates, dyslexics are often treated unfairly... Readers can step into the author's shoes as he shows how writing may appear to a dyslexic... Such a book should help everyone to understand and accommodate this learning disability.' — *Nursery World*

Jessica Kingsley *Publishers*
116 Pentonville Road, London N1 9JB

Listen To Me

Communicating the Needs of People
with Profound Intellectual and Multiple Disabilities
Pat Fitton, Foreword by Harry Marsh
ISBN 1 85302 244 6 pb

'The book is intensely practical, based on Pat Fitton's experiences with her daughter Kathy. It covers diagnosis, communication, preparing and presenting information, education, residential care, mobility, equipment, benefits, hospital treatment, leisure, relationships, and caring for the carers.'
— *British Journal of Learning Disabilities*

'Pat Fitton has managed to create from a good deal of pain and slog, an inspiring volume, with a warm and essentially positive outlook which makes it difficult to put down... This is a powerful, poignant and informative book, essential reading for all parents of children with multiple disabilities and the professionals who need to communicate with them.' — *Community Care*

'I find it difficult in a conventional review to do justice to this book... It details what is required from everybody involved: parents, siblings, family carers; and also the services they should expect: education, health and social services, housing, welfare benefits and financial provision...essential reading for parents and carers...and for professionals and service providers.'
— *Professional Social Work*

'...both accessible and informative, and should be read by parents, professionals and politicians!' — *SSLA Newsletter*

'...an excellent practical guide through the complexities of advocating for a person with profound intellectual and multiple disabilities... The practical nature of the book is reflected in its straightforward language, easy-to-follow lists of ideas and strategies to try, and well-referenced chapters, containing useful contact addresses, helplines and so forth... The book should assist planners and specialists to reach many more people who do not yet know what questions to ask with more appropriate services, ideas and understanding, and should be recommended reading for anyone involved directly or indirectly with people with profound disabilities.' — *Journal of Intellectual Disability Research*

'...packed with useful information, advice and suggestions, including the wealth of detail that could only be provided by someone who has experienced the situations described. It is written in a clear, informal, highly readable style...an invaluable resource for decision makers and the providers of services.'
— *British Journal of Special Education*

Jessica Kingsley *Publishers*
116 Pentonville Road, London N1 9JB